Hard Work, Hard Times

Hard Work, Hard Times

Global Volatility and African Subjectivities

Edited by
ANNE-MARIA MAKHULU, BETH A. BUGGENHAGEN,
AND STEPHEN JACKSON

Global, Area, and International Archive
University of California Press
BERKELEY   LOS ANGELES   LONDON

The Global, Area, and International Archive (GAIA) is an initiative of International and Area Studies, University of California, Berkeley, in partnership with the University of California Press, the California Digital Library, and international research programs across the University of California system. GAIA volumes, which are published in both print and open-access digital editions, represent the best traditions of regional studies, reconfigured through fresh global, transnational, and thematic perspectives.

University of California Press, one of the most distinguished university presses in the United States, enriches lives around the world by advancing scholarship in the humanities, social sciences, and natural sciences. Its activities are supported by the UC Press Foundation and by philanthropic contributions from individuals and institutions. For more information, visit www.ucpress.edu.

University of California Press
Berkeley and Los Angeles, California

University of California Press, Ltd.
London, England

Library of Congress Cataloging-in-Publication Data

A catalog record for this book is available from the Library of Congress.

Manufactured in the United States of America

19 18 17 16 15 14 13 12 11 10
10 9 8 7 6 5 4 3 2 1

The paper used in this publication meets the minimum requirements of ANSI/NISO Z39.48–1992 (R 1997) (*Permanence of Paper*).

Contents

Preface

After Afro-Pessimism

If much current scholarship focuses on two distinct, yet interrelated, aspects of contemporary capitalism—neoliberalism and globalization—scholars of Africa must address the attendant difficulties of the postcolonial condition, as well. Questions about Africa's "place in the world," that is, at the conjuncture of the neoliberal, global, and postcolonial brought scholars working across the African continent together for a conference, *After Afro-Pessimism: Fashioning African Futures*, at Princeton University in April 2005. Acknowledging many of the challenges facing contemporary Africa—the unevenness of North-South relations, the limits on national sovereignty, and perhaps most terrifyingly, the scale of the African HIV/AIDS epidemic—the participants stressed another sort of challenge besides. While concerned to examine the experiences of ordinary Africans, and while holding to a commitment to recording and theorizing such experiences, most agreed that the discourse of African "emergency" detracted from critical work. Africa has, to all intents and purposes, become an object of intervention by development experts, World Bank officials, and NGOs keen to devise "solutions" to its many problems. This dominant paradigm has made *instrumentalizable* knowledge more or less the only form in which "Africa" can be apprehended. So much for the reveries of scholars.

The questions that we and our fellow conferees sought to pose, then, were, How might one construct worlds within and beyond the language of predicament? Was it even possible to conceive of alternative spaces in which the imaginative and social practices of African agents could bring about "other orders of reality?" Might concepts of "invisible governance," "regimes of unreality," or even religious imaginaries offer new theoretical landscapes that would accommodate ideas of African political possibility? These and similar questions defined our deliberations.

After Afro-Pessimism was inaugurated with a keynote address by Chinua Achebe, the renowned Nigerian literary figure, novelist, and poet, who had been invited to speak directly to the idea of "Afro-pessimism." Achebe's corpus has long addressed the early challenges and indeed failures of African independence and the colonial grip that remained to shape the African state into a hybrid and semi-autonomous form, and therefore could offer a genealogy of cynicism whose historical and analytical continuities with the discourses of crisis and emergency were striking.

Since April 2005, much has changed in the world, including deepening military entanglements in the Middle East, an ever-expanding "global war on [Islamist] terror," and no less than the near-collapse of the global economy in late 2008. These changes have led us (like many others) to examine not only Africa's but the United States' "place in the world." Scholars from a variety of political perspectives now openly debate whether the United States remains an imperial power or beacon of free-market capitalism, or is becoming simply one nation within a larger system, caught in the clutches of world recession. Even former U.S. Treasury Secretary Alan Greenspan, an architect of the Washington Consensus and one of the fiercest defenders of free-market ideology, recently conceded that perhaps he had gone too far in advocating extreme deregulation. As a meltdown in the mortgage market, which brought down several titans of finance capital in early September 2008, turned into a credit crisis, and then the American economic downturn went global, one could no longer speak of the African continent as a place uniquely and exclusively plagued by volatility, or, for that matter, corruption. For financial and, indeed, moral crisis seemed to have spread to every corner of the globe. As the wars in Iraq and Afghanistan and the U.S. "war on terror" have dragged on, we have witnessed some of the most flagrant civil and human rights violations in U.S. history—most notably, at the offshore prison for terror suspects in Guantánamo Bay, Cuba—leaving many around the world to question more aggressively U.S. positions on human rights in such fraught locales as Darfur, Congo, and Ivory Coast.

The global credit crisis has been spectacular—our knowledge of its contours and proportions, scale and implications remain to some degree unknown, even as economists and financial commentators begin (as of this writing) to offer tremulous assurances that the recession is "over." The matter of preexisting disparities, to which we have all become inured, is perhaps less impressive, and yet its contours and proportions, scale and implications are surely as immense. Further, these phenomena are of course mutually implicated. It is precisely the degree of speculation and volatility in the global economy that has generated winners and losers, haves and have-nots. So what we observe in the global South—in African metropolitan centers, conurbations, and megacities—is the articulation of instability both local and global that has produced an elite with untold amounts of wealth, on the one hand, and a growing underclass attracted to the capital, opportunity, and anonymity of the city, on the other. As much as Cape Town and Dakar, to take just two examples, have seen an explosion of self-built, irregular, and impermanent housing on their peripheries, built by rural migrants seeking better lives, these urban centers are also sites for the construction of new boutiques, hotels, and casinos for the jet-set who have capitalized on global asymmetries.

These questions—of continuity and change, power, inequality, and volatility—organize this volume and direct our attention toward those politics, processes of subject formation, and enduring forms of value through which African subjects craft meaningful lives.

The original participants for *After Afro-Pessimism* included Adam Ashforth, John Comaroff, Carol Greenhouse, Brian Larkin, Charles Piot, Janet Roitman, and Jesse Shipley. To these, a great debt, intellectual and personal, is owed. Their comments and contributions gave significant shape to this book and to the central ideas in it, and we would like to express again our appreciation for their insights. The present volume includes some of these contributors and adds others. The latter joined the project as it evolved, in a sense picking up the conversation where we left off in April 2005.

The Princeton conference was made possible with the generous support of many departments, centers, and individual sponsors at Princeton University. These include the Program in African Studies, the Center for African American Studies, the Department of Anthropology, the Department of English, the Office of the President, the Council of the Humanities, the Princeton Institute for International and Regional Studies, the Princeton Society of Fellows in the Liberal Arts, the Princeton University Public Lecture Series, and the Shelby Cullom Davis Center for Historical Studies.

In developing the present volume, the editors first and foremost owe thanks to each other, and to our co-contributors, for their hard work in the hardest of times: bearing with us through long processes of submission and revision, all against the demanding backdrop of professional and personal upheavals and rites of passage. Our thanks are also due to Nathan MacBrien at the University of California, Berkeley, the editors' editor, and to a number of anonymous reviewers who gave of their time to constrain us to move the work towards intellectual synthesis. Finally, our personal acknowledgements: Beth would like to thank the College Arts and Humanities Institute at Indiana University for a semester-long fellowship that enabled her to work on this volume. Stephen sends his love and thanks to Laura, Liam, Finn, and Ciara for their forbearance and support in seeing this long project into print. Anne-Maria wishes to thank the Shelby Cullom Davis Center for Historical Studies at Princeton University for providing the space and time for work on this manuscript. She dedicates these pages to the memory of her late mother, Rosemary Sansom-Makhulu—a woman of great intellect and wit—and to her father, Walter Paul Khotso Makhulu, who persists in his tireless work with and love for a truly wondrous continent.

A.-M.M., B.A.B., and S.J.

Foreword

In Praise of Afro-Optimism:
Toward a Poetics of Survival

Simon Gikandi

This project represents and explores the implications of the cauldron in which Africans find themselves at the limits of modern culture—its premises, promises, and the inevitable disappointments that emerge when the most marginalized subjects in the world system come face to face with the most privileged. This cauldron emerges out of the series of ironies, paradoxes, or simply reversals that characterize Africans' being-in-the-world, to use a term associated with Martin Heidegger, and one that the editors and contributors to this volume constantly turn to as they try to mark out the geography of working hard in difficult times.

The paradoxical relation of African subjects and global capitalism constitutes one of the great narratives at what one may call the edge of modernity. On the one hand, African subjects, even in the battle zones of eastern Congo or northern Uganda, are known to be the most enterprising peoples in the world. They have invested heavily in the modern dictum that work liberates the self and raises its horizons of expectation. Indeed, if we accept Charles Taylor's famous claim that a key signature of modernity was the "new value put on commercial activity and money-making in the eighteenth century," then it could be said that African workers are the last economic beings in the modern sense of the word (Taylor 1992:286). It is work and the set of economic activities it generates, the modes of social organization it supports, and the variety of subjectivities that it sustains that leads Africans on perilous journeys to Europe, North America, and, most recently, India and China.

On the other hand, however, there is no guarantee that hard work leads to good times or to a higher level of human existence. For many Africans, the search for work in the European or American metropolis often leads to hard times, to diminished returns, lower expectations, and radical disenchantment. Where one would expect the African self to be enhanced by work, or vocation to lead to fulfillment, all we see are constant legal and social impediments, the often systematic and brutal blockage of desires, and ultimately what appears to be the crippling of agency. Where globalization should have opened new horizons of expectations or created alternative temporalities to deracinated localities, it only seems to reproduce familiar disabilities—poverty, isolation, and social disability.

In this context has emerged what has come to be known as Afro-pessimism—a radical sense that the ideals of progress and fulfillment associated with the narrative of modernity are doomed to fail when applied to Africa or African subjects. The play of terms suggested by the title of this book, namely the intersection of hard work and hard times, often seems to reinforce the sense that Africa is hopelessly imprisoned in its past. Increasingly, even among the people charged with mapping a new path for African development and the re-imagination of alternative futures, one hears the persistent worry that there might be something wrong with the African character. Comparisons are often made between African countries such as Ghana and Kenya and the Asian "tigers," most notably Korea and Malaysia, which were considered to be on the same level of development at independence and to have undertaken the same path to modernity: How does one explain the fact that Ghana and Kenya continue to be locked within the vicious cycle of underdevelopment while Korea and Malaysia seem to have met the standard of modernity associated with the advanced capitalist countries? The people whom Jomo Kenyatta once called the "professional friends of the African" have been busy providing answers to these questions, and many have turned it into a career; development is one of the most lucrative businesses among the impoverished (Kenyatta 1962:xviii).

But often missing in debates about development and underdevelopment, discourses that reinforce the metalanguage of Afro-pessimism even as they seek structural adjustments and transformations, is a new language for thinking about African lives as imaginative and redemptive. Analysists of the so-called African condition have no place for these vectors of African life that might point a way out of the language of crisis and failure—the role of the social imaginary, vocabularies that are derived from the lived experiences of agents, and social practices that recode the values and presuppositions of the analysts themselves. This book is remarkable precisely because it takes up these vectors and brings them to the heart of social science.

The contributions presented here stand out for acknowledging the persistence of structures and institutions but also striving to go beyond them. A starting point for the project is a recognition that it is not enough to present the most thorough ethnographic accounts of African life and assume that these will lead to a better understanding of postcolonial crisis. The editors and contributors recognize that beyond the sets of claims that have emerged from African lives observed in the field and outside the usual zones of research, analysts must seek a way out of older vocabularies and categories that already presuppose an insurmountable crisis.

To put it another way, if we presuppose that the African condition is one of perpetual crises, our modes of analysis will not simply be trapped in the language of catastrophe but will tend to confirm its existence. Afro-pessimism is hence more than a state of mind; it has become a theoretical problem. It has developed a logic or structure that has determined how Africa is conceived, imagined, or represented in the Western narrative of progress. Among a generation of Africans born a decade after independence, many coming of age in the period of postcolonial failure, signs and figures of crisis constitute what Achille Mbembe would consider to be the referential code for postcoloniality and its banality (Mbembe 2001:102).

In fact, having been surrounded for two generations by the signs of decayed institutions, the debris of a failed infrastructure, and corrupt and unjust systems of governance, it is difficult to imagine Afro-optimism as the engine that drove narratives of African identity in the age of decolonization. For this reason, the contributors to this volume are right to recognize Afro-pessimism as an existential and theoretical problem, one that threatens to sweep away the last remnants of the narrative of decolonization, which was, as Frantz Fanon aptly noted, the condition of possibility of a new African subject.

Still, figures of crisis cannot be wished away. They are the quintessential signifiers of the hard times discussed in the essays collected here. Not even dreams about hard work in Europe and America will suppress the power of pessimism about the place of the African subject in the new global order. Where the problems are real and palpable, where violence and death are constant reminders of why citizens cross boundaries in search of a better life in an imagined elsewhere, Afro-pessimism provides a much more compelling metalinguistic code than the stories of development and progress of an earlier generation. In fact, the romance of decolonization appears outdated as we increasing turn to the tragic matrix as the only logical explanation of postcolonial failure (Scott 2004).

And yet, to argue that postcolonial futures are trapped in the time and logic of empire, or to privilege Afro-pessimism as the explanatory code for the African crisis, represents not so much a singular lack of vision but a confusion of the signs of crisis with the lived experience of African actors and agents. The power of this book, then, lies in the collective effort to separate the signs of crisis as explanatory models from the lived experiences of African subjects who may find life hard but do not live in the enclosures of despair. I could go even further and argue that what is being demonstrated here is how African subjects have actually developed methods (most of them through popular culture and performance) that separate the crisis of lived experience from the imaginative goals and desires of actors and agents.

Consider, for example, the relationship between hard times (the signs of the crisis) and its reversion into alternative modes of being-in-the-world. Why is it, the editors ask, that in spite of several decades of hard times, Africans have continued to survive and have sometimes thrived in zones of war and adversity? The answers the introduction and the individual contributions present leads to nothing less than a rethinking of the nature of African knowledge and a portentous path outside the discourse of crisis. Obliged to contend with destructive circumstances and what the editors in their introduction call "contexts of sustained and deeply volatile constraint," African actors have "elaborated new modes of being-in-the-world, new forms of cultural praxis with both material and existential consequences."

When banks collapse in Africa, citizens figure out new modes of banking. When institutions of governance or justice are in crisis, citizens find detours around them. By a sleight of hand, perhaps, African subjects have been able to cope with global crisis because globalization has, for many of them, been a state of crisis. More than structures and institutions, the modern African "social imaginary" (Taylor 2004:23–24) has enabled tactics and strategies of survival that have enabled them to counter the harshness of everyday life; in turn, this has led to the fashioning of new subjectivities amidst what the editors describe as disjuncture.

This project is also an attempt to transform the vocabularies of African social life by rethinking the grammar of everyday life, the small gestures of existence (de Certeau 1984). It is significant that in the essays collected here, the forces of change or markers of agency are often to be found in sites that seem to question the tools of analysis that we have inherited from our disciplines, especially those that associate modernity and modernization with rationality and formal organization. The production of African knowledge, or knowledge about Africans, continues to face two problems, which this volume goes a long way to address. The first is the relationship between theories and explanatory frameworks and their objects of analysis. Whether we are dealing with major schemes aimed at reducing poverty or the culture of human rights, we confront a situation in which African experiences appear extraneous to the models developed to explain them.

When, for example, we talk about failed states in Africa, we assume that there is a model of a successful state and that African institutions have failed to live up to this model; rarely do we confront the essential historical fact that with rare exceptions, African states were invented at the conference of Berlin, that they were essentially colonial structures, and that even in postcoloniality, they did not have legitimacy. Painful and violent as they may be, the civil strife taking place in many African countries is an attempt to reconfigure the map drawn at Berlin. Furthermore, when we discuss the role of the state and institutions of governmentality, rarely do we listen to the voices of the governed, the stories they tell themselves, and their moral economies. We no longer seek to learn their languages, so that even when we claim to have done fieldwork among the so-called subaltern, we are reproducing a discourse that is heavily mediated by elites and other native informants.

A second problem concerns the monological nature of knowledge production in Africa. Once upon a time, in the first two decades of African independence, local institutions of knowledge production thrived. There was an Ibadan and Dar es Salaam school of history. There was a Makerere and Nairobi school of literary studies. Cheik Anta Diop's IFAN project in Dakar was different from Godfrey Wilson's Rhodes Livingstone Institute. These sites did not necessary produce knowledge that was essentially divorced from Western concerns, but in significant ways they created diverse forms of knowledge that also served as important counterpoints to the epistemological framework developed elsewhere to explain Africa. Walter Rodney's controversial *How Europe Underdeveloped Africa* could not have existed if there wasn't a Dar es Salaam school of history, a state that broadly supported the Marxist historiographic project, and a local publishing house willing to take risks with the insurgent text.

One could, of course, argue that this African knowledge was still marginal in relation to Western institutions, but it is important to note that this knowledge was not marginal in relation to Africa. So long as they worked in an African context or environment, scholars, even those wedded to European epistemologies and methodologies, functioned in a "habitual environment" that assumed an African audience (Irele 2001:xii). Africa-based scholarship was often committed to the production of knowledge for Africans. Since African institutions no longer offer significant counterpoints to knowledge that is extraneous to Africa, a book that seeks to create an alternative explanatory space for the articulation of African experiences is also producing another site of knowledge, a space where the efforts taken by Africans to contend with globalization are foregrounded and the figures of crisis, fashionable among those who make livings out of the misery of others, is put in context.

Is it significant that the informing philosophical principle of this collection is the Heidegerrian notion of "being-in-the-world"? Does this represent a turn from epistemology to ontology? None of the essays in this collection explicitly engages with Heidegger's notion of being, but this project is guided by the notion that the authors are concerned with African actors who, quoting the introduction once again, have "elaborated new modes of being-in-the-world, new forms of cultural praxis with both material and existential consequences." As a collective enterprise this book sets out bring "to light forms of being-in-the world that do not necessarily represent the kind of radical agency that many assume to be the subject of social theory."

If there is an actual turn to ontology here, then this collection has staked a significant position in social theory. How else can one study African subjects except in the conditions one finds them? The editors and contributors may not share this faith in ontological claims, but their focus on human activities, on simple acts of being, or "the everyday coping skills that form the basis of all intelligibility" is a significant one (Dreyfus 1991:3). As Heidegger put it in *Being and Time,* "Being lies in the fact that something is, and in its being as it is; in Reality; in presence-at-hand; in validity" (Heidegger 1962:26).

For those struggling to imagine and conceptualize Africa outside the rhetoric of failure and a scholarly dogma attached to old mythologies about African disability, this book will be indispensible. As it takes up acts of struggle in the informal settlements of Cape town, the genius of survival in the eastern Congo, popular culture in Ghana and Côte d'Ivoire, the politics of devotion in Mali, the global networks of Muslim traders from Senegal, this volume inscribes Africa not simply as an object of analysis or a figure of crisis, but as a subject already engaged in powerful and imaginative gestures of copying and survival. Social science has given us powerful and compelling studies of postcolonial failure, but it has not adequately recognized the poetics of survival that animates African being in hard times. This book provides a solid analysis of what these hard times are and the challenges they present, but it also foregrounds the poetic and imaginative ways in which African subjects seek a future outside the prison house of late capitalism.

1. Introduction

Anne-Maria Makhulu, Beth A. Buggenhagen,
and Stephen Jackson

> This is to argue, therefore, for a certain kind of creativity. It is
> still free-floating, however, unless we can specify the human base
> from which it springs and its particular form of work on the world,
> its form of praxis.
>
> PAUL WILLIS (1981:123)

By early 2007 the fishermen of Los Cristianos, in the Spanish Canaries, were all too accustomed to seeing members of the Red Cross delivering first aid to hundreds of young West African "castaways" huddled on the nearby beach (Wynter 2006).[1] European tourists, by contrast, were stunned to see narrow boats packed with young migrants coming on shore, not least because *pirogues*—long, open craft, painted with vivid Muslim iconography—were clearly built for fishing in domestic waters and had never been intended as transoceanic vessels, nor, for that matter, for trade in human cargo.

This new Atlantic route, the journey from the West African coast to the Canaries, has been compared by Senegalese intellectuals to the Middle Passage (see Harrow 2007), underscoring the magnitude of the exodus from Africa's mainland as much as the loss of life from drowning, hypothermia, and psychosis along the way.[2] Yet while in West Africa, local leaders and NGOs sought to turn the tide of "Europe madness" (Godfrey 2006), among migrants who entertained the dangerous journey to the North, many carefully weighed the risks and potential returns the Atlantic passage promised: employment, the extension of state welfare, public health-care, and schooling, to mention only a few benefits of European asylum. And since at home overfishing of local waters by French, Japanese, and Chinese trawlers (Sy 2006)—negative portents of global capital and its vast reach—had eviscerated the livelihoods of many and had deepened an already pervasive sense of insecurity, the decision to take to the high seas seemed not without merit.[3]

Though diminishing opportunities in Senegal and elsewhere along the Atlantic may have encouraged some to monopolize on the emergent transatlantic trade—and here we refer specifically to those *agents* of this

1

new commerce—not all traffickers (*passeurs*), or the passengers in their care, issued from West African shores. Many who persisted in the risky journey came from places across the globe equally beset by the ravages of market capitalism. Despite appearances, then, this was not exclusively an African migration, but rather a movement of displaced populations crossing the continent and drawing from as far afield as Pakistan and Sri Lanka (Bilton 2006). Yet such migrations have come to be affixed to the image of desperate Africans—"twenty-first-century savages," perhaps, banging at the doors of European civilization and thereby replaying enduring stereotypes of dependency and helplessness. Why, despite its *longue durée* incorporation into global circuits of labor, capital and commodities, Africa remains particularly marked by such enduring images of "marginality" is one question that concerns us in this introduction, and which is woven throughout the contributions to this volume.

Two sorts of opportunists converged: those who chose to risk life and limb to enter Europe in search of work and new prospects, and those who chose the passage itself as a means of social mobility, turning to human trafficking as a brutal mode of production. Opportunists, perhaps; nevertheless, the interests of each—traffickers and those who they afforded passage—responded to the vagaries of the world system.

The relationship between hardship and productive activity is central to this volume. In a variety of ways, and for a number of reasons—including Cold War and post–Cold War machinations both internal and external, structural adjustment and other neoliberal nostrums imposed by the Bretton Woods institutions, thwarted or abortive "democratizations," and proliferating, often resource-based conflicts—many contemporary African societies have, by now, had to struggle through several decades' worth of "hard times." Obliged to contend with these contexts of sustained and deeply volatile constraint, to survive—and even, for some, to prosper within them—the African actors with whom our authors are concerned have elaborated new modes of being-in-the-world, new forms of cultural praxis with both material and existential consequences. These forms, as this introduction and our authors together will go on to argue, do not arise as a deliberate and deterministic form of response. As Willis (1981:4) argues, these arise "not simply as a set of transferred internal structures . . . nor as the passive result of the action of dominant ideology downwards . . . but at least in part as the product of collective human praxis."

Being-in-the-world within such tight constraints makes for "hard work" indeed. What does it mean to arrive at the gates of Fortress Europe having chanced the hazards of the ocean crossing? While some Senegalese almost immediately drew a comparison between the journey to the Canaries and the much older Middle Passage, the parallels did not end there. The effort to reach Europe's borders certainly reinscribed a relationship between North and South forged in the Atlantic slave trade and long sustained in the uneven relations that persisted after abolition, it hinted at a vestigial colonial dependency, and finally it suggested that efforts at reclaiming social and economic membership on a global scale were a corollary of Africa's political and economic exclusion, which has been and remains profound. However, this claiming of global membership and a parallel rejection of local attachments—some Senegalese concealed their official citizenship, casting their national identity cards into the deep waters[4]—turned on a paradox.

On the one hand, we likely can agree that global flows of images, technologies, currencies, commodities, and not least people have vastly accelerated in the last several decades, symptomatic of a whole web of new convergences and connections qualitatively different from the ones recently decolonized African nations sought to make as they joined the community of nations in the post–World War II era. This acceleration has encouraged the dissolution of old boundaries, state borders, and even national economies (LiPuma and Lee 2004). And yet newer forms of exclusion and disconnection have emerged simultaneously. James Ferguson, writing of the infamous case of two young Guinean boys whose bodies were recovered from the landing gear of a plane headed to Brussels from Conakry in August 1999 (Ferguson 2006; also see Bayart 2000),[5] has rightly argued that quite apart from the apparent "porousness" (Taussig cited in Ferguson) of borders, there is a very real, concrete, and insurmountable set of obstacles to crossing them. The frontier of the First World the boys sought to travel across "was anything but 'unreal' or 'elusive'" (Ferguson 2006:166). Then again, other aspects of these times—these neoliberal times inclined, of late, to meltdown and possible dissolution—suggest that our global regime is configured through a series of discordant categories: connection and disconnection, admission and inadmission, opening and closure.

Consider the discourse of global "integration"—*market* integration, that is, and less the assimilation of populations through free and unfettered movement unless, of course, such migrations directly serve the needs of capital (Hardt and Negri 2000). Policies of "deregulation," which imply an unobstructed passage for commodities and flows of capital in a world primed in the generation of exchange values, are one way in which markets are integrated. But deregulatory policy is uneven. Some national markets are forced to relinquish sovereign control, as in the case of oil producing nations like Angola, Nigeria, and Sudan, while others continue to hide behind a web of protections. In the Democratic Republic of Congo (DRC), the deregulation of the industrial mining sector during the 1980s, encouraged by the World Bank, laid the ground for the violent atomization of natural resource exploitation (around diamonds, gold, tantalum, and many other commodities) during Congo's decade of conflict, beginning in 1996. Not the least striking effect of this radical "opening up" of the Congolese economy was the immediacy with which price shifts on international metal markets were experienced viscerally by artisanal miners on the ground in eastern DRC (Jackson, this volume; see also 2002). The United States' agricultural export policy represents another example of unevenness; hedge funds another. These operate in an almost entirely deregulated space, effectively superseding and exceeding national borders altogether. Thus, while the old command economy is gone, organizations like the WTO have, in a sense, taken its place adjudicating "the system of exchange more than others" (Blunt 2004:320).

Further, where demands for austerity in the governance and oversight of Third World nations meet First World disregard for profligate national spending, we can only wonder at the distinction between rhetoric and reality. Nor do such oppositions between First and Third Worlds, North and South even begin to broach the utterly deregulated space in which credit derivatives function as vehicles of capital transfer—lightning fast, more or less untraceable, and, as Warren Buffett has observed, circulating with deadly force as "financial weapons of mass destruction." What is certain is that we live in a world in which the overall system of command operates through inconsistency, and that those inconsistencies play a hand in producing stark oppositions between haves and have-nots, between the wealthiest and poorest nations, between those empowered to seize control of the global order and those who appear, at least, to be mere bystanders.

This volume, then, sets out to explore the contexts and motivations behind the often drastic measures taken by Africans to contend with large-scale economic and political transformations on the continent and beyond, whether driven by structural adjustment, cycles of regulation and deregulation (with their globalizing aftershocks), the push to "open" democratic space to the uncertain winds of "democratization," the increasingly rapid and prolific movements of commodities, arms and people, or the global impact of the West's "war on terror." To this end, presented in this volume are seven ethnographic cases that speak to the variety of tactical modes of being-in-the-world people adopt within contexts of "hard times"—when fiscal austerity, deriving from neoliberalist imperatives, mix with post–Cold War and postcolonial politics, all too often marked by an upsurge in violence.

We argue that these cases together address a number of contemporary theoretical debates in anthropology and African studies. Should we be thinking about "crisis," "state failure," "instability," or "social breakdown" as somehow directly determining particular practices among African actors, or is there a case to be made for highlighting a diverse set of activities that might in and of themselves provide insights into the conditions generally associated with neoliberal policies in Africa at a time of global and local volatility? Are these practices merely "coping strategies," or do they have the potential to transform the conditions in which they first emerged (see Tostensen et al. 2001; Vigh 2008)? And in what ways can a detailed examination (through "thick description") of such everyday pragmatics lead to a clearer understanding of how new forms of subjectivity and self-sovereignty are fashioned?

FASHIONING NEW SUBJECTIVITIES AMID DISJUNCTURE

While the essays in this volume argue against discourses of African marginality, they all, in different ways, start from a concern with the disjunctures and contradictions of the contemporary *dispositifs* of power—between the emergent "global order" and individual states, particularly in Africa, and between those states and their citizenries—and the kinds of pragmatics that these engender and reward. In Togo, for example, "'lotto visa' has become a major cultural event in the last ten years," as Togolese attempt to secure passage to the United States for themselves, their spouses, and children, through the U.S. Department of State Diversity Lottery held to increase the number of immigrants from underrepresented countries within the global South (Piot, this volume). Meanwhile, Murid Senegalese traders who travel between Brooklyn and Dakar build complex chains of exchange—regularly converting commodities and currency—and thereby defying import-export tariffs, on the one hand, and the undesired attentions of immigration and customs authorities, on the other (Buggenhagen, this volume). Efforts to surmount the many impediments to the unrestricted movement of people and things is perhaps all the more extraordinary for the ways in which the transmogrification of value, so central to Murid trade networks—in Marx's famous dictum, "buying in order to sell"—spans a vast transatlantic geography.

There is often a spatial and scalar logic to these practices of survival. In the eastern DRC, afflicted by more than fifteen years of violent instability, dynamic processes of repackaging, reinvention, division, multiplication, and disaggregation of already limited resources take place within the broader context of a societal involution,[6] an "inward and involved elaboration of cultural forms—whether economic, organizational, political, or symbolic—within overall stasis or, even, decline" (Jackson, this volume). An essential ingenuity (even a "genius") is at work on the part of Congolese who succeed in making what Guyer describes as "marginal gains" (2004), even as postwar Congo remains wracked with volatility. In South Africa, similarly, joblessness and homelessness—stark realities of the post-apartheid neoliberal order—encourage hyperpragmatism in matters of money, household thrift, and austere self-discipline (Makhulu, this volume). Here, too, survival relies on practices of division, subdivision, and repackaging of preexisting commodities and resources, while innovations in money lending practices have steadily indebted many. Debt remains a particularly important instrument for South Africa's poor, even in an era in which credit derivatives have desubstantiated the global financial sector. Far distant from the gleaming office towers and converted warehouses of Canary Wharf and Wall Street, poor Capetonians mobilize debt vehicles of their own, albeit on a minute scale. They do so in efforts to bridge shortfalls in household income, much as Murid traders juggle commodities and money, through an infinitesimal division of preexisting units of credit.

The "hard work" of concern to us speaks to aspects of social, physical, economic, spiritual, and imaginative labor and highlights the ways in which daily productive activity, amidst volatility and constraint, always involves political stakes. The vivid world conjured by Ghanaian hiplife music, for example, is profoundly pragmatic (Shipley, this volume). Its subjects are mercurial and performative and yet at the same time measured in their assessments of the limits of the possible. Ghanaian youth are no longer wed to the old modernist master narrative—to history as dialectical materialism—and their contemporary time dimension seems to bank on a future without a specific endpoint. In a time-space seemingly defined through indirection or an absent telos, their music, as much as their actions, raises important questions about the nature of the political subject in the postcolonial world.

The sartorial and religious practices amongst groups of Malian Muslim women (Schulz, this volume), the "transgressive" poetics—musical, stylistic, political—of hiplife's stars and audience (Shipley), and the volatile politics of street mobilizations in the recent civil war in Côte d'Ivoire (McGovern): these separate phenomena might appear to stand in radical contrast to one another. But in each instance, the actors at hand are engaged in a deliberate form of "self-writing," fashioning new self-sovereignties and political subjectivities within structures and moments of constriction. The context for these meaningful practices is not only a deepening financial crunch felt across much of Africa, but also a recognition that the liberalization of the state and, most importantly, its forms of media (such as radio and television) have not resulted in the forms of transparency and equity promulgated by advocates of the intertwining of democratic reforms and free markets. Within such rapidly transforming contexts, then, Malian women are subtly exploring the potentials and limits of their changing dispositions within Islamic public discourse and their otherwise conventional relationships to piety and moral conduct, implicitly critiquing political and religious authority. Ghanaian musicians are testing the boundaries of multiple social realms through a sensual (and yet often also censorious) politics. In Côte d'Ivoire, one can trace a "genealogy of violent play" (McGovern, this volume) in the parallels between the emergence of *coupé décalé*—a trickster club music emerging among the Ivorian diaspora in European nightclubs and reimported to Abidjan—and the staged violence of Ivorian youth militias. Both spheres, dance and delinquency, have provided young Ivorians an "ability to carve out spaces of *jouissance* in the face of diminished opportunity and real precarity." The metacommunicative frame of "play" has allowed both to prosper aesthetically and economically within a context of radical constraint.

TESTING THE LIMITS: CREATIVITY AMID CONSTRAINT

> People do not always resist the constraints in which they find themselves, nor can they reinvent themselves freely in cultural constructions of their own choosing. Culture refashioning and culture change go forward continually under variable, but also highly determinate, circumstances. These may further creativity or inhibit it, prompt resistance or dissipate it.
>
> ERIC WOLF (1997:xiii)

A common feature on display in each of these different contexts is a sense of "testing the limits" of the possible, of exploring through everyday practice and imagination a (sometimes tentative) emancipatory politics of the self, shaping and reshaping the African subject, one that remains, at times, surely somewhat "inchoate" (see Smith and Mantz 2007:73). In any given week, a resident of Goma in the DRC might just as well serve in one or another local militia as work for an NGO (Jackson, this volume).

"Polyvalence"—becoming multipurpose—is a natural response, a subject in open stance toward the constraints and opportunities of a world turned upside down by protracted conflict, volatile politics, and economic turbulence. The contemporary Ghanaian public sphere produces subjects keen to test their self-definitions against their image of global hip-hop, with its bling and bluster. Even as it remains impossible to realize the dreams of fast cars and large mansions, young Ghanaians, well aware of their circumstances and adjusting accordingly, nonetheless dream on, engaging fantasies of connection to global currents and currencies (Shipley, this volume).

Malian women organizing within Islamic NGOs and other movements, meanwhile, also embody a very careful assessment of the possible—a pragmatic politics of religiosity—that reaches only as far as the boundary of modern Islam in Mali will allow. The effect is in some fashion subtly to reshape and redefine their role *as* women and as subjects of Islamic theology (Schulz, this volume). Côte d'Ivoire's violent street politicians, meanwhile, demonstrate an ironically heightened and "playful" understanding of the violence in which they engage. Winkingly, they know that this "metacommunicative bracketing of violent political action" (McGovern, this volume) frees a person or group to undertake acts they would otherwise condemn. Unlike in other conflicts nearby in the region, they push the boundaries imposed by the metacommunicative frame but rarely cross them.

Collectively, then, the essays here bring to light forms of being-in-the-world that do not necessarily represent the kind of radical agency that many assume to be the subject of social theory—heroic and enterprising, not least thoroughly individual. Instead, our contributions present forms of collective praxis with ambiguous consequences for the contexts in which they arise.

The book's aim is thus to theorize the social experiences and political imperatives of our interlocutors based on the ethnographic insights of our contributors. Common themes and problematics organize the essays. Exodus and (im)migration are one set of strategies and signal a desire for global membership often in circumstances in which the national space no longer affords adequate care or security. By contrast, in those instances in which people choose of necessity to stay put, practices of fragmentation and division do a certain kind of work for people living in conditions of grave scarcity. And we see the division and repackaging of commodities and other objects of daily consumption both in the domestic domain and in local markets and transatlantic networks. Bundling and rebundling on scales large and small appear consistent with the logic of capital. Thus, on the one hand the redefinition of citizenship and belonging plays a key role in what Bayart (2000) has described as Africa's relations of extraversion—the continent's and its people's extension out into the global order[7]—and, on the other, the creation of new commodity chains and opportunities for cash earnings that rely on an explicit calculus of the possible.

HEROICS OR DESPERATION IN A VOLATILE WORLD?

The story of exodus from West Africa to the Canaries that opened this introduction marks a first, brief account of the problem of Africa's "place-in-the-world" (Ferguson 2006) and the kinds of uneven relations between North and South it highlights. Indeed, as we shall see, what Africans "do" when faced with material scarcity, political instability, and cultural break-down is by no means straightforward—neither as an empirical nor as a theoretical matter.

Heroics or mere desperation: how ought we to think about and theorize emergent practices of survival that appear simultaneously to flirt with and deceive death? Are these merely desperate measures in response to hard times? Or is there a way of thinking about acts of desperation as *inspired*, calculated, tactical, or even strategic? Can we understand such practices as creative, and if so, can these constitute a "particular form of work on the world, [a] form of *praxis*" (Willis 1981:123, emphasis ours)? These questions stem from a certain latent anxiety of which we are as guilty as any scholars who try to make sense of a world in which social action seems to have taken on a certain indirection or inefficacy, particularly since the end of the Cold War, or of history, in Fukuyama's felicitous phrase. As the concrete in social theory has purportedly been extinguished, somehow politics itself has been replaced with a certain fascination or flirtation with death—the death of certainty, social determination, the master narrative, and even or perhaps most of all, the Subject. And while structuralism has demonstrated "its magisterial impasse" (Trouillot 2003:10) little has emerged to replace its grandiose, if at times paradoxical, framing of history and structure. To cite Neil Smith: "The Enlightenment is dead, Marxism is dead, the working class movement is dead . . . and the author does not feel very well either" (Smith cited in Harvey 1989:325).

We also find ourselves unable entirely to reconcile emergent practices of survival, with which this collection is concerned, with the unfolding of world history, which was intended to emerge by stages, one logically following the next, only to be confounded by working-class struggle. In the era of post-wage work, post-Fordism, and the neoliberal state (however unstable this particular formation might be of late), working-class politics are harder to locate, as are reasonable alternatives. Consider for a moment Mike Davis's recent claim that urbanization—which has been historically linked to the search for work, to proletarianization, and to industry—has for the first time since the industrial revolution become disarticulated. People across the globe continue to make the urban pilgrimage—to settle in what he refers to as "slums"—and yet those migrations happen mostly in the *absence* of wage work (Davis 2006).

The irony is that Marx—grandfather of the structuralism we seem so ready to dismiss—long ago expressed an interest, above and beyond his commitment to working-class struggle, with the minutiae of lived experience. He argued this was a source of radical potential for historical transformation, given the ways in which the everyday encounters of men and women with the objective world offered myriad opportunities for self-constitution (cf. Lüdtke 1995). Surely, this insight has important implications for a theory of survival, "acts of desperation" in the view of some, which might signify a form of practical activity. In the *German Ideology*, Marx argued that the imperative to satisfy basic needs led to the historic invention of the means to satisfy such needs through production, a process that in itself constituted a "historical act." But this "instrument of satisfaction . . . leads to new needs," and to the remaking of social relationships in the daily lives of men and women (Marx and Engels 1970:48–49; cf. Meillassoux 1981). So perhaps it is time to constitute a theory of survival and to address very seriously the consequences of the proposition that survival is a kind of fundamental ethical position.

While those who left West African shores, casting their official citizenship papers into the waters, might seem desperate, at home those who embarked on the journey to the Canaries were referred to in Senegal at least with some deference as *candidats*. They were nominated by families and neighborhoods where people saved collectively, sometimes for years at a time, to raise fares ranging from 400,000 to 500,000 CFA ($800–1,000) (Harrow 2007), often relying on rotating credit unions organized by and among women—a formula frequently heralded by NGOs as a panacea for African development (Makhulu, this volume). Such carefully crafted and long-term strategies stand in contrast to images of "emergency," the result not of panic but perseverance and striving over time to realize "marginal gains" (Guyer 2004). In short, these would seem to represent practices of subject formation and self-fashioning through financial management strategies that are currently so central to the culture of global capitalism. And here we wish to stress the critical significance of the *cultural* as much as the economic. Jane Guyer has astutely observed that the preoccupation with money in everyday life, particularly for the world's most economically marginalized, is a practice so habituated it is necessarily cultural and not simply mathematical. Indeed, "money is probably the single most important 'thing/good' in ordinary people's ordinary lives. Thinking about it, planning, consulting about and paying bills, not to mention worrying (that is producing a folk theory), takes more time and imagination than much else" (Guyer 1995:5–6).

In other words, that Africans face dire circumstances and respond with long-term and often ingenious plans speaks less to a putative crisis or breakdown outside capitalism's proper domain than to a set of long-term practices that aim to renegotiate the terms of austerity within that domain. Yet according to the discourse of NGOs seeking to expand microfinance and Grameen-style banking, especially among women left behind by migrants, one would have the mistaken impression that African women and men had engaged very little in micro-level financial management prior to the interventions of foreign donors (Stiansen and Guyer 1999:1). More generally, the international consensus—that is, the consensus of so-called experts, the media, and policy wonks—assumes that Africans have limited capacities of foresight and long-term vision. And yet clearly perseverance in the management of money to achieve forms of long-term social value, even during periods of mass volatility, stands not only as a response to crisis but as an end in itself producing new and unfolding forms, and, ultimately, generating new subjectivities and new politics, as each of the contributions to this volume demonstrates.

Having suggested, then, that the central *dramatis personae* of this volume more-or-less simultaneously embrace pragmatism and acts of the imagination—we acknowledge this may seem a contrarian even paradoxical view. Yet David Harvey, at least, sees these as mutually complementary endeavors, *required* even, for the work of the political to take hold. Of course the acts of imagination to which Harvey is committed are hardly those that transfix the hiplife artists and their fans who are the subject of Shipley's essay (see also Lipsitz 2006). Further, Ghanaian youth, as Shipley demonstrates, are likely to be fairly "sensible" about the conditions of their existence. Rather, Harvey is invested in those imaginative leaps that construct the possible, namely the "concrete potentialities and capacities immanent in what we already have" (Merrifield 2002:153). We think this particular recognition moves us somewhere important analytically, which is to say we stand behind the claim that the "creativity" we identify in the practices of transatlantic Murid traders, informal loan officers in Cape Town's squatter settlements, Ivorian youth, and Congolese powerbrokers, to mention a few, constitute "a kind of production" (Willis 1981:124). Further, although the kind of productive work African actors engage in achieves only "partial resolutions, recombinations, limited transformations" (ibid.), this is less significant than the fact that these have consequences, albeit uncertain ones, for the social order. While we do not have any notion how these stories will end, given a protracted history of attempts by Africans to "impose some form of control or closure on the world[s]" (Comaroff 1985:13) they experience, we can be certain that efforts to hedge against hard times will proliferate and persist.

ENCOUNTERING VOLATILITY

Notwithstanding our concern to examine the responses that people make to, and within the terms set by, prolonged and protracted periods of political, economic, and social constraint, the contributors to this volume each provide refutations of the proposition that "crisis x induces response y." Indeed, as we collectively argue, the very category of "crisis x" is not an adequately rich, nuanced, or politically and historically grounded understanding of the conditions and constraints within which the kinds of improvisation and innovation that interest us so centrally unfold. Rather, as we have suggested, the contributors explore a variety of tactical modes of life that arise within contexts of sustained volatility and long-term constraint on the political, economic, and social planes in contemporary Africa, and they ask what these can tell us collectively about how citizens of the continent have fashioned new subjectivities, new manners of "being-in-the-world."

As most of us carried out ethnographic research in the two key decades in which Africa, south of the Sahara, was most afflicted by the ravages of neoliberal adjustment, we think it necessary to say a few words about the neoliberal before we proceed. In acknowledging the concept's discursive and practical value we hope to move some distance beyond the claim that neoliberalism is "everything," or that what it subsumes are mere epiphenomena. As much as the global financial crisis of 2008 created uncertainty in the markets, it also created uncertainty about what it was that had broken down and what would come to replace it. Nor was it apparent that privatization and deregulation, important instruments of neoliberalism and the alleged causes of the meltdown, had been as extensive or as total in their reach as many purported them to be. Additionally, though efforts to comprehend the arcane operations of derivatives or subprime mortgages seemed to reflect a knowledge gap—though the U.S. Federal Reserve intervened in the crisis, did it really grasp the depth of the financial fallout or even the practical implications of a government bailout? For that matter, had neoliberalism met its limit? Immanuel Wallerstein argues that such debates are mere smoke and mirrors, that worrying about subprime mortgages obfuscates much larger cycles of boom and bust, and that even the current crisis should be considered a "short-term event," in the sense Fernand Braudel implied (see Arrighi 1994), that is to say, a short-term event within a much longer cycle of accumulation and collapse.[8]

The difficulty in identifying the root causes of the recent "global economic crisis" doubtless stems in part from an inability to articulate *what* neoliberalism is. For many, the term is overused and underspecified, for others worse still *over*specified, analytically weakened by its very capacity to subsume everything. Rather than dispute these diametrically opposed viewpoints, we think our project might be better served by focusing on the *uneven* purchase the term may have not only for our contributors, but more generally for almost anyone who chooses to use it. What we can agree on is that in the last several decades the capitalist world economy has been determined by a set of specific political and economic principles, while the degree of their penetration has been different in different national and regional contexts.[9] In other words, we are not concerned simply with the uneven uptick of the term but with its uneven effect. Indeed, some of our contributors would argue that in the contexts in which they work neoliberalism provides a backdrop against which other, more immediate pressures impinge: a violent postcolonial crisis that is at once one of identity and of authority, as in the cases of Côte d'Ivoire (McGovern) or the DRC (Jackson), or a latent political contest between institutionalized Islam and the transition to multipartyism, in the case of Mali (Schulz).

Indeed, even though the "neoliberal" narrowly defined consists in a series of economic policies, these have always and everywhere implied at least a de facto theory of the political. This is as true of the neoconservatives and their preoccupation with "freedom" and "free markets" in L. Paul Bremer's Iraq as it was, two centuries before, in the eighteenth-century England of Locke and Smith, whose ideas regarding free markets and the social contract (or the civil polity) necessarily theorized the economic and the political together (Locke 1980; Smith 1977). In the post–Cold War conjuncture, democratization, good governance, and multipartyism in the former colonial world have collectively constituted the "Washington Consensus," touted as the remedy to war, violence, and civil unrest, most particularly for conflicts that have emerged alongside the introduction of new market fundamentalisms and yet often enough have been understood in essentialist terms.[10] What this has signified for Africans in particular is in major part the subject of this collection.

One final point concerns the recent volatility in the global financial markets (Miyazaki 2007; Zaloom 2006; also see Makhulu, this volume). True, the collapse of Lehman Brothers, the Fannie Mae and Freddie Mac takeovers, the AIG bailout, the temporary freeze in credit markets, and the regulation and restructuring of investment banks have together highlighted the failures of neoliberalism, that is to say, at a technical level, and for that matter as a problem of an algorithmic sort (see Bernstein 2005). The $700 billion government bailout in the United States and the seizure of banking institutions worldwide left many U.S. pundits in 2009 arguing that we were witnessing a brand of economic socialism reminiscent of a bygone era. Yet even as those critics of "big government" contend that it is not the responsibility of the state to bail out banks or for that matter homeowners, we would question the underlying assumption that the "state" and "capital" have operated as independently of each other as free-market proponents have maintained, at least since the fiscal crises of the 1970s. As we have already suggested, it is not clear that neoliberalism ever operated by the ideals it espoused. To declare something so protean at an end is perhaps to miss its persistent ability for transmogrification. Just as we can be certain that Africans will persist in their efforts to shore up risk, we can be equally certain that instability, blind faith, superstition, and greed—to name only a few "explanations" for the current financial crisis—are not particularly African.

LIVING ON THE MARGINS

Sometimes the actors in this volume are engaged in specific practices in direct response to the predicaments they face. Other times, they are doing so precisely in spite of them. How they articulate those predicaments as moments of crisis is of central concern to our contributors, who seek to understand and to convey the questions that Africans are asking themselves about social, political, financial, and moral worlds. Thus, we look across sub-Saharan Africa to track different situations of constraint and different responses to such constraints, paying particular attention to the varied social, cultural, and moral horizons that order lived experience. What these contexts share is a certain indirection (see Shipley, this volume) that characterizes the post–Cold War moment everywhere, not least in Africa. And indeed, we would not be the first to cite the eclipsing of a political era in which Cold War allegiances and varied independence struggles allowed the political field to be delineated in far starker terms than is possible today (for example, see Kellogg 1987; Lash and Urry 1987; Harvey 1989; Fukuyama 1992; Derrida 1994; Sennett 2006; Comaroff and Comaroff 2000). The current climate involves a range of new social movements, multiple and often fractured identities, and struggles that seem to hinge on forms of politics less easily defined than they might once have been. Finally, we want to suggest that it is therefore unclear—to us as much as it may be to our interlocutors—the degree of one-to-one correspondence between circumstances and the hard work necessary to transcend those circumstances.

A number of scholars have posited that Africa's problems stem from its relatively marginal position in the world system (see, for example, Arrighi 2002; van de Walle 2001; Castells 1996). By contrast, we emphasize the forms of radical *inclusion*, albeit partial, unequal, and uneven (Ferguson 2006; Bayart 2000; Bond 2006a), that determine the continent's place-in-the-world. Historically a major source of raw materials—Congolese copper and uranium, Nigerian oil, Angolan diamonds, to list only a few—Africa's "failures" of economic integration have arisen less from any actual disarticulation from the global system than from a perceived incapacity to transmogrify raw materials into manufactured goods: to transform the object potential of coltan into cell phones, pulp into paper, or coffee beans into caffeinated brew. Moreover, the system of exchange has been historically controlled from beyond the continent's borders, thereby dictating the value of commodities produced in Africa. The price of coffee, after all, is determined not in Kenya or Tanzania but on global commodity exchanges.

As a consequence, Africa's place in the global commodity chain has been understood as structurally irrelevant, following Castells (1996), while the absence of any significant manufacturing sector (with the notable exception of South Africa's) has been judged indexical of the continent's location outside capitalism. But these uneven relations with the so-called "outside," relations that necessarily sanction all manner of predatory accumulation within resource-rich enclaves (Watts 2006), define an obvious site of *articulation* rather than exclusion. This has been the case at least since the emergence of the Atlantic slave trade. Indeed, arguably Africa is and has long been at the center of a confluence of global forces marked by a shift in modes of extraction through heightened militarization and a growing focus on corporate capital devoted to the production of oil, energy, and armaments (Smith 2004). As James Ferguson has observed, "it is worth asking whether Africa's combination of privately secured mineral-extraction enclaves and weakly governed humanitarian hinterlands might constitute *not* a lamentably immature form of globalization but, rather, a quite advanced and sophisticated mutation of it" (Ferguson 2005:380). Such niche economies are defined through instability, that is, both in terms of the internal dynamics that regularly give rise to the use of private security firms (Singer 2003), but also given general conditions of volatility that make those niches possible in the first place. Hence, counter to the policy imperative to create optimal circumstances for markets, specifically through practices of good governance, it may in fact be the case that free markets operate just as well in the near total *absence* of any form of governance whatsoever. Has Africa been a harbinger of things to come; has it foretold of the kinds of volatility that have recently come to define the financial markets?

While civil war may have destroyed many African economies, others have been constituted precisely *through* prolonged conditions of instability (Marchal 2004:115). For example, the ongoing political and economic crisis in the DRC has in some measure facilitated the extraction of coltan and diamonds and led to a lively cross-border trade in everything from precious metals to everyday necessities such as milk (Jackson, this volume). In Senegal, successive economic crises have been responsible in part for environmental devastation and fiscal restructuring, which, in their turn, have given rise to Murid parallel circuits, regionally and internationally, providing inexpensive consumer items and foodstuffs in times of high inflation and fiscal austerity (Buggenhagen, this volume).

INTERNAL UNEVENNESS

So far, we have stressed the uneven relations between sub-Saharan Africa and the former colonial metropolitan centers—those sites of industry, economy, and political domination, beyond the immediate sightlines of the African scene. Those relations between North and South—asymmetrical in every sense and the nature of which Andre Gunder Frank (1981) contended was in fact the condition of possibility of development in the North—are important to the story we and our contributors would like to tell, but by themselves they are largely insufficient. Africa has also been dogged by *internal* unevenness, and, specifically, by hierarchies of wealth that have emerged from the particular neoliberal regimes that have unfolded in each national context in the past twenty years or more. An apparent paradox: in many regions of the global South technology is available, yet somehow unevenly deployed. It is not uncommon to live with degraded roads on the one hand and cutting-edge cell phone networks on the other. These are the grounds on which struggles are fought over material survival as well as symbolic, ritual, and practical experience. Further, these are spaces in which conventional relations of wage and work, and labor and production, have for the most part dissolved, leaving in their place rather more immaterial forms of both money and commodities (see Makhulu, this volume).

Consider Senegal as one such illustration. This was the first African nation to undergo structural adjustment, in 1985. While some of those reforms were reversed during the early 1990s, beginning in 1994, and obeying IMF and World Bank prescriptions, Senegal achieved consistent GDP growth nearing 5 percent or more per annum (World Bank 2003). The new neoliberal moment has been marked by "Alternance," the defeat of some twenty years of rule by the Partie Socialiste in favor of President Abdoulaye Wade's 2000 campaign platform of economic liberalization, largely favored by young Senegalese who imagine these policies would earn them a share of the spoils. Upon his 2007 reelection, Wade moved aggressively to attract further foreign capital to Senegal. He struck deals for a new national airport project, led by the Saudi Binladin Group (Flynn 2007); a free-enterprise zone project driven by Dubai World that would extend across 10,000 hectares near the new Dakar International Airport (Rahman 2007); and sold new rights to iron-ore extraction in the southeast of the country to Arcelor Mittal, the world's largest steel producer, this in hopes of supplying China's growing need for metal ore.

In short, this is a country that has actually followed the neoliberal script. And from this perspective, the Senegalese and other West Africans who have made the perilous overseas journey in search of employment in Barcelona's construction industry[11] may have done so precisely given the new wealth being accumulated in Dakar—wealth to which ordinary Senegalese have little or no access. For indeed, it is not just Western capitalists and Chinese oil companies who are accumulating vast amounts of capital in the context of national instability. As the case of Dakar, among others, shows, there are always pockets of affluence amid the great fiscal austerity felt by the majority. In Dakar at least, the uneven effects of these developments are epitomized by the wall being built along the coastal highway, the Route de la Corniche. Here a steel barrier separates a growing French, Lebanese, Chinese, and Senegalese elite class of traders, business people, and politicians residing in beachside villas from the masses who reside in the *quartiers populaires*. All too clearly, "the millennial moment has passed without a palpable payback" (Comaroff and Comaroff 1999a:284) for those who must look on at the signs and symptoms of conspicuous consumption from the immiserated margins.

Of late, David Harvey has suggested we rethink global inequalities in terms of "accumulation by dispossession"—a mode of accumulation characterized by heightened levels of capital at one pole and deepening poverty at the other (see Harvey 2003; Frank 1981; Amin 1976; Rodney 1972). Further, many claim that such asymmetries are historically unprecedented (see Bond 2006a; Ferguson 2006; Klein 2007; Luxemburg 2003). To be sure, given the fast truck in luxury goods, and their images and signs, wealth appears ever more proximate, but it remains mostly inaccessible to the vast majority. And yet things are not quite as they seem: those who do hold the signs of wealth are just as likely to possess debt in equal measure, as the demise of Lehman Brothers and other big financial houses has foretold. In South Africa, where the national economy has been exponentially financialized since the end of apartheid, these claims ring perhaps truest; they do so too for the ordinary man who is more indebted today than ever before (Makhulu, this volume). South African society is also one of the most unequal in the world, and as the gap between rich and poor grows, policy interest in questions of "relative poverty" has grown (see Pillay 2006). It is also apparent from the South African case that wealth disparity is a great destabilizer, leading to civic unrest. And while the debate about violent crime rages, there are indications that property crime in particular has emerged as a mechanism of redistribution in the absence of any systematically implemented official policy of reallocation (see Steinberg 2001; Comaroff and Comaroff 2006).

ETHNOGRAPHY ON AN AWKWARD SCALE:
OUT OF SPACE AND OUT OF TIME

> This returns us to the problem of power in the motivation of
> historical practice itself—power material and symbolic, both
> concentrated and dispersed in the various domains of social action.
> For, ultimately, the logic of such sociocultural responses on the
> part of the oppressed resides in their attempts to impose some
> form of control or closure on the world. Their efficacy, however,
> both as efforts to subvert structures of domination and as cryptic
> but passionate statements of the human spirit, remains a matter
> of some controversy.
>
> JEAN COMAROFF (1985:13)

Hard Work, Hard Times is, then, concerned with how processes of expansion, innovation, and "productive technique" unfold in contexts of collapse, and how such processes enable practical investment in enduring forms of value. For many of our contributors, their ethnographic insights hinge precisely on exploring practices, subject formations, and modes of African being-in-the-world responsible for engendering substantively new cultural forms, even within the constraints of civil unrest or financial contraction. This has meant addressing ourselves to the task of thick description (Geertz 1973a), of accounting for lives lived amidst economic and political volatility as much as uneven, patchwork infrastructure.

This "thick description" had, necessarily, to be conducted on an "awkward scale" (Comaroff and Comaroff 1999a), standing analytically athwart local, national, continent-wide and global threads in order to capture their warp and weft in each context. The kind of "work on the world" that is possible from a Ghanaian locus, for example, differs radically from the sorts of productive techniques at the disposal of Congolese (now more than ever faced with deep and violent political instability). For some African actors the preoccupation with productive techniques of overcoming derives from the imposition of neoliberal policies and the fiscal austerity these require. This is certainly the case in South Africa and to some degree in Senegal and Ghana. Others will argue that the overarching framework of constraint in which African subjects operate arises out of a set of post–Cold War aftershocks, as "democratization" and the demise of the one-party state have given way to deep instabilities in the face of efforts to establish multipartyism. This is likely true of the DRC and Côte d'Ivoire, where an abundance of parties and acronyms to match suggests less a healthy system of representation than a proliferation of symptoms in the diseased body politic. Ivorians certainly have much to say about post–Cold War conflict. But of course violence comes in many forms, and by another measure South Africa, which is generally held up as a postcolonial success story, figures as a prescient tale of the continuities between colonial and postcolonial orders in which formerly sanctioned modes of violence have been transformed—"democratized," if you will—in the face of neoliberalism's grave disproportions of wealth and poverty.

Each of the essays in this volume, then, explores different slices at the issues presented above, as witnessed in a range of circumstances and milieus. Charles Piot considers the irregularities of the Togolese state and its relationship with the general population—at once repressive and weak, present yet incapacitated, and seemingly on the brink of dissolution or retreat. Piot argues that following several "false" coup attempts, withdrawal of World Bank and IMF funding, and efforts to liberalize Togolese markets in the post–Cold War period, this small West African nation became a shell of its former self. In the last decade or so, the U.S.

visa lottery has become increasingly significant for Togolese who aspire to emigration from West Africa, and many use the lottery in a bid to secure safe passage to the United States for themselves and their families. Indeed the U.S. Department of State Diversity Lottery figures prominently in fantasies of new lives and new prospects elsewhere.

Togolese must navigate the ever-shifting U.S. immigration and homeland security bureaucracy while at the same time negotiating rights in persons concerning which spouse and which children will accompany them. Here kinship and political economy collide as Togolese recipients of the lottery visa seek to gain by strategically accessing those multiple scales of value that are in play in the borderland spaces between West Africa and the United States.

> As with Atlantic African economic phenomena generally, "lotto visa" is an enormously inventive, entrepreneurial border practice, which has generated its own scales of value and pricing, and produced far-reaching networks of debt, rank, and clientage. These borrow from—though also innovate upon—conventional scales of value, price, rank, and debt. It is also a practice that bears the imprint of the post–Cold War neoliberal moment and its structural adjustments in West Africa, a moment of crisis that has fostered, among other things, cultures of duplicity and identity fabrication. As such, the green card lottery entails a set of practices that are symptomatic of Togo's place of relative "abjection" and marginalization—to borrow James Ferguson's phrase (Ferguson 1999)—from today's global economy, and might be read as a desperate attempt by Togolese at inclusion. . . . ["Lotto visa" draws on] all the resources and imaginaries of the moment, those of the post–Cold War conjuncture—of its felt crisis, of the eviscerated though-still-dictatorial state, of social death and the emptiness of citizenship under such conditions, of a sprawling transnational diaspora and the desires and longings it creates, of informationalism and its new technologies—to produce a generative fantasy about exile and citizenship and global membership. (Piot, this volume)

Stephen Jackson focuses on dynamic processes in the broader context of Kivutien involution—whether economic, organizational, political, or symbolic—within overall stasis or, even, decline. His discussion opens up a new analytic space in which to consider survival strategies operating against the backdrop of civil unrest, and specifically how such strategies have a tendency to take on spatial or "fractal" qualities. Readers are introduced to a lifeworld within and yet somehow beyond the long shadow cast by civil war, where the *Système D* (or *système de se débrouiller*)—a mode of fending for oneself—is a driving force in daily life. Here people are not merely "making do," they are actively debating the changing forms of the social person and social reproduction more generally. Hence, even while acknowledging a lengthy Congolese agon, Jackson's essay tells a compelling story about the ways in which African agents daily make possible the "continuation of creativity within collapse." Moreover, while the temporality of crisis always entails a short *durée*, Jackson argues (De Boeck 1996) that the "Congolese crisis of make believe" is part of a much longer historical sequence in which the gulf between what centralized forms of power do and what they say they do has provoked an ingrained skepticism and a space of productive opportunity. At Jackson's urging, then, we return to the site of the everyday without resort to celebratory language, acknowledging the ways in which the very real predicaments of ordinary life tend to impose forms of kindness and cruelty, concern and indifference.

In New York City, Beth Buggenhagen describes not entirely dissimilar activities amongst Muridiyya traveling between Brooklyn and Dakar who, she proposes, must build complex chains of value exchange—converting commodities and currency at every turn—thereby defying tariffs, on the one hand, and the undesired attentions of officials, on the other. Efforts to surmount the many impediments to the unrestricted movement of people and things is perhaps all the more extraordinary for the ways in which Murid transmogrifications of value, as already mentioned, span such vast transoceanic space. At the outset Buggenhagen describes the relationship between Murid soteriology—salvation through "sweat" (*naq*), previously generated by work in agricultural communes in service of the shaykh—and contemporary Muridiyya who direct their "sweat" outward to the global marketplace. Playing on the strengths of this tight-knit religious alliance and intertwining religious and commercial imperatives, Murid sidewalk traders in New York blur the distinction between activities deemed merely "illegal" and those deemed "terrorist," particularly in the post-9/11 context. Indeed, without such inventiveness Muridiyya fall prey more often than not to criminalization, arrest, and, worse still, to accusations of aiding terrorist networks based primarily in the Middle East.

As Buggenhagen's contribution shows, while Murid disciples defy attempts at the imposition of regulatory authority, weaving cargo and currency through official and unofficial spaces within the global economy, such practices do not necessarily undermine the state form itself (cf. Roitman 2005:18–19; Larkin 2004:297). In challenging legal regulations, globally and nationally, to stake out the slippery boundaries of licit, illicit, and, we would add, "terrorist" trade (cf. Roitman 2005), Muridiyya, like many other Africans, render the relationship between state and subject more complex, ambiguous, and multivalent rather than eviscerating it entirely. Thus, instead of emerging in the context of what scholars have called weak (Reno 1995), failed, failing (Kraxberger 2005), or even collapsed states (Zartman 1995), Murid economic activities, whether based in peanut monoculture or transnational trade, remain absolutely integral to the state itself precisely because they substitute for its diminishing resource distribution functions.

Anne-Maria Makhulu's essay probes the predominantly spatial or fractal logic of economic survival in South Africa. Unemployment, homelessness, and other stark realities of the post-apartheid neoliberal order have encouraged extreme financial pragmatism and austerity, enacted by dividing, subdividing, and repackaging preexisting commodities and resources. This is as true of urban market women who trade in small items such as individual sweets and chewing gums, cigarettes, and loose oranges, as it is of large contractors in the construction industry. A similar logic is at work in the formal post-apartheid housing sector. Privatized under the new post-1994 neoliberal regime, responsibility for the delivery of so-called public or low-income housing has been transferred to private corporations and in turn to those to whom large companies outsource contracts (in itself an act of subdivision and replication). Much as Senegalese Muridiyya act through complex private networks to redistribute resources—in a sense, operating as a religious corporation—South African private interests represent the state in matters of basic social goods such as shelter. But the consequences of this new market fundamentalism have been stark as housing size has radically decreased, while construction costs have soared. It is noteworthy that prices on the South African property market skyrocketed during the 1997–2004 period, in part an indication of broader, global speculation in real estate, which hit South Africa with a particular severity. Indeed, South Africa's revaluations were the world's highest, on the order of a 200-percent cumulative increase (see Bond 2006a:22). Thus, housing provision as one feature of a larger post-apartheid restitution process is now regulated less by the state than by the economy (cf. Hayek 1944). Other peculiar distortions have arisen to complicate the everyday struggles of ordinary South Africans. Debt, and the trade in debt, is one. In an era in which derivitization and securitization have effectively desubstantiated the global financial sector, debt remains a particularly important commodity for those at the grassroots. Poor Capetonians mobilize debt in order to shore up the inevitable shortfalls in household income, much as Murid traders juggle commodities and money, through an infinitesimal division of preexisting units of credit.

In a striking analytical move, Makhulu analogizes the financial strategies of Cape Town's squatter communities to those of Wall Street traders dealing in derivatives and now toxic securities. Residents of the Cape Flats invest their energies and passions in community saving schemes known as *umgalelo*. Within these tight networks, families scrimp and save, elaborating complex financial strategies that combine peer pressure, the cultivation of austerity, deferred gratification, and an almost religious asceticism with a keen calculus of cost, benefit, and risk. Families that save in *umgalelos* are engaged in a daily and seemingly unending struggle just to "get by" within a post-apartheid state characterized by a strong degree of what Makhulu identifies as "ideological incoherence"—sometimes pretending to neoliberal reform while continuing to provide some measure of a social safety net, sometimes speaking the language of the liberation movement while cleaving to the imperatives of the IMF. Within this uncertain terrain, those whose conditions of life "may be abject [are nonetheless] pragmatic subjects," necessarily working within abjection and "steadily redefining its conditions at every turn, exquisitely remaking the world around them, and at the same time debating the limits and limitations of their own conditions of possibility" (Makhulu, this volume).

We suggest that these different examples of repackaging, division, and reparceling are consistent with a broader neoliberal logic that appears to subject everything from credit instruments to real estate to routine fragmentation and dematerialization and must therefore be considered spatial in dimension. With the deterritorialization of sites of production, the fracturing of national space, and a general hypermobility of persons, capital, and things (Hardt and Negri 2000), the spatial has taken on a critical if phantasmagoric significance in the contemporary moment.

Time and tempo, temporality and history have undergone parallel but distinct transformations. For one, as many theorists have recently argued, and as we suggested at the beginning of this introduction, this is an era typified by the death of old certainties (Derrida 1994; Fukuyama 1992; Graeber 2001, to name but a few paradigmatic discussions) that range from ideology, history, the Subject, and even to grand theory. Of concern to the contributors to this collection are the ways in which African actors either seek to recuperate or reject outright conventional notions of teleology and historical efficacy, charting new courses in the face of structural ambivalence and ambiguity in a world after communism, after revolution, after the dissolution of utopian fantasies—opting at times for straightforward pragmatism, at times instead embracing risk and radical contingency.

Jesse Shipley's work on Ghanaian hiplife gestures at a deeply ontological sense of the world at its most post-teleological. His subjects are versatile, performative, and protean, and yet at the same time disposed to orient themselves to the world *sensibly* and to acknowledge their own "state of existence." No longer wed to the old modernist master narrative—to history as dialectical materialism—their contemporary temporality also seems to bank on a future without a specific endpoint. The analytical horizon of this changing temporality is a "crisis" both immediate *and* protracted: "crisis" here, as actually experienced, tends to have delimited temporal boundaries, but beyond Africa, African "crisis" seems permanent, ongoing, timeless (always with us), while the West remains (effortlessly) stable, productive, and capable of playing a hand in the resolution of Africa's predicament through intervention of one sort or another. To be sure, even this certainty, that is, the West's supreme sense of competency, has most recently dissolved. Taken together, these space-time dimensions seem to imply something distinctive about the current conjuncture, not least an eclectic sedimentation of different forms, a layering of different time-spaces, one on top of the other, often in incommensurate and yet co-present ways.

What "practices of self" are at stake in the making of African subjects, and what futures might these bring into being? How should we understand the localized forces and global visions that are generative of the transnational circuits of persons, goods, and ideas, and what impact might these have on social, literary, and other expressive forms at *home*, in the African societies from which they emanate? Shipley takes up these questions with respect to political agency and hiplife's emergence. Not merely a form of African popular music, hiplife draws its popularity from its ability to articulate concerns among youth about accumulation and masculine virtue within the neoliberal state. Not merely a new form of popular cultural expression, hiplife emerges out of Ghanaian "public oratory traditions of proverbial indirect speech from Akan chiefly courts" and translocal circuits of artistic expression spanning the Atlantic. It combines "older forms of highlife popular music and traditional storytelling and formal proverbial oratory, with hip-hop musical sampling, scratching, and rap lyricism." Here gender is key to hiplife's success as social critique precisely because it stands in contrast to female expression in Gospel music. Taken together the two artistic figurations demonstrate a concern for the production of persons, of wealth, and of social forms of family. Shipley leaves us with a vital question: "If the global market becomes the metaphor and economic structure of political hegemony, can the terms of market-driven, individuated accumulation reshape [African] critical agency?" (Shipley, this volume). In these times such questions challenge us to think about the ways in which ideas of social security and prosperity, well-being and welfare, have reentered the public debate, and yet to what degree these are realizable is difficult to say.

In her contribution, Dorothea Schulz examines the possibilities for a gendered critique of Malian political and religious authorities, and the process of subject formation from within the long shadow that these cast. Focusing less on questions of agency than political subjectivity, Schulz suggests that sartorial and religious practices among Malian Muslim women play an important if subtle role in their changing dispositions within Islamic public discourse. Taking as her fields of inquiry Islam's recent move to the heart of public controversy in Mali and the centrality of women to this process, she engages current critiques of "agency" that have come to dominate anthropological theorizing (Asad 2003). She suggests that despite the heightened presence of women in public ritual, there are clear limits to the political effects of their presence. In so doing, Schulz productively interrogates what can appear so appealing about religiously inspired discourses in (at least nominally) post-authoritarian African state politics.

In analyzing Muslim women's moral quests (and the sartorial and ritual forms these quests take) as one among many competing registers of political subjectivity in Mali's public sphere, Schulz not only moves us beyond a prevalent scholarly preoccupation with Muslim women's dress and the power inequalities this dress allegedly reflects, she also highlights the paradoxical nature of the developing dynamics of Muslim women's political interventions in Mali. In contrast with those analysts who suggest these demonstrate increasing public representation and participation (see for example Navaro-Yashin 2002; Göle 1996, 2002; Cinar 1998), she proposes that they defy reductive, linear interpretation and argues for careful exploration of the nexus between the reconfiguration of central parameters of political intervention and control, gender dynamics, and changing notions of political and religious subjectivity.

Finally, Mike McGovern discerns an Ivorian teleological concern with a decolonization that never took place, or that must, at least, be completed. The idiosyncratic terms of the relationship between postindependence Côte d'Ivoire under Houphouët-Boigny and France, its former colonial power, engendered in Ivorian street youth a revolutionary fervor, a leveling imperative that "was so bitter in large part because it had been so long delayed" (McGovern, this volume). The violence of the student activists broke forth within a space and time marked by "postcolonial malaise (a malaise aggravated by poverty, pervasive violence, and xenophobia)," but "counterbalanced by play" (ibid). His contribution, like Jackson's, stresses the violent edges and expressions that must be weighed against the emancipatory possibilities of the tactics considered in this collection.

It is at once striking and a matter of common sense that African subjects continue to produce, to aspire, and to fantasize while laboring under incredible hardships, and from within contexts of volatility and constraint that render the business of social reproduction daunting. Perhaps it is this unique affective disposition, above all, that not so much distinguishes this moment from a prior historical conjuncture as insists it remains a distinctive feature of the present. The neoliberal moment is, of course, one of hyphenation—a second coming, so to speak, haunted by the liberalism from which it follows. The same holds true for those other, enduring couplets that, shackled uneasily together, continue to haunt the global present: the postcolonial, the post–Cold War, the post-authoritarian. It is hard to argue at all convincingly for a radical break or discontinuity with the past. At the same time, the kinds of temporal and spatial transformations we have described, basic dimensions of human experience, no less, seem to indicate that things are not quite as they were.

For such new moments, new theories are needed. As Duffield argues, "Rather than the developmental rhetoric of scarcity or breakdown, one has to address the possibility that protracted instability is symptomatic of new and expanding forms of political economy; a function of economic change rather than a developmental malaise. It is difficult for the development model of conflict to convey such a sense of innovative expansion" (Duffield 1998:51). The materialist claims of Duffield's argument, our essays show, have their mirror in the cultural and imaginative sphere, too. It is not just "political economy" that is expanding in new ways, but moral and imaginative economy, as well.

We do not seek to deny the many challenges facing contemporary African societies—the deeply unequal terms of North-South relations, the equivalently unbalanced nature of relations within the continent, the limits of political and religious authority, the constraints of economic regulation and debt service, to name just a few. But we assert that in efforts to encapsulate the African situation that mobilizing the concept of "crisis" flattens and diminishes the ambiguities of the lived world (see, for example, UNDP 2006; cf. Thomas 2006).[12] New theories aiming to capture this ambiguity must refuse teleologies in the same way that the subjects of this volume do in their multiple ways. They must take detailed account of the myriad tactics that contemporary Africans employ to carve out domains of material and existential possibility for themselves within ongoing agonistic socioeconomic contexts. And they must be attentive to the capacity to fantasize, which, while never an escape from the hard politics of bare life, seems undeniably to motivate so many practices of resistance, submission, complicity, and transcendence. Aspiration drives both deliberate and unwitting efforts to transform the immediate and volatile worlds in which the subjects of this collection live and struggle.

2. The Search for Economic Sovereignty

Anne-Maria Makhulu

Since South Africa's first democratic elections in 1994 much has changed, both in the content of political and social life and in the ways in which post-apartheid discourse has come to reframe the contemporary South African situation. A propos discourse, a few examples may be especially illuminating: consider, for one, the marked shift from the Marxist-Leninist-speak embodied in the Freedom Charter—a manifesto for revolution drafted in 1955—and the (neo)liberal-legal language of the new constitution, through which certain aspirations of the old charter *might* be realized (stress here on *might*). Or as a corollary, the relatively new emphasis on rights talk as a means by which citizens *might* make specific claims on the state (again the stress on the tentative is important), or the apparent refocusing of concerns surrounding inequalities in South African society, both under the law and in terms of access to opportunities and capital. The grossly uneven distribution of resources—whether in housing, land, or money—has latterly come to be understood in broad class terms rather than as race discrimination, as was the case under apartheid (Nattrass and Seekings 2001; also see Seekings and Nattrass 2005).

These concerns with political ideology, law, and rights operate in the main on a broad discursive plane tapping directly into the national debate about the post-apartheid condition. Yet perhaps more compelling are the ways in which "conversations"—beyond the sphere of officially sanctioned talk—reflect a yearning for the recent past, even while condemning the racist and segregationist logic that underwrote it.

If before 1994, access to housing, jobs, and other benefits of a "free" society were denied Blacks en masse, it was possible, at least rhetorically, to point to the apartheid regime's policies of racial exclusion as culprits for widespread poverty, particularly for the black majority. But with the expansion of the black middle class after 1994, discourses of poverty and race changed, highlighting a peculiar relationship of the present to the past in South Africa, where of late the *idea* of wage labor (in its apartheid guise) has enjoyed a resurgence even as the conditions of its possibility have collapsed under the constraints of a new liberalism.

For all that it denied Africans license to work where and when they chose, the old system of wage labor promised jobs. In stark contrast, the new neoliberal agenda sanctions economic growth at any cost, even at the expense of job losses. Little wonder that the old wage-labor system should come to be perceived as a solution to the neoliberal impasse in South Africa, an impasse defined primarily through its confusing dual imperatives of restitution and privatization. Thus, on the one hand expressions of need and, perhaps even more significantly, of *desire*—few are immune to fantasies of wealth and conspicuous consumption—echo erratic market speculation; on the other, more modestly, hopes of fulfilling basic needs are increasingly associated in the popular imagination with a concept of work that had far greater currency in the past. As if in the debate about employment there might be a way to resolve the rather peculiar terms and constraints of a post-apartheid ontology.

Admittedly, this idea of the laboring subject is something of an anachronism and depends on an older theory of labor, one that was once realized through travel to urban areas from the countryside and through access to wage work, though inevitably mediated by the old system of pass laws. This yearning for apartheid, presumably sans political repression—a desire for "sweat" as a precondition of material security—is simply no longer realizable in an era in which urbanization and employment have been disarticulated, not only in South Africa, but worldwide (see Davis 2006). But the new concern with work in times of very high unemployment also stems from the increasing debt burden in most households as a consequence of diminishing real wages and rising inflation.[1] Indeed, debt and indebtedness have substantially increased much as they have elsewhere in the world (see the introduction to this volume), not least in the United States, thereby not only desubstantiating the concrete world of material objects, such as homes—both as the brick–and-mortar basis of fundamental security and as its metaphorical foundation, too—but also the epistemological certainties that came with older relations of wage and work.

So where does contemporary South Africa sit in this broader historical schema? As the culmination of a long struggle for freedom, fought both within and beyond South Africa's borders, democratization doubtless settled the matter of colonial racism—putting to rest a very long history of repression. Yet South Africa's new democracy emerged more or less against the backdrop of shifts in the world system, not least in light of the collapse of communism, and the associated deepening crisis of the liberal state. Just as a new world order dawned, throwing in question the very nature of the political, so the post-apartheid state adopted economic reforms that sought to rapidly deregulate markets, privatize state assets, and as a consequence undercut any future comprehensive social welfare strategy (see Makhulu 2010)—which is not to deny conspicuous efforts in the areas of housing provision, public education, healthcare, and social grants executed as part of the project of national reconstruction.

This essay makes two fundamental lines of argument relating specifically to the problems of South Africa's partial transition. I first highlight some of the ways in which the poor, in one township on the outskirts of Cape Town, shore up household budgets against the ravages of the market and at the same time continue to imagine futures, even as the possibility of such futures is circumscribed by new conditions of deprivation. I focus specifically on the financial coping strategies of households and the ways in which "money struggles" (Guyer, Denzer, and Agbaje 2002) are foundational to aspirations to social reproduction. Further, I define households as a complex set of extended kin relations and moral obligations—fundamentally, as in many parts of the world, where people break bread together—that in South Africa at least confront the "crisis-ridden intersection of kinship and political economy" (White 2001:458).

My second line of argument concerns the concept of sovereignty (see Hardt and Negri 2000; cf. Agamben 1998, 2005). While questions of law and power are central to the recent scholarship on sovereignty, it is striking the degree to which this renewed interest seems to have been coincident with a growing concern for the future of the nation-state—historically the location of sovereign power. Under pressure from transnational capital and its associated circulation of people and things, national boundaries have become both increasingly porous and more strictly policed, creating new barriers to precisely the kinds of movements late capitalism requires. In part, obstacles to the mobility of both persons and objects (but particularly persons) come not only from hypervigilant border policing but in the kinds of ethnic or cultural citizenship claims that deny membership to some and grant it to others (see the introduction to this volume; also see Piot, this volume; Ferguson 2006; Geschiere and Jackson 2006; Ceuppens and Geschiere 2005). In brief, the nation-state seems to be at a historic crossroads—neither entirely eclipsed nor entirely without compromise.

There are, of course, other modalities of membership, which the exclusive focus on *political* autonomy or sovereignty ignores. So, just as postapartheid politics have been redirected toward a neoliberal agenda, class membership and sodalities have been harder to articulate with the demise of an older global labor politics. In this essay, then, I focus, perhaps perversely, on what I term "economic sovereignty" as a way of reconnecting conceptions of politics and economy, just as the early political economists intended, and thereby to reconceive the social contract and free markets in terms broadly "civil social," even while rejecting the liberal project it assumes (cf. Smith 1977).

As much as I am concerned with the possibilities for economic autonomy at the individual and household levels, such considerations must also address larger forces, for problems of sovereignty derive, as LiPuma and Lee (2004:4) have recently described, from flows of capital, "which become instrumental in compromising the sovereignty of national economies." Thus, the pages that follow involve a thinking on two planes simultaneously—one, individual households, the other, global financial markets. This conjuncture of family and finance suggests, I hope, a new course for grappling with the complexities of the current global order, not least in the face of the recent financial crisis (see the introduction to this volume).

THE POLITICS OF BARE LIFE

On the outskirts of Cape Town, a series of adjoining settlements dot the landscape, varying in size and infrastructure from small informal encampments along Lansdowne Road, the main arterial road leading from the Cape Flats to the city, to much larger formal townships set back from the N2 motorway. This sandy wasteland leading to the Atlantic Ocean has historically been a dumping ground for those forcibly removed by previous regimes; such is the story of the Flats' oldest township, Langa, founded in 1923, and designed to accommodate African workers relocated from Ndabeni. Successive waves of deportations of Blacks and Coloureds during the 1960s, 1970s, and 1980s rid the core of the city of "non-Whites" and saw the expansion of townships and informal settlements across the Flats. Even today, driving down the N2 motorway, it is this legacy that is most visible: the grossly disparate amenities across Coloured and African townships, the overcrowding, the seemingly unregulated squatting in backyards, and the ever-persistent racial zoning of space, which, while no longer a matter of law, nevertheless remains a matter of course.

Since 1994 many areas of the Flats have been upgraded in situ, entailing the temporary relocation of local residents to nearby "transit camps," often little more than open spaces lacking adequate running water and electricity, while bulk earthworks and houses are completed in the designated project area. For the first time, communities fall within clearly demarcated municipal ward boundaries linked to electoral roll and census records, and although these boundaries have shifted some with each local and national election, in the main their official status is relatively secure. In fifteen years the old revolutionary politics have receded; the new routines (civic meetings and forums) signal at once the practical procedural workings of democracy and, to some degree, an empty formalism, too (see Negri 1999 in Comaroff and Comaroff 2000:292). The neoliberal regime, of course, has played a part in the structuring of public life, and what were formerly organic bodies that sought to redirect grassroots activism under apartheid have reorganized as community organs. These draw attention to values of transparency, public participation, and compliance with rate payments (see Chaskalson, Jochelson, and Seekings 1987) in tandem with the rollout of new housing, educational, and health programs.

In 2006, Mrs. Mfeketo and her husband, their four children, and a granddaughter lived in a small Reconstruction and Development Programme (RDP) house[2] set back from the main road leading out of Lower Crossroads, previously a small informal settlement and now boasting a population of a little under 30,000.[3] The house was organized around a central living space, two bedrooms, and a kitchen. While the front of the house was built from brick, the rooms in the rear were pieced together from the remains of a much older structure, mostly assembled from corrugated iron, cardboard, and plastic sheeting. This part of the house dated back to the 1970s, when the Mfeketos lived in Old Crossroads (today a separate township a mile down the road). In the townships and squatter areas the recycling of homes has long been a survival strategy in a city characterized by movement and displacement—"movement" less in the sense of a particular and liberating urban experience, as Raymond Williams (1973:6) invoked, than as an expression of social vulnerability.

Practically speaking, then, homes are often an amalgam of new and old, bricks and mortar, cardboard and tarpaulin, and they signal both the legacy of housing restrictions and newer challenges to adequate shelter arising from the policies of the current dispensation.[4] Indeed, since democratization in 1994, efforts to deliver housing have been slowed by both technical and political impediments. Provincial budgets have been either over- or under-spent, public funds have gone to private contractors operating with minimal state oversight (despite the rhetoric of audit culture and transparency), and generally, notwithstanding government claims about targets—in housing, that is, one million homes in the first ten years of democracy—enormous backlogs have amassed while the quality of completed homes has been questionable. The Western Cape faces particularly grave shortages; in 2010 the overall provincial backlog was estimated at 500,000 households, with a rate of increase much higher than elsewhere. The City of Cape Town alone estimates that 400,000 households are eligible for subsidized housing, although only 310,000 appear on the city's housing database.

Obstacles to housing provision are a consequence of both past and present policies, of course. Yet while apartheid explicitly promoted housing scarcity through reductions to the black social wage, neoliberalism has tended to encourage poverty enabling or alleviating policies that seek less to replace slums and shantytowns than to "improve" them as a "less ambitious goal of public and private intervention" (Davis 2006:71). This is more-or-less consistent with the movement away from top-down reformist strategies of the postwar period and toward "championing privatization of housing supply . . . and micro-entrepreneurial solutions to urban poverty" (ibid.; also see de Soto 2000). Such interventions have very limited impact, while presaging the state's withdrawal from the development field, leaving private individuals to address the shortcomings of national reconstruction.

In 2006 Mrs. Mfeketo ran a sweet and snack shop from home and could most often be found preparing small fried foods and seasoned chicken feet, which her husband then sold from a stand in the front yard, along with loose cigarettes, small packets of crisps, and an assortment of sweets. This "survival" business provided the family with its main source of income, bringing in the equivalent of a few dollars a day.[5] For many residents of Lower Crossroads, "informal" businesses have come to substitute almost entirely for wage-paying work, both raising questions about the salience of the "informal" (Roitman 1990; also see Sayer and Walker 1992) as a useful analytic category, and forcing the state to adopt the rhetoric of parallel economic structures, not dissimilar from the older Marxist conception of dual economy. Strangely, nineteenth and twenty-first century South Africa seem to share a great deal in this regard. In *The Origins of Totalitarianism*, Hannah Arendt wrote of the concept of superfluity, of workers drawn to South Africa in the nineteenth century by the gold rush and industrial revolution, who without local conditions of white wage labor would have enjoyed little "use or function" (Arendt 1994:189) in the formal labor market.[6] Today, the exponential growth of the informal sector speaks to a broader regional and continent-wide phenomenon, as well—to a form of globalization that necessarily depends on "capital flows and markets [at] once lightning fast, [patchy] and incomplete" (Ferguson 2006:49), and to unevenness both within and between regions (Ferguson 2005:380).

Mr. Mfeketo lost his job in a leather tannery in December 1999 thanks to downsizing. Even then, five years into South Africa's democratic transition, unemployment rates were rapidly increasing (reaching 38.6 percent in 1998),[7] and by the end of that first decade approximately one million jobs had been shed in mining, manufacturing, and agriculture. These retrenchments were consistent with the state's implementation of structural reforms (self-imposed and in line with World Bank and IMF policies), whereas privatization and deregulation saw the financial sector expand to 20 percent of the national economy even while employing only 1 percent of the workforce.[8]

Since the 1970s, intensifying financial circuits of capital have coincided with increasing levels of uneven development, not only in South Africa but worldwide (Bond 2000; see also Arrighi 1994; Harvey 2003). In Asia aggressive hedge funds and IMF deflationary policies brought economies there to the brink, resulting in widespread bankruptcies and poverty during the late 1990s. As devastating as the crisis itself may have been, a growing consciousness of "the relative capacity of some to command the system of exchange more than others" (Blunt 2004:320) drove a deepening loss of confidence. And during the same period, South Africa saw widespread retrenchments as the poor resorted to stark survivalist strategies while the state ostensibly "democratized" poverty alleviation programs by devolving its social welfare responsibilities.

And yet South Africa is not so easily read as a clear-cut "neoliberal" case. For even as the 1990s saw the push to privatize, the state continued to offer social grants, including pensions and child support payments. Further, since democratization the number of grant recipients has actually increased from 2.6 million in 1994 to 6.8 million in 2002 (Bond 2006b:148). Thus, from one perspective contraction and devolution have been matched by opposite and paradoxical tendencies, doubtless partially conditioned by the legacy of apartheid racial discrimination that left a vast majority of South Africans underserved by the state and to which the new black majority government has rightly sought to respond. This predicament has given rise to a variety of possible readings, among them that social grants are merely a Band-Aid in light of official refusal to acknowledge the broader context of inequality in South African society. Further, critics argue, the expansion of the social wage has been offset by increasing costs for utilities such as water and electricity—a function of the privatization of basic needs—and of education, which though purportedly free is subsidized by the poor through mandatory tuition fees and expenditures on books and uniforms.

Whatever the nature of the polemic, many South Africans are heavily dependent on state subsidies, which are central to processes of social reproduction. At age 65 Mr. Mfeketo began collecting a state pension amounting to R800 a month (approximately U.S.$85),[9] while three Mfeketo children were of working age but remained jobless and a fourth child was still attending school. In the Mfeketo household and many others like it, state pensions have become a primary source of income.

A recent national study[10] has gone some way to unraveling the practices through which heavily indebted households shore up finances in the absence of steady wage work, and with heavy reliance on informal economic activity and social grants. This gap, what economists call the "wage puzzle," is negotiated via a dizzying array of both formal and informal financial instruments, which enable survival from one financial year to the next. The study showcases a combination of mechanisms for saving, banking, borrowing, lending, and channeling money into socially reproductive labor. These include bank accounts, pensions, insurance, store credit and credit cards, retirement savings, and debt administration, as well as savings schemes, burial societies, and loan sharking. As in many parts of the world, popular rotating credit and savings schemes offer the advantages of increased purchasing power (because members pool resources when looking to make large household purchases) and fairly consistent saving through group incentives. The study rightly observes that while poor households may have very little money, "this [doesn't] mean that they [don't] manage what they have."

Back in 2006, Mrs. Mfeketo belonged to a savings scheme along with nine other members. Thandu 'Xolo (Lover of Peace) was a formal association with a written constitution and strictly enforced regulations. The group made monthly contributions of R30 (approximately U.S.$3) per member over eleven months, January through November. December was set aside as a time for cashing out and preparing for the coming year: paying annual school fees, buying uniforms and books, making the journey to the rural areas, and attending to general home maintenance, including roofing and repainting. The "December holidays" were associated not so much with religious celebrations per se (even though people referred to giving Christmas gifts) as with both the ritual and practical reproduction of the household, perhaps best symbolized by the circumcision of young men. Indeed, trips to the rural Eastern Cape were indissociable from the desire to see young boys enter circumcision schools (*abakwetha*) close to familial homesteads. In so doing, families effectively renewed connections between town and country and lifeworlds separated by hundreds of miles. Young boys destined to become "new men" (*amakrwala*) spoke of circumcision as a critical rite of passage, which facilitated a necessary generational transition.

The savings group had a fixed deposit[11] or savings account and three of the members served as co-signatories, going to the bank after monthly meetings to deposit contributions. The co-signatories were also responsible for notifying the bank of large withdrawals (usually in anticipation of December), maintaining the association ledger, and guaranteeing a minimum balance in the association's account. To the uninitiated, these collective savings groups (*umgalelo*) seem to present no particular advantages over individual banking. But almost universally, participants argue that saving together is much more rewarding, in a double sense. Members who pool resources in a fixed deposit or savings account see their savings appreciate incrementally with interest earnings, as compared to the much smaller sums they might deposit individually and on which they would be ineligible to earn interest. The interest earnings on fixed accounts are approximately 7.0–7.3 percent, high for the United States but in keeping with South Africa's higher inflationary pressures, which include a relatively weak currency, rising input costs such as labor in the productive sectors, high demand for certain goods that outstrip supply, and the relatively high cost of specific imports, among them oil and electricity.[12] While the state has mandated regulatory changes requiring banks to offer accounts to the very poor, "Mzansi" accounts (for very small depositors) tend to charge very high fees. In part, those who bank together do so to avoid the penalties and maximum balance restrictions on such accounts, but they also seek out the interest earnings, which Mzansi account holders are disqualified from earning.

Finally, perhaps just as significant is that group deposits made by members of collective savings schemes demand a very particular form of fiscal discipline: the group restricts the withdrawal of funds, in so doing redirecting consumer desire and ensuring the security of the domestic balance sheet. Discipline is sustained through peer pressure and the logic of delayed gratification. And in this way, lump sums of money are converted into a steady trickle—what Karl Polanyi (2001) described as reciprocative systems, or "redistribution writ small."

Of course, these activities depend on the constitution of a certain kind of self-regulating subject: a "responsible and moral individual and economic-rational actor" (Lemke 2001:201). Members often spoke of "belt-tightening" strategies, consistent with discourses of self-empowerment that have become pervasive in the context of the devolution of state welfare functions onto private institutions. While such behaviors are easily read as compensations for the market's failure to provide, the logic of self-imposed austerity is as much a means through which neoliberal subjects actively propose alternatives to the impossible conditions in which they find themselves. The search for financial autonomy or economic sovereignty, albeit achieved through relatively conventional means—through saving, delayed gratification, and abstention—suggests an entirely new order of value in relation to the absence of formal work. If wage and labor were the horizon against which struggles for material survival were previously weighed, today another kind of labor is invested in the forging of relations of borrowing, lending, and the extension of credit (a point to which I will return below). Thus, though narratives of frugality and self-restraint expose the limits of social reproduction, they also highlight the myriad ways in which subjects act within and upon the constraints of neoliberalism, and in doing so reshape and elaborate both the practices of austerity as well as the kinds of subjects they seek to become.

Hence, these new kinds of subjects—shaped not so much by practices of consumption as by self-abnegation (or negative consumption)—are not only moral or rational but have a highly pragmatic orientation (Comaroff and Comaroff 1997:66) to the lived world. Against the grain of theories of consumption, consumer culture, and desire as a site of active self-definition (see, for example, Benjamin 1999; Baudrillard 1998), I would argue that those who must *deny* desire are not simply subjected or somehow lacking in capacities of self-realization.[13] The circumstances of their lives are doubtless abject, but pragmatic subjects necessarily work *within* abjection (as the introduction to this volume discusses), steadily redefining its conditions at every turn, painstakingly remaking the world around them, and at the same time debating the limits and limitations of their own conditions of possibility.

Mrs. Mfeketo's *umgalelo* had been in operation for almost fifteen years when I first met her. Established in Old Crossroads, the scheme moved when its members were relocated to a transit camp in Lower Crossroads in the early 1990s amid on-the-ground conflict against the state, rumors of a democratic transition, and efforts on the part of the apartheid regime to relocate and remove squatters in a final bid for urban containment and management of African populations. Not all such schemes are this stable, of course, and many function without formal banking instruments. Instead, participants make contributions to one another on a rotating basis throughout the year and recipients have discretion in the use of funds.[14] Both schemes have their advantages, although generally those making use of the banking system are more successful and tend to have greater longevity. The Mfeketos certainly had reaped small but meaningful benefits over time. The seats in the living room, kitchen unit, fridge, bed, school fees, and uniforms all had been paid for through Mrs. Mfeketo's hard work and diligence.

Much as I have suggested that the self-imposition of austerity might be understood as consistent with a new neoliberal logic—a mode of self-regulation, of "savings as 'spirit' or 'moral' discipline" (Khan and Pieterse 2004:30)—the broader historical context in which acts of abstention and austerity are enacted is also critical to understanding responses to current hardships.[15] Savings schemes in South Africa date back at least to the nineteenth century, and although they emerged in conjunction with proletarianization and wage work when Africans had only limited access to formal banking institutions, in the post-apartheid era the schemes have not lost their relevance despite the introduction of banking for the poor.[16] Under current conditions the schemes have taken on a very clear purpose, namely, to surmount the seemingly impossible challenges of life on the economic margins. Yet in so doing they have tended to replicate the very neoliberal logic that justified their necessity in the first place. One might even venture to say that the Thandu 'Xolo scheme was concrete evidence of the relative "successes" of self-adjustment, something the South African state itself has embraced in order to fall in line with World Bank and IMF policy. Indeed, savings schemes have tended to reinscribe principles of micro-entrepreneurialism central both to personal gain in limited circumstances *and* to the larger project of privatization and devolution in which the attribution of individual capacities denies that larger structures play a part in determining personal fortune or misfortune.

FROM DEATH OF THE SUBJECT TO DEBT AND THE SUBJECT

In what follows I address practices and stratagems of economic survival that signal a new materialism. Specifically, I consider the place of *debt* in an economic system increasingly organized around credit instruments, both formal and informal, and how the fact of debt at one order of magnitude prefigures a set of relations of debt and indebtedness at another. In the face of the current global financial crisis debt has taken on historic importance, and yet little has been said about the indebtedness of the poor (see the introduction to this volume).

Like the Mfeketo family, the Mjwanas resided in Lower Crossroads, which (as I have previously suggested) is an economically depressed, formerly working-class community of some 30,000 people, now deeply afflicted by high levels of unemployment. However, the Mjwanas' circumstances were additionally stricken. Indeed, I want to argue that theorizing poverty requires far greater nuance in understanding the *degrees* and levels of impoverishment that are generally masked by the development literature and even poverty eradication strategies. In 2006, Mrs. Nomalady Mjwana belonged to a large savings scheme some forty members strong. It was based in Old Crossroads and had been in operation since the late 1980s, when it convened in Boystown (otherwise known as Section 5), named for a boys' reformatory located there when the area was still partially given over to farming. The group, Masibonisane (Let's Help Each Other Advance), met weekly at Sikilela Primary School. While contributions were made throughout the year, the group generally recessed during January when people traveled to the Eastern Cape. As with Mrs. Mfeketo's group the focus on the December holidays signaled something quite apart from the notion of "holiday" defined in terms of bourgeois leisure time, gift-giving, and so forth. Rather, December was time to accomplish the very hard work of social reproduction: of making family, raising children and bringing them to maturity, dealing with the demands of the dead most often based in the rural areas (largely through ritual sacrifice), and attending to the many material demands of domestic life. *Umgalelos* are explicitly a mechanism for achieving the goals of social reproduction by enabling young boys' initiation into adulthood, the construction of rural homesteads, and investment in children's education through school fee payments and the purchase of books and uniforms.

Masibonisane's weekly contributions of R10 were significantly smaller than those in other schemes, but were made more frequently, given the limited regular income flowing into member households, including child support grants. The Mjwanas' arranged their payments around the timing of earnings from Mr. Mjwana's casual gardening job and the small food stand where Mrs. Mjwana worked a few days a week. As a consequence, Nomalady contributed R30 weekly and made additional payments on behalf of several of her children: Bongiwe (a twenty-five-year-old daughter), Phumlani (a twenty-three-year-old son), Phelokazi (a thirteen-year-old daughter), and Nasiphi (a ten-year-old daughter). The incentive to contribute on her children's behalf (a practice in which many women engaged), and which suggested competitive giving, increased potential contributions and earnings in the scheme. Thus, ideally Nomalady's contributions totaled

R150 per week, plus a R2 "transport contribution," which covered the costs of cosignatories and other members who took turns traveling to the bank to make deposits into a fixed account. Annual contributions were registered in two separate ledgers, maintained by two members specially appointed to the task. The ledgers reflected identical transactions—contributions, deposits, and in some cases money owed, as well as additional transactions or *matshonisa* (loan sharking). A third ledger recorded "transport money" entries only.

The Masibonisane constitution stipulated that contributions were made regularly, that meetings were attended and began punctually, and that absent members sent on a formal apology delivered by another member. These binding rules encouraged consistency and overall group stability. Again, self-discipline, moral rectitude, and self-imposed fiscal restraint characterized the ideal subject who could be a member of such a scheme.

Nomalady ran a sweet stand on one of the major thoroughfares feeding off the R300 motorway and across the road from a local wholesale supermarket. She worked there every other day, usually Monday, Wednesday, Friday, and the weekend. Depending on business, most days she made anywhere from R50 to R70 in profits;[17] she sold not only sweets but crisps, yogurt, and occasionally fruit. The R200–250 she made each week was not always sufficient to cover her target weekly contribution of R152. When Nomalady couldn't make the whole contribution in one go she found ways to catch up by the end of the month. Strategies included participating in so-called *gooi-gooi*, or unstable "in-and-out" schemes (pyramid or Ponzi schemes)[18] where money could be rapidly recuperated, as well as loan sharking. Members of the scheme who either needed additional funds or wished to make extra money would lend to friends and other, poorer neighbors. Indeed, Nomalady had been known to lend at very high interest rates and saw in the high risk of default the potential for maximizing profits by charging upward of 50 percent interest on loans, which if recuperated yielded further profits through interest earnings from the bank.[19] Alternatively, members also could borrow from the scheme itself—that is, once at least R400 worth of contributions had been made for the year. Clearly, the notion of risk was at least in principle offset by the promise of its securitization. In much the same way as derivatives *derive* their value from other assets, one form of contribution might be offset by contributions made elsewhere or by the practice of lending to others, backed by the security of membership in the association.

At the end of any given year the three co-signatories presented the scheme's ledgers to the bank and withdrew funds for all its members, leaving a small amount on deposit for purposes of keeping the account open. Nomalady withdrew close to R7,600 at the end of 2005. This money was used for transporting family members to the Transkei for the December holidays, the slaughter of a cow for a family celebration, the refencing of the homestead, groceries, school fees and uniforms for the following year, the initiation of a young man in the extended family, and finally the repainting of the family's shack in Lower Crossroads. Other sources of income that year included Mr. Mjwana's income from casual gardening work. He was 58, preretirement age, and worked from time to time. In addition, one of the younger children, under 14, continued to receive a child support grant of R180 a month.[20] Yet, ultimately, it was Mrs. Mjwana's careful management of limited resources—her persistent redistributive and reciprocative care—that won the day, ensuring that at year's end the labor of social reproduction might continue into the following.

THE MATTER OF RISK

> At each stage, risks can be converted into securities, sliced up, repackaged, sold on and sliced up again. The endless opportunities to write contracts in underlying debt instruments explains why the outstanding value of credit-derivatives contracts has rocketed to $26 trillion—$9 trillion more than six months ago, and seven times as much as in 2003.
>
> *THE ECONOMIST* (2006)

> No progressive observer of the US economy can fail to be startled by the high level of debt borne by the bulk of the population. These are folk who borrow not for luxury, but for survival.
>
> VIJAY PRASHAD (2003:4)

At first glance a comparison of households on the margins of Cape Town and global financial markets might seem implausible. And yet attributes of each are remarkably similar in that they seek to ensure survival on the one hand and profit maximization on the other. What these apparently different institutions and practices arguably share are assumptions about the nature of value and the possibilities of its realization. If the poor are prone to spiraling debt and depend on loan sharking and other brokerage relations that offer credible, if limited, solutions to the fundamentally nongenerative nature of post–wage work activities, the "casino economy, with its financial speculation and fictitious capital formation (much of it unbacked by any growth in real production)" (Harvey 1989:332) replicates some of the very same strategic misrecognitions. Both imply a faith bordering on the occult: faith in the generative properties of transactions involving either money or capital, and faith that value can be conjured from what is largely immaterial, such that the old formula by which money was converted into commodities and commodities into money prime (M-C-M'; or "buying in order to sell," as Marx put it) has been supplanted by the surreal prospect of capital generating more capital, somehow unmediated by the commodity production process. What indeed is required to construct a world contingent on the realization of M-M'? Only very recently, there was an almost religious faith in the capacities of fictitious capital, yet as the global credit crisis has revealed there are of course limits to its magical properties. That collateralized debt obligations cannot, in a whole chain of such obligations, generate infinite quantities of surplus value has been for some a disturbing revelation.

Marx was not unaware of the potential of money markets, of course. His "general formula for capital" concluded with the case of *interest*-bearing capital. That is, a mode of circulation in which the intermediate stage was lost and money begot money, or as he characterized it "money which [was] worth more money, value which [was] greater than itself" (Marx 1990:257). Yet Marx's primary emphasis on productive forces and the relations of production as the mechanisms driving world history made the sphere of circulation a less likely focus, at least as a relative matter. The prominence of finance capital in the twenty-first century, however, can hardly be sidestepped, nor the sphere of circulation that makes it so generative. Indeed, the reemergence of circulation "as the cutting edge of capitalism" has transformed aspects of our modern market economy in quite radical ways given the decoupling of capital from sites of production and the ways in which circulation has reorganized state functions (LiPuma and Lee 2004:9).

While such "cultures of circulation," following Lee and LiPuma (2002), signal the amplification of circuits of finance capital, and while such circuits and their velocity may distinguish the contemporary conjuncture, the apparent absence of "real production" also marks a mystification rather than the actual dissolution of the commodity, namely abstracted labor value, in the M-C-M' formulation. Still, labor's apparent disappearance— that is, through a series of geographical displacements (what Arrighi [2004] and others have termed "spatial fixes")[21]—is paralleled by the very real experience of absent wage work and the concomitant spiraling of extremes of wealth and poverty. In such circumstances lived experience is radically altered too. In a world peculiarly defined by both promise and powerlessness poor people survive in part because of a certain optimal pragmatism, but they also do so by engineering fiscal stratagems that, to all intents and purposes, have no material basis. Thus loan sharking and other precarious financial arrangements for securing income rely as much on stealth as forms of magical thinking. This thinking refuses the immanent possibility of failure or, in the case of money lending, the distinct probability that clients will default on repayments. Fantastical stories abound, most often to account for the inexplicable successes of a few in the face of a roller-coaster economy. It is said that those who beat the odds no doubt sell their souls to the devil, devise Faustian pacts, or consort with witches. In rural South Africa, for example, farmers perceived to profit despite bad weather, blight, and low commodity prices do so, it is argued, because they benefit from the free labor of zombies in their employ—armies of which descend into the fields by moonlight and reap profits for their masters.

But just as zombies come to haunt their owners, following them everywhere "like unruly shadows [o]r the alienated essence of their own labor" (Comaroff and Comaroff 1999b:803), bad investments and the debt they create haunt their investors too. For financial markets are equally prone to what I will call mythical thinking, which is to say they assume, particularly in environments in which certain instruments function outside the reach of regulators and the "velocity of capital" stands in for "real money," that profits can be arbitraged in the lag between investment and return. So again, just as zombies persist in reminding their masters of their savage exploitation, so investing in certain sectors carries enormous risks. Trading in credit is one such case, as we have learned in the face of the credit crunch. As levels of default increase sharply and the credit cycle comes full circle even the most resilient investors meet their downfall: "On the one hand there can be no doubt that financial product innovations and especially new debt instruments associated with new information, communications and technology simply permit a greater debt load without necessarily endangering consumer finances" (Bond 2006a:21). On the other hand, as the subprime mortgage market's collapse has shown, there are limits to the debt burdens both individuals and formal institutions can bear. And as Patrick Bond has recently suggested, savings rates have fallen concomitantly, in the United States slumping to 3 percent across households.

Marx's primary object of de-reification was surely the commodity. One way to debunk the notion of value as intrinsic to the thing itself was to show the ways in which commodities were implicated in a network of social relations including, most fundamentally, the labor process. In this way, the thing-ness of the commodity was set against the process of labor alienation of which it was a direct and immediate outcome. Marx argued that this process was concealed by the science of political economy, which instead construed value as a series of formulas. These bore "the unmistakable stamp of belonging to a social formation in which the process of production has mastery over man, instead of the opposite, [and] appear[s] to the political economists' bourgeois consciousness to be as much a self-evidently and nature-imposed necessity as productive labour itself" (Marx 1990:174–75).

My point in rehearsing Marx's well-known critique of commodity fetishism is the following: at least in some formalist sense, both finance capital and other informal transactions that assume capital and money, respectively, as central to their endeavors dissolve M-C-M' into M-M'. It is particularly striking then that in two entirely distinct sectors of the economy—the one financial, the other "informal," for want of a better term—wage work is more or less dissolute. In the one instance fewer and fewer actual workers are required to drive the culture of circulation—again, consider the financialization of the South African economy since 1994 and the fact that it employs a meager 1 percent of the workforce—and the crisis of unemployment has given rise to an ever-expanding informal sector, as manifest expression of a crisis of redundancy. This "crisis," so to speak, masks instead a more permanent condition in which a mechanism that produces "superfluous" populations is itself constituted by that very superfluity, rendering superfluity (borrowing from Arendt [1994] and more recently Mbembe [2004]) necessary rather than extraneous to the system as a whole. There is, in addition, an almost parallel faith that the financial speculations of the poor and global marketeers share in common: indeed, both presume the possibilities of profit. These come in a variety of forms. In the case of small informal savings and lending schemes they are expressed as the proliferation of complex arrangements of relations between lenders and borrowers—relations that are often multilayered, duplicative, and even exponential—while in the financial markets the invention of increasingly arcane instruments of speculation multiply much for the same reasons.

In each instance, when one scheme or instrument is exhausted new ones must be devised: innovations that will optimize possibilities for gain. This impetus to innovation is nothing new, of course. Marx and, indeed, Luxemburg were keen to show the ways in which capitalism required ever more novel outlets for accumulation—for perpetuating accumulation over time after the process of "original" or "primitive" accumulation had been satisfied. For Luxemburg in particular, imperialism, as the political expression of the accumulation of capital (Luxemburg 2003:426), constituted the key historical process through which accumulation might succeed, even as she dissented some from Marx's rather schematic view of expanded reproduction (see Marx 1990; cf. Luxemburg 2003).

To be sure, what neither could have anticipated were the new technologies that would serve the process of accumulation, what Harvey has recently called "accumulation by dispossession" (Harvey 2003), a process characterized by extremes of accumulation at one pole and poverty at the other, nor as surely, the role Wall Street and other markets might play in continually seeking new alternatives to financial instruments and sectors that had been previously exhausted. Remarking on the shift from industrial to financial trade in New York City in the late 1980s, at a critical conjuncture in the underwriting of new financial instruments, the *New York Times* noted, "New York has constructed 75 new factories to house the debt production and distribution machine. These towers of granite and glass shine through the night as some of this generation's most talented professionals invent new instruments of debt to fit every imagined need: Perpetual Floating Rate Notes, Yield Curve Notes and Dual Currency Notes, to name a few, now traded as casually as the stock of the Standard Oil Company once was" (Scardino 1987 in Harvey 1989:331).

Thus, if stock options were the invention of the 1970s, the derivitization of markets ushered in a whole new paradigm in financial transactions in the decade that followed, while hedge funds and the trade in risk (namely credit derivatives) exploded on the scene in the millennium (Das 2006).[22] These last assumed a disproportionate role in the transformation of what was both imaginable and possible, as banks, for example, no longer held onto mortgage loans but instead sold a parcel of such loans to a third party or "special purpose vehicle." The SPV "issued bonds in the market to raise the cash" (Das 2006:282). And what came to be referred to as "mortgage backed securities" constituted, within fewer than two decades, an enormous new market. This complex dance between risk (that is, credit) and its securitization (through repackaging and resale) operates on any number of distinct scales—as much in the financial markets as imitatively within smaller, informal institutions such as savings associations where money and credit are managed in equal measure (see the essays by Buggenhagen and Jackson in this volume). The current logic suggests new openings for risk taking and investment, and in the absence of genuine acknowledgment of the role of abstracted labor value, debt seems to increasingly occupy that narrow and claustrophobic space between M and M'.

CONCLUSION: SQUATTING AS POLITICS

What, then, of families like the Mfeketos and Mjwanas, who seek daily to secure a future and to gain some sort of economic autonomy? The central thrust of this essay has argued that against the backdrop of growing austerity, ordinary South Africans have found creative if challenging ways to work within the structures of possibility and impossibility the new South Africa presents them. And in this constant negotiation of the neoliberal conjuncture the "family" has been particularly critical to local institutions while survival practices such as the *umgalelo* have directly sustained efforts at social reproduction.

On a broader social and civic level, grassroots responses to the current dispensation have come in a variety of forms. Organizing against the privatization of basic needs and stressing instead the decommodification of access to water, electricity, and other services (Desai and Pithouse 2004) has been one. Housing has been a populist cause as well. Indeed, across South Africa emergent post-apartheid political struggles have coalesced around issues of everyday survival. The state has responded in less than predictable ways, further evidence of the confusing and complex linkages between state and capital that seem to gesture at the core essence of neoliberalism. As Sharma and Gupta have recently suggested (2006:277), it seems that neoliberalism "works by multiplying sites for regulation and domination through the creation of autonomous entities of government that are not part of the formal state apparatus and are guided by enterprise logic."

I have also tried to argue that politics and economy are worth rethinking in terms of their analytical linkages, but particularly in view of the turn to a materialist politics in contexts such as South Africa's where responses to deregulation and privatization on the part of the poor have been less uniform than one might first imagine. Thus, as against some mythical economic form that imprints itself onto the subjectivities of the most marginal in the global society, in fact, different responses and modes of subjectification have resulted. Further, the imaginings and fantasies of poor Capetonians do not merely rest on the attempt to gain some kind of financial hold year to year but assume the possibility of a future and therefore the capacity to initiate young men, to rebuild rural homesteads, and the like. Equally, there are fantastical and largely speculative conjurings of wealth and influence, derived from popular soap-opera idealizations, of the entrepreneur as national hero, as well as the very concrete manifestation of a small but nevertheless new black bourgeois class. On the other hand, the ongoing fantasy of a past, economically sound yet politically repressive, proposes the model of wage work as an alternative to the impasse of the present. This is really a highly concrete vision, and assumes with it the re-materialization of now largely elusive benefits such as brick and mortar homes as against those tenuously held together given the vagaries of the current deregulated construction industry. Recall that I began by noting that the Mfeketos' home was built from bricks, cement, corrugated iron, and tarpaulin—an amalgam of old and new, of pre-post- and post-apartheid.

Above all, the search for economic sovereignty rests on perspectives and affective dispositions towards risk, in much the same way that hedging and securitization immunize investors against loss (in the best case scenario, that is). Funerals are a national pastime suggesting that life in South Africa remains precarious, even while democratization has introduced a new, if often ambivalent, respect for the rule of law, human rights, and racial equality. The AIDS epidemic has played a significant part in shifting the country's demography: at last count the World Health Organization's estimate of life expectancy had dropped to 50 years for men and 52 for women; further, an estimated 1,000 die of AIDS-related illness every day across the country.[23] The relatively high incidence of violent crime in South Africa is much debated too. Some argue for the redistributive function of crime in a society historically marked by grave inequality, others reckon on a moral dimension suggesting that a generalized mistrust of the law, stemming from the old system of apartheid, has laid the groundwork for a rash of crime.[24] Whatever the case, South Africa is afflicted by all manner of risks and people die unnatural and untimely deaths for all sorts of reasons, not least on the way to and from funerals in a country with one of the highest driving-related fatality rates in the world.

Again, the neoliberal logic which dictates a moral subject who seeks self-betterment through hard work and a rational economic subject who can figure the calculus of profit through survivalist strategies highlights possible linkages between neoliberalism and "self-empowerment," between a neoliberal subject both empowered and simultaneously complicit in the project of neoliberalization; likewise a subject keen to hedge, to arbitrage, and indeed to embrace debt and additional risk, precisely as a way of ensuring against the ultimate risk of total destitution.

3.   "It Seems to Be Going"

The Genius of Survival in Wartime DR Congo

Stephen Jackson

> The [African] continent is *turning inwards on itself* in a very
> serious way.
>
> ACHILLE MBEMBE (2001)

> Here—oh, yes—she knew very well: to be alive was already
> to display genius.
>
> SONY LABOU TANSI (1990)

Through a decade of war and volatility in the Kivu provinces (at the eastern edge of the Democratic Republic of the Congo—formerly Zaire), people somehow clung to the sense of humor and unceasing playfulness with language for which they are renowned. Kivutiens would seldom provide a straight answer to the regular French greeting "Ça va?" (how's it going?). Amongst the defiantly humorous responses were: "Ça ira un jour!" (one day it will go!); "Ça peut aller . . ." [it might be going/it could go]; or "Ça va au rythme du pays!" (it goes to the rhythm of the country!). One reply freighted with deliberate ambiguity was "Ça va avec tolérance zéro!" (it goes with zero tolerance!), a double pun against the violence with which the RCD (Rassemblement Congolais pour la Démocratie) rebels who dominated the Kivus[1] met any sign of dissent, and against the degree to which, under the RCD, economic margins for ordinary Congolese had contracted to nothing. One might also hear "au rythme de la guerre" (to the rhythm of the war) or even "au rythme du RCD." Once, eschewing words altogether, a friend responded with a single gesture: a sinusoid penciled in the air with his right hand, a roller coaster of uncertainty.

But by far the most frequent answer was "Ça semble aller . . ."—it seems (or appears) to be going. The ambiguity was deliberate—"things give the appearance of progressing[2] or 'simulate' progress; maybe things are going, maybe they aren't"; "I really don't know"; or "I really couldn't commit."

A CRISIS OF MEANINGFULNESS:
MAKE BELIEVE AND MAKE TO SEEM

In July 1999 the RCD planned mass celebrations in Goma, North Kivu, for the thirty-ninth anniversary of Congo's independence from Belgian colonial rule. Militarily controlling much of the eastern third of Congo but aware they were despised by most Kivutiens, the administration ordered parades and commanded attendance. Most people I spoke with preferred to remain at home and, as they coyly put it, "meditate." "What have we got to celebrate? And what would we celebrate with?" The RCD announced a kermesse—a fair for the display of local produce and crafts.[3] In response, anonymous tracts passed from hand to hand amongst Kivutiens calling for a boycott. The RCD quickly conceded. The kermesse was abandoned. Goma's bars and nightclubs were instead invited to establish temporary franchises on the supposed fairgrounds. The middle classes came to drink, dance, and eat barbecue for a night or two. But the "high" entry fee (approximately U.S.$0.50) meant few among the general population could afford a visit.

An RCD banner dominated the entryway. But only a small stall nearby distributed RCD leaflets and most fairgoers ignored it. On the night I treated my motorcycle-taxi man, Dieumerci, to a visit, the crowd was thin, though the music was pulsing. I commented that it seemed at least something was moving again in the town, for the first time in a long while. "Do you know what this is?" Dieumerci retorted with irritation:

> All of this is just an imitation, an imitation of you whites . . . It's all
> just a poor imitation of Westerners. Before you came, we walked
> around butt-naked, with only *cache-sexes* on us. See these clothes I am
> wearing, these jeans, this t-shirt? They're all made in the West too.
> Without you we wouldn't be anything. It is only because of the West
> that we have ever been able to take any kind of step forward. Without
> you there would be no development here.

Like most Kivutiens, Dieumerci read the kermesse as a symbol of the hollowed-out nature of Congolese political culture. Its nadir had been achieved, perhaps, by the RCD, but the hollowing out had begun long ago. In Dieumerci's eyes, political events—whether "dialogues" with civil society or official "celebrations"—were poker games. The stakes were symbolic capital, such as the political credibility of political parties or rebel movements versus opposition drawn from local elites or civil society, and the tactics were bluff and bluster, show and make believe. Ordinary Kivutiens could decode such politicking with practiced cynicism. But they were often playing along, too, conniving with it. According to Filip De Boeck (1996:92), "The rupture between discourse, action and structure is total. The Zairean reality, deeply marked by a crisis of meaningfulness or leading sense, has gradually turned into a world in which fact and fiction are interchangeable . . . The *faire croire* [make believe] and the *faire semblant* [make to seem, make to resemble] have taken over from reality."[4]

Over the long term, the state itself—its structures and institutions, its emblems and its symbolic patrimony—was systematically pillaged, unbundled, repackaged, and resold by those governing. Against such a backdrop, "connivance" with power became naturalized as the "postcolonial work *par excellence*" (Werbner 1996:2), engendering opportunity (as well as difficulty) and "myriad ways in which ordinary people bridle, trick, and actually toy with power instead of confronting it directly."

This political culture of make believe is first glimpsed in *longue durée* historical processes. Jan Vansina, for example, offers intriguing hints of involution, imitation, and the gulf between semblance and substance deep in the precolonial history of the Kivus:[5]

> On the western slopes all along the mountains bordering the uplands of Maniema in the area west of Lakes Kivu and Edward, the forests harbored tiny principalities ruled by a *mwámi*. . . . They strike us as theater-like states, because their miniscule size was matched by elaborate rules for succession, accession to the throne, and royal burial, by a complex titulature surrounding the royal office, and by intricate royal rituals and a plethora of emblems, as if these district-sized kingdoms were the equals of the great kingdoms that lay beyond the rift itself. These societies are in part *involuted reminiscences* of what others farther east had been before large states appeared in the great lakes area, in part *imitation* of these kingdoms, and in part quite original *elaborations*. (Vansina 1990:185; emphasis added)

Later, the Arab slave trade penetrated as far as Maniema in the Kivus, providing graphic instruction in the intimate connections among power, profit, and predatory violence. Later again, under the banner of King Leopold's "Congo Free State," Congolese learned a further drastic lesson about the gap between official utterances and the brute reality of political power. Smiling, regal declarations of civilizing intent were undercut by the piles of severed hands on rubber plantations, when slaves filling the royal purse failed to make their quotas.

Later still, under Mobutu Sese Seko, Zaire experienced thirty years of what Michael Schatzberg (1988:1) has described as Janus-faced dictatorship: "Zaire has two faces: one smiles, the other snarls; one exudes paternal confidence and caring, the other is insecure and oppressive." Cold War Realpolitik provided Mobutu with a free pass to rule as a latter-day Sun King, conjuring up illusions of divinely inspired progress, development as deus ex machina. The president's godlike image descended daily through the clouds on Zairean TV while economic life imploded and political discourse further hollowed out.

In August 1992 currents of democratization seemingly sweeping the continent forced Mobutu to permit the organization of a Conférence Nationale Souveraine. Its delegates voted to strip him of executive power, to adopt a provisional constitution of transition, and to change the country's name back to Congo. Another sharp lesson about the gap between rhetoric and Realpolitik was provided when, despite all their rhetoric about democratizing Africa, the international community backed Mobutu in completely ignoring these actions. In stark contrast five years later, when Laurent-Désiré Kabila proclaimed himself president at the head of a ramshackle foreign-backed insurrection and renamed the country, the international community woke up and took note, quickly moving to support the new ruler (Nzongola-Ntalaja 2002:1). And finally, when Kabila split from the neighboring countries (Rwanda and Uganda) who had backed his rebellion and these raised a new force against him (the RCD), the international community remained aloof as the country split and war swallowed millions of lives.

In short, the consistent, *longue durée* contradiction between what centralized power (be it colonial or postcolonial, national or international) *said* and what it *did* engendered a yawning gulf in political culture. As De Boeck suggests, recourse to the *faire semblant* and the *faire croire* became the reflex for both the elites and the masses.

"Make believe" (*faire croire*) is, of course, intimately related to "make to seem" or "make to resemble" (*faire semblant*). Dieumerci's complaint against the kermesse was that it palely imitated the Western Other and thus, by implication, lacked both authenticity and, more importantly, quality. Etymologically, *faire semblant* is closely related to *facsimile*, to create a copy, to simulate and thus, potentially, to dissimulate. Accusations of inauthenticity and dissimulation multiply across my fieldnotes from this period: in accusations about "false" or "duplicitous" claims of Congolese nationality (Jackson 2007); in accusations that Rwanda was seeking to organize a "parody of secession" in the Kivus; or that the Banyamulenge, Congolese Tutsi rebelling in 2002 against Rwandan Tutsi, were merely engaged in staging *un montage*—a set-up, a fakery. Stoller, theorizing mimesis as a pivotal political tactic in the postcolony, suggests its power "derives from its multisensorial affecting presence" (Stoller 1995:195). But in the kermesse, and more broadly in Congolese political culture since the waning of Mobutu, mimesis often *fails* to affect. The imitation fails to capture the population because it is transparent, banal, laughable, because it is just a "poor imitation," something shoddy.

Nor is mimicry always a laughing matter. Taussig reminds us of the proximity between the desire to imitate the Other and to erase him, between the "mimetic faculty" and the capacity for "genocidal terror"—recalling Horkheimer and Adorno's assertion that "there is no anti-Semite who does not basically want to imitate his mental image of a Jew, which is composed of mimetic ciphers" (cited in Taussig 1993:66–67). The *géno-cidaire* may begin by wishing to impersonate his fantasy of the Other, but if he cannot convincingly pull it off, the failure of make believe, of simulation and dissimulation, can directly engender first abjection and then an explosive violence.

"MAKING DO," "POLYVALENCE," AND "LIVING IN THE AIR"

Though the practice of survival through turning your hand to what you could long predates Mobutu, it is he who is said to have baptized it. Was the president lamenting or winking in the 1970s when he diagnosed as "le mal Zairois" (the Zairean disease) the fact that "everything is for sale, everything is bought in our country" (Callaghy 1984:190)? Even then, his prescription for popular survival was notorious: "débrouillez-vous!"— "make do," or "fend for yourself."[6]

In response to more than a century of increasingly volatile political make believe, Congolese of all stripes have been obliged to hone their reflexes. Flexibility and the ability to self-promote have become critical to both survival and prosperity in the Congo. The imperative of making do (*se débrouiller*)—sometimes celebrated, sometimes scorned, but always much debated by Congolese themselves as a category of their lifeworld (see also McGovern, this volume, for an Ivorian comparison)—has operated for decades in multiple sectors and across class, gender, and identity group, productively exploiting the gulf between semblance and substance through mimesis and facsimile. Through it, individual Congolese have not only survived. They have elevated *débrouillardise* (resourcefulness) to an art form, an ethic, through it actively debating the changing forms of the social person and social reproduction more generally.

In 1999, Filbert—a Congolese cameraman I met on a ferry on Lac

Kivu—offered to make a video about my fieldwork. I told him that I was trying to understand the Congolese way of life. He retorted, "Well, that's going to be difficult! The Congolese lives in the air. He doesn't have a fixed position!"[7] Only in his mid-twenties, Filbert had already been an auto mechanic, a driver, and a gold miner, before trying for a career in video production:

> We live only a third of life here. Me, I'm multipurpose [*polyvalent*]. Would you condemn me for that? For you, if you were to leave your country there is somebody that would notice. If I were to leave, nobody would notice, nobody would care. There wouldn't even be anyone who would record the event!

In his "polyvalence," he was joined by customs officials who were also smugglers, militia fighters who collaborated with their enemies to export minerals to the global market, teachers who were farmers who were traditional healers, churchmen who represented extremist factions, soldiers who switched sides merely because they wanted "to get back to work," youth who moved from agriculture to mining to armed banditry and back in a matter of months, and civilian administrators who created opposition militias before defecting to the ranks of the RCD (and vice versa) (Jackson 2003b; for comparison, see Buggenhagen, this volume, and Piot, this volume, for "jostling" within the "informal sector"). Everyone wore multiple hats and carried several business cards, at least one of which seemed to represent a local NGO, one of the newest means of getting by (Jackson 2004).

In short, negotiating and managing multiple identities, allegiances, affinities and profiles had become daily habit. Hedging your bets and balancing your portfolio of societal debts and obligations become critical life skills when, as the Congolese novelist Labou Tansi so strikingly put it, to be alive is already to display "genius." Such trickster entrepreneurialism became a source of pride in Congo, a lifestyle, a cultural value, and a political act. It also acquired a set of humorous and richly suggestive epithets: the "Eleventh Commandment"; "Article Quinze" (the mythical "fifteenth" article of the constitution);[8] or *débrouillardise* (resourcefulness) or simply *Système D*.[9]

A single theory of causation for the emergence of such rich practices of improvisation, negotiation, and flexibility would be hopelessly reductionist—as reductionist, perhaps, as the term *crisis* to which such ingrained practices of improvisation might then be construed as the inevitable response (against which the introduction to this volume argues). From the global literature one can infer at least three related streams of causal thinking about the emergence of such practices. First, one can read the emergence of flexibility as representing the core operational logic of late capitalism (Harvey 1989), crossed with that logic's effects on citizenship because of migration, diasporas, and transnational flows (Ong 1999), and/or complicated by the business arena's saturation with biomedicalized discourses of corporate health founded in "immunity" and resistance to "infection" (Martin 1994).

A second stream reads the flexibility in lifestyles and strategies as quintessentially *postcolonial*. Life in the postcolony is beset with indeterminacy, entanglement, ambiguity, and uncertainty (Nordstrom 1997; Appadurai 1999; Werbner 1996). The postcolonial *dispositif* then demands and begets improvisation:

> [T]he postcolony is made up not of one "public space" but of several, each having its own logic yet liable to be entangled with other logics when operating in certain contexts; hence, the postcolonial subject has to learn to bargain in this conceptual marketplace. Further, subjects in the postcolony also have to have marked ability to manage not just a single identity, but several—flexible enough to negotiate as and when necessary. (Mbembe 2001:104)

A third stream theorizes flexibility and improvisation as deriving directly from contexts of radical volatility and uncertainty. Such "unstable places" demand that individuals learn "to function effectively while familiar hegemonic relations are suspended, visibly deconstructed, and recirculated as parts" (Greenhouse 2002:5; see also 1996). These are "crises, by definition, [which] involve conditions in which people (including the state's agents) must improvise with the elements of their social and political technologies and cope with a variety of unexpected disruptions and opportunities." Through them, "improvisation even in previously unimaginable circumstances makes meaning itself a mode of social action and not merely a reaction."

At least in the Congolese context, these separate streams of literature must not be taken as mutually exclusive but as characterizing successive, mutually reinforcing waves of influence that, together, have intensified an already established set of reflexes. "We live mysteriously," Filbert the cameraman told me, a half-smile on his lips as we concluded our conversation. Neither resisting nor actively collaborating, Congolese have been obliged over the *longue durée* to collude and connive with power, forcing a smile, playing along, meanwhile vigorously pursuing other agendas: straight survival for the many, enormous status, wealth, and power for the few. In the face of every new proclamation, initiative, or opposition countermove, people became used to asking two key questions. The first was, what's really behind this? Nothing was ever what it appeared on the surface. The second was, what's in it for me? Everything—historical inheritance, cultural forms, identity categories and networks, material resources, political movements and symbols, and more—became negotiable.

To theorize practice this way swings dangerously close to a vulgar economism, the kind dismissed by Geertz as the assumption that "down deep, culture is shallow; society runs on the energies of want" (Geertz 1984:516). But I do not mean to argue that the Congolese externalize and exogenize their culture or identity in order to sell out. Rather, as Bob White (2000:49) has argued, in Congo "ideas of personhood are not necessarily based on the Western model of an essential 'true' self which is opposed to an externalized world outside of the self, and is necessarily compromised or tainted by exposure to the forces of the market." For Congo was always already in the global market—through slavery, through the extractive violence of the colonial rubber trade, through the "everything's for sale" ethic of *Mobutisme* and Zaire's place in the Cold War. Congo has remained in violently intimate contact with the "global" for several centuries (see the introduction to this volume). Thus, Congolese flexibilization begins not with *late* capitalism but with its earliest manifestations, intensifies through colonialism, further increases under the duress of *Mobutisme*, Realpolitik, and late capitalism (particularly under structural adjustment), and explodes in the radical instability and uncertainty of the civil war. No wonder *polyvalence* became something to celebrate.

"A LITTLE NOTHING"

"Everybody has had to become a bit predatory" because of the war, a senior UN official in the Kivus told me in 2002. "There is a whole microeconomy of repackaging, reselling, disaggregating all the products, where everyone adds their 20 *francs congolais*." A Congolese aid worker described how families in her *quartier* "just sell a sack of charcoal to survive." The sacks were broken up into kilo parcels and resold. Others broke these down further into packages of just a few bricks and resold them for "un petit rien" (a little nothing). Markets were now being held in the evening rather than, as traditionally, the morning because it took all day to scrape together any money with which to buy food. Produce was sold in smaller and smaller units—a pen-cap of salt, one eighth of an onion, a paper twist of peanuts. "Think of the 'Qaddafis,'"[10] resumed the UN official, "who sell their petrol a liter at a time on the street when the stations will only sell units of five or ten liters at a time. It's not a question of convenience, it is complete absence of margin, the absence of ability of anyone to invest ahead in a large quantity."

For some, the Rwandan border offered micro-margins. Dieumerci gave what he earned every day to his cousin to pay off the loan on his motorbike, keeping less than 50 U.S. cents with which to eat. On the side, he smuggled milk. He would collect empty mineral water bottles from friends employed at aid workers' houses. Then he would cross the border to Rwanda with a 20-liter jerrican and buy fresh milk from farmers down from the hills (buying in a shop would have eliminated his margin). Crossing back again he would drop 20 Congolese francs to the border officials to look the other way, decant the milk into the bottles, sell them, and "after all of that, I gain a little nothing." Filling the jerrican cost $10: over a day or two he could sell the repackaged milk for $14–15 (135 Congolese francs per liter) to people from his neighborhood.

Asked how he survived on so little, Dieumerci laughed, saying he was comparatively "middle-class . . . I ration myself to 100 *francs congolais* [at that time, a little less than a dollar] a day. I eat only at midday and the evening, at home or sometimes in an *nganda* [street restaurant]: 70 *francs congolais* buys you some beans and rice, or beans and bananas. Meat and foufou [manioc paste] is about 100 *francs congolais*. I don't eat in *La Pelouse* [a well-known *nganda*]! I find cheaper places, but still clean . . ."

THE MICRO-DIVISION OF POLITICAL AND OTHER FORMS OF CAPITAL

This pervasive economy of division, subdivision, and micro-division provides, I contend, a productive metaphor for theorizing other spheres of Congolese life, too. For it is not only economic capital—goods, reserves, resources—that was being subdivided and recycled in this fashion, but other forms of "capital" too (political, symbolic, social, even cultural). Alongside the miners (for diamonds, gold, tantalum, and other minerals in which the DRC is rich) and the money traders in the so-called informal economy,[11] one must also consider the political and military realm (the proliferation of one-man militia armies and rebel movements), the spiritual (the burgeoning of new churches), the developmental (the mushrooming of local NGOs), and the discursive (the acceleration of the rumor mill and the production of anonymous tracts).

My argument is that activity in all of these separate spheres exemplifies the creative imperative to recycle existing forms (political, cultural, economic) in the hope of both *making a margin* and *making sense*. In thinking about the DRC one needs, therefore, to find a way of balancing a description of a prolonged and bitter social agon with a proper account of the enormous, if inward, creativity that has accompanied it. If violence destroys, it also engenders multiple forms of production, economic and cultural. Forms proliferate and multiply opportunistically even as they subdivide. At stake is both survival and meaning.

Consider, for example, the trajectory of eastern Congo's RCD rebels, who precipitated the 1998 war with an attempted coup mounted from Goma. From the beginning, this was a movement born of opportunity, not ideology. By the frank admission of some in its senior ranks,[12] it never possessed a coherent political project beyond the seizure of national power. When that proved impossible—by late summer 1999—the RCD began to splinter. Rivalries between its patron states, Uganda and Rwanda, over rich mineral deposits erupted into all-out fighting in Kisangani, with hundreds of casualties. The RCD split, split, and split again. Its first titular leader, Ernest Wamba-dia-Wamba, fled to Ugandan protection and the remainder, now rechristened RCD-Goma, reshuffled. Jokes quickly circulated at the RCD's expense. As one friend in Goma put it, "You know that *orchestre* [Congolese dance music group], Wenge Musica, who have split into all these different *ailes* [wings], Wenge Musica Aile Paris and so on? Well, it is just like that . . . Not the RCD, but the RCDs, plural—from wings to feathers . . ."

Soon, RCD-Goma, RCD-ML (Mouvement de Libération), RCD-National, RCD-Originel, RCD-Congo, and the RCD (period) vied for supremacy. Each fought to stake claim to the diminishing symbolic capital attached to the initials. Organizational mimesis became the order of the day: each new faction marshaled letterheads, cabinets, spokesmen, simulating governmentality. Political style trumped substance. Around Ituri, in northeastern Congo, three separate RCD subfactions contended, each exacting separate permissions for travel ("visas") and commerce ("licenses"). In July 2002, RCD-Goma spokesman Kin-Kiey Mulumba split away to form RCD-Congo, claiming, "The RCD, that's us . . . RCD-Goma has put itself out of the game" (Agence France Press 2002).

This fission proved deadly. In the race to the bottom, the smaller the movement, the less its dwindling legitimacy and the stronger its repression. The smaller the territory each controlled, the more its determination to wring from it what it could through the now infamous Congolese war economy of gold, diamonds, coltan, tin, coffee, and other lootable commodities (Jackson 2001). Each bargained with military godfathers in Rwanda or Uganda for protection, struck transient deals with former foes, or promised protection to this or that marginalized ethnic group, playing up fears of genocide in return for the temporary opportunity to mine and plunder.

This schismogenesis was mirrored within the RCD's proximate opponents, the Mayi-Mayi militias. "In general, we are nationalists; we fight for a noble cause," a spokesman for Mayi-Mayi "General" Padiri[13] told me in 2002. But this much-vaunted "popular resistance" never resembled the unitary national movement its propagandists claimed. *Mayi-Mayi* is better understood as the contemporary recycling of a long-standing (as early as the Mulelist rebellion of the 1960s and further)[14] Central African repertoire of agrarian insurrection relying on magical technology to confer immunity to gunfire. *Mayi* is a Congolese variant of the Kiswahili *maji* (water). *Mayi-Mayi* is a war cry referencing two kinds of water: holy water, with which fighters are ritually "baptized" before battle, conferring invincibility; and the water into which bullets fired at the "baptized" turn. Belief in the efficacy of this technology remains pervasive throughout the Kivus, rendering barriers to entry remarkably low in what might be dubbed the militia industry. Mayi-Mayi deaths, which were frequent, were popularly ascribed to violations of taboos or imprecision in baptismal rituals. Mayi-Mayi movements proliferated. Beginning with a Nyanga/ Hunde militia to protect autochthon interests in the early 1990s, ten years later the number of factions had reached double digits, presenting less a challenge to the RCD than to each other, vying to control mineral-rich terrain. Here, rather than a micro-division of an original unity, the Mayi-Mayi phenomenon is best understood as the frantic multiplication of an original type: the rapid creation of multiple facsimiles until underlying similarity of purpose or form is all but erased and the symbolic capital inherent in *Mayi-Mayi* risks depletion (underlining that the *productive* resource of violence can reach an endpoint when seams of both meaning and material are overmined).

Less violently, NGOs in the Kivus followed a similar trajectory (Jackson 2003b, 2004). Beginning in the late 1980s, a small number of development, human rights, and democratization groups emerged in the narrow political space opened up as a result of external pressure to democratize and internal retrenchment of state services. By the early 1990s analysts were approvingly noting the Kivus as somewhere "development without the state" was advancing (Streiffeler 1994). But the 1994 refugee crisis—when a million

Hutus spilled across the border after genocide in Rwanda, followed belatedly by millions of dollars of initially undirected aid—produced booming demand for local NGO partners and so these too began to proliferate. True to form, Kivutiens simultaneously generated multiple new organizations and fashioned richly dismissive epithets for them: "mushroom NGOs" (*ONGs champignons*) which spring up over night to avail of the manure (money) thrown over them; "momentary NGOs" (*ONGs momentanées*), "spontaneous" and "occasional" NGOs, "hobby NGOs," "prostitute" or "fictitious" NGOs, "satellite NGOs," and so on.

THE FAILURE OF "STATE FAILURE"

The atrophying organs of the Congolese state offered another opportune field for multiplication and micro-division, in which operations and authority could be disaggregated, parceled out, and resold. In 2000, while still collecting field materials on the war economy, I met Rose, a customs official at Bukavu airport, South Kivu, as I disembarked from a cargo flight from Walikale, a major centre of coltan (tantalum ore) production. Smiling, Rose asked to search my bags. She seemed a little disappointed not to find any mineral samples. In lieu of a uniform, Rose was resplendent in a colorful blouse tagged with motifs of tropical fruit and the motto *Wamama—Tuendelee Article 15*—"Women, Let's Go Article 15!" Here was a state functionary in clothes unashamedly enjoining women to fend for themselves, with a nod and a wink toward the discourse of the gender and development movement. Rose lived day to day not through her official salary (long unpaid) but through "fees," "taxes," and "Fantas" (small bribes, named for the drinks they might purchase) she could leverage, wearing her official hat, on goods illicitly transiting through the airport. At least some of these unofficial flows she also assisted in organizing.

The predatory nature of *Mobutiste* Zaire's police, army, and officialdom of all kinds has been much remarked upon.[15] But that they were predatory implies, of course, that they were anything but absent. State administrators not only remained constant presences in Kivutien life until the advent of war in 1998, many of them at low to medium levels in the hierarchy remained in place *during* it. The same customs and immigration officials always greeted me at the Rwanda-Congo border whether Goma was under Kabila or the RCD. Several had, I suspect, held the same positions under Mobutu and I doubt any future regime change will dislodge them. When I first met them, their salaries had gone unpaid for the better part of a

decade and they lived from what they could levy on those crossing the
border.

Similarly, through the same decade-long ructions, the morning rumble
of traffic in Goma's streets (as in Kinshasa) was presided over by traffic
police in uniforms the patriotic yellow and blue of the Congolese flag.
Similarly unpaid for months or years, they divided their efforts between
aiding the regular flow of traffic through the main boulevards and pulling
vehicles over to the side of the road to shake their drivers down for the
most minor of infractions.

Under the RCD, the local courts were still quasi-functional, hearing
complaints and trying civil cases. "Licensing" and "taxation" of petty
commerce continued. The "armed forces" and "police" continued shaking
people down much as they had in the past, though the paranoia and repression of the RCD perhaps afforded them even more excuses than before.
And customary authority—a highly politicized institution under Mobutu,
reciprocally assimilated to the centralized state (De Boeck 1996)—continued a complex and strategically ambiguous stance, both embodying and
resisting the authority of the Kinshasa government and/or the RCD rebels.

In short, the state of the state throughout the *Mobutiste* (early 1960s–
mid-1997) and post-*Mobutiste* (since mid-1997) eras shows a perhaps surprising degree of continuity. Throughout the period of RCD control of the
Kivus, the degree of direct violence that individuals suffered increased
enormously. Mortality rates rose concomitantly to unprecedented levels—
four million or more are thought to have died countrywide as a result
of the conflict (Coghlan, Brennan, Ngoy, et al. 2006). But many of the
everyday points of interface between ordinary people and those acting in
the name of the state remained much as they had under Mobutu.

An examination of Congo-Zaire's long-term crisis must focus, therefore, on how the "smiling, snarling" state (Schatzberg 1988) and the "conniving" postcolonial subject (Mbembe 2001) grew together in a strange,
mutually suspicious and yet codependent political culture, each appearing
to sustain the other as both inexorably exhausted the room for maneuver. Examining the involution of a shared but fractious political culture
as a whole—rather than focusing on the "trompe-l'oeil" of the state
(Bayart, Ellis, and Hibou 1999:19)—is likely to provide a clearer view
of the historical trajectory of "crisis." Much might be learned through a
biographical study of such minor functionaries of the supposedly "failed"
state who continue to believe that the state is still made importantly
and materially *present* through their work. These would argue that their
débrouillardise, rather than representing the state's corruption or "col-

lapse," maintained its salience to the lives of citizens during prolonged periods of uncertainty.

Unfortunately, Congo/Zaire has figured as a central analytical object in attempts by political scientists to derive an analytical category of "failed" or "collapsed state."[16] Interrogated against the lived reality of Kivutien life under the RCD occupation, these categories provide few answers and suffer from a variety of analytical failings. First, in attempting to compare such widely contrasting African "crises" as Somalia, Rwanda, and the DRC, theorists of state failure/collapse have been obliged to produce long *symptomologies* rather than tight taxonomies, ones which venture well beyond the weakness of centralized governmentality. To single out—a little unfairly—just one recent theorist, Robert Rotberg suggests that the characteristics of state failure include violence of an "enduring character," much of it "directed at the existing government," often combining demands for autonomy of an "enflamed character" with "criminal violence;" "disharmonies between communities," and an inability to protect the citizenry who "depend on states and central governments to secure their persons and free them from fear." Instead, failed states "prey on their own constituents" or fail to "control their borders." They are marked by institutional weaknesses, with legislatures that are merely "rubber-stamping machines" for the executive, a bureaucracy that has "lost its sense of professional responsibility," and a highly politicized military "devoid of the esprit that they once demonstrated." Infrastructure deteriorates or is destroyed, and "the effective educational and health systems are privatized." A nation-state "also fails when it loses legitimacy—when it forfeits the 'mandate of heaven'" (Rotberg 2003:5–9).[17] And so on. So all-encompassing is this diagnostic that one is tempted to ask if any state on Earth would survive its diagnosis with a clean bill of health.[18]

Second, in asserting that a particular state has "failed," such diagnoses themselves fail to identify those for whom it continues to work: extractive political elites, middlemen, paramilitary opportunists, entrepreneurs who avail of the compromised institutions adventitiously to leverage profit (Jackson 2005). For these, such states are a remarkable success, and the label of "failure" misdirects our attention from how mutated forms of state administration serve their ends.

Third, and most directly pertinent to this essay's concerns, notions of state failure or collapse (or the newest term of art, state "fragility")[19] are inadequate to capture the sense of radical expansion, production, and creation that prolonged societal uncertainty engenders across multiple sectors of existence. This point has been well captured by theorists as different as James Ferguson (2005)—

> It is worth asking whether Africa's combination of privately secured mineral-extraction enclaves and weakly governed humanitarian hinterlands might constitute not a lamentably immature form of globalization but, rather, a quite advanced and sophisticated mutation of it . . .

—and Mark Duffield (1998):

> Rather than the developmental rhetoric of scarcity or breakdown, one has to address the possibility that protracted instability is symptomatic of new and expanding forms of political economy; a function of economic change rather than a developmental malaise. It is difficult for the development model of conflict to convey such a sense of innovative expansion.

INVOLUTION AND CREATIVITY IN THE DR CONGO

The state failure/collapse metaphor is certainly inadequate to capture the strange and expansive creativity within the drawn-out societal agon through which the people of the DR Congo have endured. Analysts would do better, I contend, to work from an earlier, Geertzian metaphor that teetered precariously on the edge of crisis: that of involution. Congo's violent societal trajectory has been involutionary, in Geertz' sense of "culture patterns which, like Gothic architecture or Maori carving, having reached a definitive form, continued nonetheless to develop by becoming internally more complicated" (Geertz 1984:514). Involution invokes an energetic, intricate, but *inward* and involved elaboration of cultural forms—whether economic, organizational, political, or symbolic—within overall stasis or, even, decline. From a purely terminological point of view involution might thus be seen as the opposite of evolution, or perhaps of development itself (etymologically related to devolution)[20]—involution as the anti-teleology, perhaps, since it entails an ever more frantic response to the challenges of *survival in the present* rather than dreams of building for the future.

The involution metaphor is presently enjoying a quiet revival in the social sciences. Khuri (1978) diagnosed "social involution" as Lebanon's civil war gained momentum and the bases of production deteriorated, drawing more and more people into the war's vortex. Frick McKean (1989) decries "cultural involution" in the syncretic balance between tradition and economic modernization in Indonesian tourism. Africans and Native Americans adapting their cultural forms to respond to forced displacement are displaying involution, suggests Weist (1995). Curvilinear development of this kind is visible in the "disappearing" organizational identity of the French gay movement (Duyvendak 1995), the "involutionary" economic privatization of post-Soviet Russia (Burawoy, Krotov, and Lytkina 2000), the tactical alliances between drug traffickers and guerrillas in the "political involution" of Colombia's violence (Sánchez 2001), or the indefinite patrimonialism of the Chinese Communist Party (Lü 2000). In all these ways scholars are productively reworking Geertz's original (1963) thesis on agricultural involution in Indonesia to theorize what might be styled as an *introvertive turn* in organizational and societal forms.

Across these widely differing contexts and inquiries, overarching similarities can be detected. Involution responds to constrained space and margin for maneuver by engendering great, but inward, creativity. It often forces recourse to the so-called traditional, accompanied by elevated levels of (often violent) economic predation. It is vortex-like, sucking more and more people into its processes—yet its progress can go almost unnoticed. Most of all, involution contains the seeds of its own inevitable crisis, Geertz's "terrible impasse" when internal complexification "runs out of space between the lines" (Geertz 1984:515). In that involution is, itself, a response to incipient crisis, this raises the possibility that involution may collapse into crisis *within* crisis. Survival under such circumstances is truly an act of "genius," as Tansi (1990) writes. Congolese creativity amid volatility has been great, but inward, and ambiguous. On the one hand it has represented the only chance for a great many Congolese, and political and personal advance for a rather smaller number. On the other, involution may merely delay a later, looming implosion/explosion.

Involution also implies—in case this could be in doubt—that though official global economic narratives frequently write Africa out of the picture (Guyer, cited in Ferguson 1999), the twists and turns of globalization are deeply etched into everyday African experience (see the introduction to this volume). Ferguson (1999:236), mulling over the "disappointed expectations" of Zambian copper miners—and, himself, mining Kristeva and Borneman—remarks that globalization has rendered Africa "abject": "thrown aside, expelled, or discarded."

Whether this captures Copperbelt Zambians' sense of their relation to the global, it does not encapsulate the complex lived reality of those working the Kivus' coltan, just a little further north. Between 1999 and 2001, a tenfold increase in the spot price of tantalum (a vital ingredient in microelectronics, including, in particular, cell phones) on international metal markets had an immediate and galvanizing effect on artisanal production in the Kivus—where some of the world's richest deposits are found (Jackson 2001, 2002, 2003a). Young men threw themselves into digging, while a complex and shifting network of commercial and military actors, both Congolese and foreign (particularly Rwandan and Ugandan) dominated the higher levels of the commodity chain, often violently. Then, in 2001, the international price plummeted as rapidly as it had climbed. A frantic reorganization followed in which actors at all levels were squeezed out. Some turned to other commodities, some lost everything. Those at the bottom of the chain were often left with nothing.

This price-driven arc of frantic activity followed by sudden contraction refutes the notion that Africa and Africans are marginalized from the global. Kivutiens, at least, continue to endure an intimate exposure to global market forces, directly and dramatically experiencing shifts and changes in global demand over which they have no control.

If Fergusonian/Kristevan theorizations do not entirely capture this reality, however, other theoretical variations on abjection do. Michael-André Bernstein, in his breathtaking examination of the dark side of Saturnalia, *Bitter Carnival* (1992), writes of abjection not as complete expulsion to the margins and irrelevance, but as confinement to a location just "under the floorboards." This, Bernstein tells us, is a truer rendering in English of Dostoevsky's "underground" Man, the epitome of the literary abject hero. Bernstein's approach to interpreting abjection is, indeed, primarily literary, strongly influenced by a Bakhtinian interest in genres and conventions. Abjection, he suggests, is "always governed by the mapping of prior literary modes." It must be understood as a social relation, one that is dialogic and experienced through conversation, but one taking place on profoundly unequal terms. It is in this sense that one can construe Africa's—and Africans'—relations with globalization also as a profoundly unequal conversation, something of a dialogue of the deaf. This dialogue includes unequal exchanges about development, modernity, modernization, democracy, governance, debt versus good financial husbandry, and so on. Each of these ("we have them," says the West, "and you don't, but you need them!") reinforce abjection dialogically, and constitute their own, established, metanarrative modes of technocratic discourse, with an effect analogous to the weight that pre-existing genres and modes place on abject heroes in contemporary literature.

Confined "under the floorboards," the abject is held, in Bernstein's terms, in "a tenuous and partial resistance to the normative," without its own place from which to speak, contained wholly within power. Congo's and Africa's abjection cannot be imagined as distinct from global arrangements—rather, they should be understood as held inferior but intimate to those arrangements. Within this radically unequal global "conversation," one then can interpret Congolese involution as a question of tactics, not strategy, in de Certeau's sense. Tactics are enacted from within the space controlled by power: they do not work outside it (de Certeau 1984).

Wartime Congo saw the room for maneuver diminish almost to a vanishing point, forcing a tactical introversion, a frenetic reworking and reworking of available material rather than producing anew entirely, very much in line with Mbembe's diagnosis that the African continent has been *"turning inwards on itself* in a very serious way." Great creativity is at stake. But this creativity is in some sense *involuted.* It involves an ever more frantic process of internal complexification while overall cultural forms remain unchanged or even begin to atrophy (Geertz 1984). As war—which itself stagnated and turned violently inward—constrains the space for agency more and more, so desperate inventiveness also turns in on itself. All forms of capital, material (gems, metal ore, tropical hardwood, agricultural produce, land . . .) or cultural/symbolic (tradition, history, identity, alliance or enmity, rite, religious organization . . .), are pressed into the service of elite profit or peasant survival.

Crisis forces improvisation; but can improvisation infinitely defer the effects of crisis? At what point do processes of politico-cultural introversion and involution lead to implosion? Might this be when the "make believe" of political actors becomes *beyond* belief, when the different forms of capital appear too depleted and populations become critically uncertain about what can and cannot be credited? Might this be the trigger moment at which extreme violence breaks out from below?

The term *crisis* (or *emergency*, which humanitarians seem to prefer) is, in this way, rendered even more than usually problematic. How long can a crisis be asserted to persist before the term itself becomes devoid of teleological sense? The prolonged involution of the Kivus appears on the one hand to be the logical outcome of long-term processes delving back to the colonial and precolonial eras. On the other, the crisis is also of recent genesis, emanating from successive conflicts over the last ten years. A chronic, ongoing, and ever-deepening difficulty has in effect been overlaid by a set of largely exogenous difficulties that intensified and accelerated it.

In such a complicated picture, it is impossible to argue completely for either historical continuity or rupture. Within the Kivus, during the years of conflict, this overarching indeterminacy has manifested itself in two contrasting varieties of pessimism about the future, and one modest optimism. According to the first pessimism, involution could continue more or less indefinitely since Congo's resources—not just economic capital, but human, political, and so on—are so vast as to be almost inexhaustible. As a Kiswahili proverb, frequently quoted in the Kivus, has it, "you never finish eating the meat of an elephant" (*nyama tembo kula hawezi kumaliza*). This depicts Congo as a vast carcass state, to be picked over by predators and scavengers long into the future, Prometheus bound to the rock, his torment unchanging, constant, and daily renewed.

In the other pessimism, implosion is seen as dangerously near, the various resources that could be creatively reworked to delay the inevitable almost depleted. As one Kivutien priest described the impasse to me in 1999: "It is a kind of swollen abscess and it will have to burst one day . . . It will lead to nothing except dead bodies . . ."

The texture of *both* pessimisms about torment amid the potential for plenty is captured in a rumor circulating in Kinshasa in 2007. It tells of a giant magic snake—a boa or python, it seems—which vomits money. The story goes that the snake was given to a prominent diamond dealer from the Central Kasai provinces by his marabout, from whom he had asked financial help. The catch—there's always a catch—is that however much cash the snake would vomit on any particular day, it all had to be spent by the end of that same day or the magic (and the snake) would die. On some days, the snake would vomit as much as $100,000. "And it's no mean task to spend that much in a single day even in Kinshasa, Monsieur, let me tell you!" said my Kinois friend who related the story.

In short, the seemingly fantastic and bottomless ability to plumb the Congolese patrimony for money—whether through coltan, military campaigning, religious or developmental missionizing, or plain old "grand corruption"—might, in the end, prove self-defeating, leading to the loss of magic (the disenchantment of postmodernity and late capitalism?) or, worse still, to violent eruption.

A CODA AND A PUNCH LINE

But there remains modest optimism, too. Improbably, and despite more than four million deaths, the Congolese have carried on. In Sun City, South Africa, in 2002, a shaky peace agreement was cobbled together between the multiple belligerents. It resulted in an unwieldy transition government—the "1+4"—with a president (Joseph Kabila, who succeeded his assassinated father in 2001) and four vice presidents (including one representing each main belligerent army). The transition eventually led to historic mid-2006 elections, the first for more than forty years, in which

Joseph Kabila was confirmed as president. Increasingly forceful military operations by a large United Nations peacekeeping presence, in conjunction with new, integrated Congolese army (the FARDC) reduced but could not eliminate the predations of the armed groups. These turned inward still further, exacting renewed violence against the local populations in the smaller and smaller territories they controlled. Meanwhile, the FARDC rapidly replaced the armed groups to become the principle violator of human rights in the country.

In economic terms, while 2006, the final year of the transition, reported more than 6 percent growth in GDP, this represented little more than the usual rebound in an economy's receipts after war. As the year closed, much more pertinently for most Congolese, inflation was running close to 20 percent, prices of basic commodities were soaring above already elevated levels, and the Congolese franc-to-dollar exchange rate was slipping precipitously. The daily struggle to eke out a survival livelihood continued. In cities across the country, the traffic police still turned out daily in their yellow and blue, and the Qaddafis hawked their petrol by the side of the road.

The elections saw massive public participation. But mistrust of the *faire semblant* remains alive and well. The elections promised change and were met with ringing international endorsements as "free and fair." But many Congolese still viewed them with an understandable caution and suspicion, discounting them as a trickery and a trumpery, a façade through which the West was seeking to impose its choice of president, a "foreigner's foreigner"—for Joseph Kabila has been subject to the same accusations of non-authenticity and non-nationality that have dogged other African leaders in recent years (Jackson 2006). In political terms, the elections bred new parties and electoral alliances that were described as "marriages against nature"—a Tutsi running on the MLC ticket (a rebel movement that had opposed the RCD) in North Kivu; Nzanga Mobutu, the former dictator's son, allying himself with Joseph Kabila, son of the man who overthrew him. All the while, the armed groups in the east—the Mayi-Mayi and others—continued to split and re-form (though the RCDs, plural, imploded at the polls).

At a conference in New York toward the end of 2005, I introduced a Nigerian colleague to a Congolese friend:

> *Nigerian colleague:* You're from Congo? Congratulations: things are going better there now, no?
>
> *Congolese friend:* Well, there is the *semblance* of improvement . . .

Things still only *seem* to be going. For the DRC to emerge from its long involutionary impasse will take more than the passage to democratic elections or even the slow betterment of the macroeconomy and the regeneration of livelihoods. Success will hinge on a longer and much more fundamental regeneration and revaluation from within of everyday Congolese political culture, reversing a very long and involved history of the *faire semblant* and the *faire croire*.

4. This Is Play

Popular Culture and Politics in Côte d'Ivoire

Mike McGovern

Cross your wrists in front [as if shackled]
Cross your wrists behind
Guantanamo . . . Souba!
Oh you, my brother, oh you who create these problems—
　Guantanamo!
Even if you've done nothing, you can find yourself there—
　Guantanamo!
You who do menial jobs there [abroad], you'd better watch out—
　Guantanamo!
You who are working, you can find yourself in—Guantanamo!
Pray to God that you're not too late—Guantanamo!
When you're there everyone will forget you
Your friends will give your wife an STD rather than watch over
　your family.
[Finally] you'll be freed, paid for the mistake that was made—
　Guantanamo!
Claude Bassolé!

DJ ZIDANE

PRELUDE

Every era has its soundtrack. The first years of the new millennium, marked for many by the events of September 11 and the United States government's disastrous response, were marked by rather different events in Côte d'Ivoire, as the formerly stable country's self-image was rocked by a coup d'état on Christmas Eve, 1999. 2000 was a "terrible year" that culminated in deeply flawed presidential and legislative elections accompanied by carnage and the increasing use of rape as a weapon of political terror (Le Pape and Vidal 2002). The situation reached its nadir with an attempted coup-turned-rebellion on September 19, 2002. This rebellion, which pitted cashiered soldiers from the country's north against the sitting government, soon transformed into a de facto partition of the country.

Despite the suffering and distraction caused by these events, Ivorians remained vitally engaged with world events. They also continued to live their lives in all their mundane details, eating, making love, and hustling for a living. Seen from the outside, quotidian life seems suspended in "war zones." Inside, it is apparent that babies do not stop crying when they are hungry, smokers do not cease to crave cigarettes, and people still drink and dance during lulls in the fighting. Certainly this has been the case in Côte d'Ivoire.

In this essay I explore several dimensions of everyday life by way of an examination of Ivorian popular music. On the one hand, this allows me to make a rhetorical point in keeping with the overarching theme of this book: in Côte d'Ivoire, as in other parts of Africa, creativity continues not only "beyond" crisis, but alongside and *inside* it, while popular culture itself remains a kind of work undertaken in hard times. This proposition leads to the empirical core of this essay, which is an analysis of shifts within Ivorian popular culture and within Ivorian politics, and of the links between the two.

During the period of civil conflict Côte d'Ivoire's soundtrack undoubt-edly has been *coupé décalé*—a music with Ivorian roots and strong Congolese influences—born in the African nightclubs of Paris and now one of the most widespread forms of popular music on the continent. *Coupé décalé* is party music: the rhythms are supremely danceable and the form has spawned dozens of subgenres, each with its own dance. "Guantanamo" is one of these. The lyrics quoted in the opening epigraph are testament to Ivorians' continuing engagement with global events; they may also be a kind of oblique commentary on the precariousness of living in Côte d'Ivoire.

Most of the rest of the lyrics (beginning with "Claude Bassolé!" the name of a *coupé décalé* record producer) are forms of "throwing" (White 2008)—"shout outs" to various in-group members of the *coupé décalé* community, its producers, patrons, singers, and celebrities. As in many *coupé décalé* songs, most of the lyrics are metacommunicative:[1] Listen to me, I'm singing; yes, I'm on your stereo system. Yes, I know those others you've been listening to, too. We all have money—look how much money! This may seem frivolous in the context of a song about what many have come to call the Global War *of* Terror. And yet, how much does one need to say about the American prison in Guantánamo Bay, Cuba? The song is wonderfully succinct. Even if you have a job and have done nothing wrong, you might just find yourself there. No sooner will you arrive than you will be forgotten and forsaken by your erstwhile friends and family. Combined with dance, in which dancers respond to the commands, "Cross your wrists in front!"—everyone crosses their wrists as if manacled—

"Cross your wrists behind!"—we put our wrists together behind our backs—"Guantanamo" condenses the essential knowledge the weak have of their own vulnerability to the organized violence of the state. *Coupé décalé* also ekes out what little transcendence there is to be had in such circumstances: the song and its dance underline not only the control each of us has over our own bodies as pleasure-making machines,[2] but also the ability we have as meaning-making machines to look directly at torture and illegal detention and belittle it, dancing with arms satirically crossed behind our backs at the edge of the abyss.

This, I propose, is the soundtrack of the contemporary Ivorian conflict. I use it here as a window on that conflict because it shows one way that the links between artistic production and political, economic, racial and gendered formations are never deterministic in the way an older Marxist approach might have it. They are, rather, linked by what Raymond Williams (1977) called "structures of feeling;" those subtle and shifting ways of thinking about and representing the world that shape, rather than determine, the products of creative life and political decisions.

A GENEALOGY OF VIOLENT PLAY

The Republic of Côte d'Ivoire has long been the richest nation in West Africa, aside from post–oil boom Nigeria. Unlike Nigeria, Angola, or other mineral-rich states where most citizens have seen little benefit from the fabulous profits derived from their underground wealth, many Ivorians did benefit from the "Ivorian miracle" of the 1960s and 1970s.[3] Because Ivorian wealth was built upon plantation agriculture that led hundreds of thousands of small and medium holders and some 2,000 large holders to produce 40 percent of the world's cocoa, a significant tranche of the population benefited directly from cash-crop agriculture, and most Ivorians saw significant increases in their access to education, healthcare, paved roads, electricity, and potable water during the first quarter-century of independence (1960–85).

Côte d'Ivoire has also been a magnet for immigrants from neighboring countries. Some of the enticements have been purely economic, as Côte d'Ivoire quickly became richer than most of its neighbors. However, there are other, less tangible benefits to living in Côte d'Ivoire. Particularly in Abidjan, the attraction may be much the same as the attraction of moving to London, Paris, or New York City for people coming from provincial towns: the excitement, the anonymity, and the freedom of the city. That freedom takes many forms. It may be the freedom from the claims family members place on successful kin back home, or the freedom from certain social and religious constraints. It is also the freedom of the city—the possibility of reinventing oneself, the encompassing promise of social license.[4]

These freedoms are perhaps most attractive to young people—those old enough to make a living for themselves but not yet constrained by the responsibilities that come with spouses and children.[5] Young people are a central element on both sides of the Ivorian conflict, and war-making in this region has been a means of upward mobility and intergenerational jostling since at least the nineteenth century. Youth respond to the cues of and work within conditions of possibility that have been set by their elders, but at the same time, participation in Abidjan's violent street politics is one of the ways that young people—especially young men—have carved out spaces of self-expression, enjoyment, and freedom in the city, just as their opposite numbers have created a rural version of the same freedoms by joining the rebellion in the country's north. The similarities between these two groups of Ivorian youth pose a significant question: while the Ivorian war has been portrayed as primarily a battle between ethno-religious groups, is it perhaps more accurate to understand the conflict as an intergenerational struggle?

There appears in the words and acts of many of the Ivorian conflict's protagonists a pronounced sense of play. To call such things as street protests, lootings, and virulent xenophobic speech "play" may seem perverse, given that these acts are often accompanied by considerable violence and suffering. However, I use the term in the sense developed in the anthropological and sociological literatures (Simmel 1971; Huizinga 1950; Bateson 1972). This literature emphasizes the "metacommunicative" aspect of play in order to show how it can frame an event or utterance in such a way that those who are culturally fluent can understand it to be set apart from ordinary life. In this sense, play quotes "real" life and can even appear identical. The stakes are nonetheless different.

This urban social dynamic, I argue, relies on young people—mostly young men, often unemployed or underemployed—looking for "where the action is," to use the title of Erving Goffman's generative 1967 essay (Goffman 1967). Such young men, poor, bored, filled with desire fed by lubricious music videos, consumerist fantasies, and the soft pornography televised on Ivorian satellite television, seek the consequential, risky terrain of combat to try their chances and to fashion new selves (Banégas 2006). As Goffman writes, those most likely to try their luck in such violent activity are those who "have not been tightly woven into organizational structures. Presumably among them these fateful activities will be least disruptive and the most tolerable; it is a case of having little to lose, or little to lose yet, *a case of being well organized for disorganization.* The study of corner gangs of aggressive, alienated urban youth provides an illustration" (Goffman 1967:212, emphasis mine).

In the last sections of this essay, I suggest some ways that the "play" frame has helped to limit the damage done in the Ivorian war at the same time that it cannot be tightly controlled by those who would cast themselves as its producers. The consequences of a "play" scenario spun out of control may quickly turn ugly, as the case study of "deadly play" presented later in this essay suggests. However, one of the characteristics of the Ivorian conflict has been that the occasional explosions of violence are often deflated and de-escalated very quickly. This is possible, I argue, because many of the protagonists understand that the violence in which they are involved has been "bracketed"—it is intended to send a message, but definitely not meant to spin out of control into a durable cycle of tit-for-tat violence.

I want to begin, however, with a description of the emergence of Abidjan's violent youth politics. It is ironic that the two figures who galvanized young men's resolve to change their situations in Côte d'Ivoire's North and South—Guillaume Soro and Charles Blé Goudé—were both English majors and sometime roommates at the University of Côte d'Ivoire's main campus in Cocody, a posh neighborhood of Abidjan. More importantly, both were heads of the Féderation Estudantine et Scolaire de Côte d'Ivoire (FESCI; Federation of Ivorian High School and University Students). Soro headed the organization from 1995 to 1998, and Blé Goudé succeeded him from 1998 to 2001. Another famous "Young Patriot," Eugène Djué, was also head of the organization from 1994 to 1995. FESCI was founded in 1990, the year of Côte d'Ivoire's first multiparty elections, and backed Laurent Gbagbo, a professor of history on the Cocody campus, who had established the Front Populaire Ivoirien (FPI) in 1982, going into exile soon thereafter.

Yacouba Konaté (2003) has described the ways that the campus politics of the 1990s spiraled toward increasing violence as the FESCI, allied with the teacher's union, increasingly mobilized its student base against the regime of then-president Félix Houphouët-Boigny. As government repression of student activists turned violent and included long periods of detention without charge,[6] the students themselves became increasingly violent. This violence was turned against a government that had come to represent a calcified structure of illegitimate rent-seeking by elders who had mortgaged the younger generation's future. It was also turned inward, with fights among students leading to deaths and even such neologisms as to "Zébiér," meaning to stone someone to death (the fate of one FESCI defector); *braiser*, meaning to burn someone alive; or *machettage*, referring to killing by machete. As Konaté writes, "weapons as dialectic had got the better of dialectics as a weapon" (60).

In the Ivorian context of diminishing cash crop income and rising demands for transparency from donors, Ivorian elites were no longer able to maintain the comfortable lifestyles to which they had become accustomed while distributing the patronage that had been the basis of an earlier generation's political legitimacy. Insurgent youths chafed against the sudden downturn in their prospects, both in the short and the long terms. Yet even this contradiction was not entirely new. Toungara (1995) wrote about much the same dynamic in the context of intergenerational competition within Côte d'Ivoire's one-party state in the 1970s and 1980s. In the 1990s, however, what was qualitatively different was the way in which Ivorian elites embraced and refashioned the neoliberal mantras of privatization and decentralization, effectively subcontracting out domains of economic activity to younger protégés and allowing them to "pay themselves." Young Ivorians were prepared to take on the opportunity, and some showed themselves especially apt at using violence and the threat of violence tactically to gain what they considered their due. As one former FESCI head told a Human Rights Watch researcher: "FESCI is the best school for leaders there is. You come out battle hardened and ready to do politics. Ours is a generation that had to come to power one day, so if you see members of FESCI rising up, our view is that it was inevitable and came later than it should have. The arrival of this class will change politics" (Human Rights Watch 2008:1).

It is not all young Ivorians who combined the sense of *débrouillardise*, or the ability to get over, with the feeling of entitlement that would allow them to characterize their accession to wealth and power as "inevitable and [coming] later than it should have." Under the structural constraints they met, it was Côte d'Ivoire's rising elite, its most ambitious and entrepreneurial university students, who granted themselves this license. This activism gradually became mixed with political and economic ambitions, too. After General Robert Gueï took power in a 1999 coup, he granted the FESCI rights to control a large portion of the stock of university housing in Abidjan. This move resembled similar ones within the security forces, where legitimate claims for structural change that would ensure a future by and for the younger generation were parried by a government increasingly squeezed by external factors yet which remained unwilling to give up the perks that had become the expected reward for arriving at the top of the political hierarchy. The FESCI turned university housing into a sizeable rent and began to shake down other students, petty traders, and the women who served prepared food on campus. Disgusted Ivorians increasingly came to play on the similarity between the organization's acronym and the term *fascist*, referring to members as *féscists*. Most Ivorians have become skeptical about the putative "patriotism" claimed by FESCI or its Young Patriot spin-offs.[7]

It is within the FESCI that such figures as Soro, Blé Goudé, and Djué learned the mechanics and the rhetoric of violent street politics. This form of political practice combined a fluency in the language of civil and human rights with the practices of organized crime, charismatic oratory with the mundane organizational skills necessary to running an institution, and a mode of self-fashioning as a political avant-garde with the supplications of an excluded generation without prospects. It is crucial to understand that this is not simply a world of *either* criminal accumulation *or* of principled "legitimate defense." Rather, the two coexisted in the actions and words of many FESCI "alumni" as they went on to take leadership positions in the political process in both the South and North of the country.

FREE MONEY: THE TRANSITION FROM *ZOUGLOU* TO *COUPÉ DÉCALÉ*

Yacouba Konaté begins his article "Génération zouglou" with a list of the national musical styles that conquered African audiences continent-wide: multiple types of music from Congo/Zaire, Ghana, Nigeria, and Guinea. He then goes on: "As for us, the children of Houphouët-Boigny, we remained skeptical: When would we have a national music? What day would we have the pleasure of hearing a music which, from its first notes, would evoke, would signify, Côte d'Ivoire from the West to the East, and from the North to the South?" (Konaté 2002:777). Konaté answers his own question. Abidjan had long been the hub of the West African recording industry, with musicians coming from Mali, Guinea, Burkina Faso, and even Zaire to record music there. Alpha Blondy's success in the 1980s and 1990s was also continent-wide, but his reggae, though lyrically Africanized, was in the classic Jamaican style. It was not until the emergence of *zouglou* in the late 1980s and 1990s that Côte d'Ivoire finally got its own national musical style.

Sung in the Abidjanais working-class French patois known as Nouchi and using *alloukou* rhythms from the Bété-speaking West of the country, *zouglou* was a popular musical form that met with broad success that even seems to have surprised its creators. At the same time that young people's dissatisfaction with Côte d'Ivoire's one-party state was crystallizing on the Cocody campus, in part through the FESCI, *zouglou* was born. The music combines social commentary with humor, portraying the tribulations of ordinary Abidjanais in their search for money, love, and enjoyment in precarious circumstances.

Like the literature of Sony Labou Tansi, Ahmadou Kourouma, and Ayei Kwei Armah, the lyrics are often ludic and lascivious. Songs tell stories of *grottos* (big men, especially those with a taste for young girls) and *gos* (girls), of prostitutes *faisant boutique son cul* (peddling their asses) (Konaté 2002:787), of *côcôs* (mooches), *mogos* (best friends), *yeres* (those who are streetwise), and *brezos, gnatas,* or *gaous* (bumpkins).[8] They are frequently humorous, as in the expression *tysoner*, which means to bite someone's ear, or *gbangban (problem) de Molière*, which is Nouchi slang for standard French. Nouchi phrases comment sardonically on politics: to *gueï robert* is to go back on one's word, just as the 1999 *putschiste* Robert Gueï did when he ran for president in 2000 after promising to step aside. *Les temps sont Gbagbo* means that times are hard and a person is broke. *Filer des AFP* is to speak untruthfully because one has an ulterior motive, as many Ivorians believe the French news agency Agence France-Presse does in its reporting on Côte d'Ivoire. A *Cube Maggi* is someone who gets involved in everyone else's business, just as the ubiquitous Maggi Cube condiment is "mixed into every sauce" in West African cuisine.[9] A *blessé(e) de guerre* is a very ugly person, whose looks are compared to one wounded in war—slang that has emerged in the context of Côte d'Ivoire's recent experience of conflict and yet still manages to find humor in it.

In addition to recounting the challenges faced by poor but industrious *gazeurs*[10] in their search for good times, *zouglou* acknowledges the realities of ethnic stereotypes without conceding anything to them. Interpreting one *zouglou* hit, Konaté asks, "How can youths whose everyday lived reality is deeply cosmopolitan fall so easily into xenophobia?" He answers his own question: "In the cosmopolitanism of the large African city, citizenship remains a fragile given."[11]

Many *zouglou* tunes recount the trials and tribulations of ordinary Ivorians who know they have the cards stacked against them. The biggest international *zouglou* hit was "Premier Gaou" by Magic System. The original video begins with a scene of a woman getting into a well-used Mercedes sedan. A young man in flip-flop sandals and a sleeveless t-shirt tries to talk to her as the car drives away. Twice in the video, his poverty is indexed by one of his flip-flops falling off as he chases the Mercedes. The story, as developed in the song, is of a struggling musician abandoned by his girlfriend, Antou, for a richer man. When he achieves some success, getting one of his songs broadcast on national radio and television, she comes back to him, once he seems a more attractive prospect than the man she had left him for. The lyrics recount: "elle dit le gaou a percé/ Attends je vais partir le couper" (She says [to herself], look, the bumpkin has achieved some success/Wait, I'm going to go back and trick him out of some of his wealth). The refrain to the song, "On dit premier gaou n'est pas gaou, oh/C'est deuxième gaou qui est gnata, oh," translates loosely as "once burned twice shy." However, this proverbial knowledge is transmitted in the vocabulary of *gaou* and its synonym, *gnata*, which are implicitly opposed to the savoir faire of the *yere*. In short, the song is a kind of bildungsroman, showing the singer's transformation from newly arrived yokel to slick urban star, his sentimental education effected by his painful first romantic deception in the big city.

After its ascendance over the course of the 1990s, *zouglou* began diversifying and transforming into *mapouka*, famous for the sensual (some would say obscene) dance that accompanied it, and later informing the development of *coupé décalé*. Simon Akindes argues that "[t]hrough the reappropriation of *reggae*, the re-invention of *zouglou* and the explosion of *mapouka* and new forms of local expression, popular music gradually became a voice for the voiceless and a mouth for the speechless, especially at a time when the myth of the 'Ivorian miracle' was quickly crumbling" (Akindes 2002:86). Most Ivorians would agree that *zouglou* was a genuinely "bottom up" popular musical genre that nonetheless seduced high school and university students in Côte d'Ivoire just at the moment that they became political forces on the Ivorian scene. *Coupé décalé*, though indirectly related to *zouglou*, is its sociological mirror image. Introduced from Europe, it is a musical and dance form created by the rich and subsequently accepted by Ivorians of various social strata. As Dominik Kohlhagen has described it, *coupé décalé* was created in 2002 not in Côte d'Ivoire but in Paris's chic African nightclubs like the Atlantis. At the beginning of 2003, shortly after its birth (and the outbreak of war in Côte d'Ivoire) the "concept" came to Abidjan (Kohlhagen 2006). While the figure of the *zouglou gazeur*, which I would translate as "reveler," has a roguish quality, it is roguish in a self-deprecating, loosely carnivalesque sense. And although the *gazeur* is successful and able to enjoy the good life, he is never too far removed from the poor and spurned boyfriend, who loses his sandal as he chases his girlfriend's new lover's car. In the new style, the figure of the *coupeur décaleur* takes the trickster side of the *gazeur* and adds something more explicitly criminal to the mix.

It is worth delving into the meanings of some of the terms that define the universe of *coupé décalé* in order to have a clearer sense of its orientation. In Nouchi, *couper* (in standard French, literally "to cut") means to embezzle, cheat, or steal.[12] *Décaler* (in standard French, to shift or unwedge) means "to scram" or "to disappear" in Ivorian patois. The figure of the *coupeur décaleur* is thus similar to the Nigerian 419 artist or Cameroonian *feyman*—a criminal who specializes in fraud, one who does not necessarily resort to violence to achieve his ends but uses the trickster's superior intelligence and shrewdness to take advantage of others.[13] Also, unlike the petty pickpocket or the heavily muscled *loubard* who might execute purse snatchings or robberies, the *coupeur décaleur* set his sights higher, using wire fraud, counterfeiting, and other skills to make a big profit (cf. Piot, this volume). As Kohlhagen has said of the original *coupeurs décaleurs:*

> Most of them succeeded financially very quickly in [sic], by not always very clear and very honest ways—that's what people say, one doesn't know exactly. Some of them have spent some time in prison but this is also rumors, it's not very clear. What is clear is that they are quite young, between I would say 25 and 35, recent arrivals, and people who succeeded in some way quite quickly after their arrival in France. (Mitter, Shipley and Kohlhagen 2007)

Coupé décalé inventors like Douk Saga and Lino Versace arrived at Parisian clubs with ready cash and began to *travailler.* In the drab, law-abiding world this word meant "to work." But in the playful space of night time *jouissance,* the *coupeurs décaleurs* "worked" by buying bottles of champagne for everyone, spreading cash around, treating DJs especially well, and they found themselves at the center of new, ephemeral networks of patronage in which they traded a portion of their wealth for a degree of fame and deference.[14] (This gives an ironic twist to the title of this volume, *Hard Work, Hard Times!*)

The founding song of the genre was "Sagacité," or "Wisdom." This is the fourth key term in the lexicon of *coupé décalé* and it, too, has seen its meaning stood on its head. The Web site nouchi.com defines the term thus:

> Sagacité (noun): In its proper meaning, the word "sagacité" means clear sightedness or insight, but in the figurative sense we might call Ivorian, "sagacité" means to maneuver by working (*travailler*—in the sense of spreading largesse) and dodging (*décaler*—running away, implicitly after committing some kind of fraud) in various countries. Example: "Hey, my brother, I'm hustling in London [now] and two days before, I hustled in Paris."

As with "Guantanamo" and "Premier Gaou," the video of "Sagacité" tells us much about the imaginative universe of the genre. Where "Premier Gaou" was filmed in Abidjan,[15] "Sagacité" is filmed in Paris. The opening scene, in front of the Prince de Galles Hotel, shows Douk Saga[16] flipping through a thick wad of 50, 100, and 200 euro notes and handing a fat tip to the (white) doorman. The video cuts quickly to Douk exchanging *bisous* with three white women in front of an FNAC music and bookstore. They are evidently seeking his autograph. After a quick cut to show him tipping yet another doorman, the camera zooms in on a group member's wrist, showing an expensive watch. Next, they climb into a Mercedes (in this case a new SL 550, not the twenty-five-year-old sedan of "Premier Gaou") and drive away, with other successive clips showing them shopping at Versace and Dolce & Gabbana. Just as with the shift in Congolese music videos, Ivorian videos in the twenty-first century have shifted away from images depicting the excitement of the African capital to images of the European capital in order to highlight the glamour and wealth of their performers.[17]

Coupé décalé thus builds upon the fantasy structure of an idealized "elsewhere" underlying much popular culture around the world. Togolese lotto visa candidates (Piot, this volume), Senegalese and other West African immigrants undertaking the risky voyage toward the Canary Islands (introduction, this volume), and Ghanaian hiplife performers critiquing the state through a hybrid performance genre that borrows from transnational hip-hop codes (Shipley, this volume) are other examples in this collection of related stances toward a place that has been imaginatively cleansed of ambivalence. There is a close kinship between the fantasy of freedom and anonymity of African capitals like Abidjan and the imagined overseas paradises where West African immigrants throw money at working-class Europeans (with the same aggressiveness buried in the gesture as in the putative charity of Euro-American "aid" to Africa) and enter into sexual congress with women of all colors by dint of their charm, style, and easy money.

There is a more prosaic history involved, too, inasmuch as the links between Abidjan and European capitals, and between Congolese dance music and *coupé décalé*, are the consequence of a very real trajectory of immigration during the 1980s and 1990s. During the Mobutu period, moderately popular Zairois musicians had difficulty getting visas to France. By coming to Abidjan, making some recordings, and playing some concerts, they were often able to get visas that were denied to them in Kinshasa. This network was intertwined with another by which bandleaders made money by bringing large retinues of musicians and dancers with them on each European tour, leaving many of them behind in Europe and then returning with a new lineup a year or two later. This network brought together music, immigration, and illegal activities at the same time that it brought Congolese influences into Ivorian popular music. *Coupé décalé* was thus the fruit of several decades of cross-fertilization, and several prominent *coupé décalé* artists are in fact of Congolese origin.[18]

In the new millennium, Ivorian music has approached, and perhaps even surpassed, Congolese music as the most popular in francophone Africa. If, as Achille Mbembe has argued, Congolese popular music "has demonstrated itself to be the most successful expression of *serenity in the face of tragedy*" (Mbembe 2006:63, emphasis in the original), then Ivorian music's rise to continental importance has taken place under similar circumstances of warfare and economic downturn. Kohlhagen argues that the hedonistic culture that has grown around *coupé décalé*, including its suspension of moral disapprobation concerning fraud, is part of Ivorians' attempts to distract themselves from a situation of war, unemployment, and lack of prospects. Yet there is more than mere distraction at stake here. The moral imagination that underpins the justification by the former FESCI leader quoted above, who conceives it normal that a student union should be a place to become "battle hardened and ready to do politics," is a reaction to the circumstances of blocked progress experienced by the country's youth. Similarly, *coupeurs décaleurs* resident in "fortress Europe," where they have difficulty gaining visas in the first instance and are often treated as less than second-class citizens when they do arrive, may consider anti-immigrant prejudice and racism sufficient justification for bilking Europeans out of their money. Undoubtedly, this is a case of people making their own history, though, to paraphrase Marx, not under conditions of their own choosing (Marx 1963 [1852]).

This raises a delicate question in the context of the relationship between creativity and crisis explored in this volume. It is easy for many of us to appreciate the creative genius that deflates the hubris of the Bush regime through a parodic recreation of Guantánamo Bay prison as a sexy song-and-dance number. It is difficult, though, to assimilate the perversion of a student union into a racketeering operation that uses rape, beatings, and even assassinations as its tactics in the same positive light. By disposition and disciplinary training, I remain interested in understanding these dynamics rather than in rendering judgments about them. However, many Ivorians express trepidation about the future, one in which an FESCI leader boasts, "So, if you see members of FESCI rising up, our view is that it was inevitable and came later than it should have. The arrival of this class will change politics."[19] Educators and others in Côte d'Ivoire fear these changes.[20] The valorization of "free money" may be part of the problem facing Côte d'Ivoire, not the solution. This uncertainty and moral ambiguity are captured as well in *coupé décalé*.

"THIS IS PLAY"

Talk about Ivorian music is one thing, its connections to youth politics another. In trying to understand the motivations and sociology of the Young Patriots, it may be helpful to ask what these young men are trying to do, and how they square the language of legitimate defense and concern for the "republican institutions" with the use of intimidation, racketeering, and xenophobic rhetoric. Spurred by Erving Goffman's essay "Where the Action Is," I want to ask *where* exactly the action might be for an unemployed twenty-seven-year-old resident of a working-class neighborhood like Koumassi or Yopougon.

Such "action" takes place within a frame that sets it apart from ordinary life. One advantage of a "play" frame, as it pertains to political speech and action, is that it renders opaque the relationship between illegal acts and personal responsibility. One might well ask what is communicated within such a frame. Charles Blé Goudé and other Young Patriots, just like the "Patriots" in the rebellion,[21] speak "the language of protest, in which one seeks a redress of grievances, and speaks to power in the supplicative voice, legitimating power by the act of speaking" (Marcus 1989:13). As previously noted, the leading Ivorian Young Patriots are university students or graduates whose path toward professional careers has been blocked by factors both local and international, and their performance of violence is, in part, a call to be included in a larger set of forces.

In addition to the kind of supplication that aims to focus attention on young people's plights, urban youth politics in Côte d'Ivoire is shaped by a strong sense of "play." There are obvious elements of play in the supplication of the Young Patriots, embodied in Blé Goudé's charismatic pop-star lifestyle and the hyperbole that characterizes much of the movement's rhetoric. Notwithstanding, it is useful to look at play as a separate dynamic in its own right and to think of play and supplication playing off one another, sometimes in balance and at other times tipping dangerously toward one or the other within an unstable, frequently violent context involving high political and monetary stakes.

Perhaps the best rendering of play comes from the anthropologist Gregory Bateson.[22] He wrote that "this phenomenon, play, could only occur if the participant organisms were capable of some degree of meta-communication, i.e., of exchanging signals which would carry the message of 'this is play'" (Bateson 1972:179). What Bateson is keen to point out is the bracketed nature of such activity, conveying the sense that "[t]hese actions in which we now engage do not denote what those actions for which they stand would denote" (ibid.:180). It is this framing that concerns us here, and the possibilities that it presents to people who would organize or participate in violent political action.

I have already noted the playful qualities of Nouchi language as well as its use in Ivorian popular music. Nouchi culture styles itself as "street," and this self-fashioning revolves around the distinction between those who are *yere,* or street-wise, and those who are *gaou,* or rural and credulous. In a masterful paper on Ivorian urban culture, Sasha Newell (n.d.) distinguishes two levels of segmentary opposition. At the first level, the Ivorian elite cultivated under Houphouët-Boigny's rule signaled its difference from the rest of the population by its appropriation of the language, dress, educational credentials, and lifestyle of the French political class. Houphouët-Boigny's success in this process—in which his own claims of equal status with French politicians was ratified by the reciprocal network of corruption that made French politicians beholden to him and vice versa—gave Ivorian elite culture a large measure of hegemonic legitimacy. Although Houphouët-Boigny's Baule ethnic group dominated the Ivorian elite, every community in the country had members in this privileged, cosmopolitan group (Bakary 1997). Newell points out that among the remaining 90 percent or more of the population, there was yet another opposition, that is, between the disabused, hustling non-elites of Abidjan and their country cousins, who were yet to acquire the cosmopolitan habits of their city-dweller counterparts.

Newell emphasizes the extent to which cohabitation in large "court-yards"[23] and the frequency of urban intermarriage across ethnic, religious, and even national lines created Abidjan's cosmopolitanism, and how Nouchi became the language of that cosmopolitan urban culture. Other registers allowed Abidjan's residents to signal the extent to which they were "in the know," not least on the fashion forefront. Those wearing the ankle-length caftan known in West Africa as a *boubou* signaled both their probable Muslim faith and their "traditional" orientation to style, while the hip and *yere* (who might be Muslim or Christian) wore jeans, baseball caps, and t-shirts or polo shirts in the American style.

Newell extends the distinction to the division of labor: "*yere* describes someone who cannot be scammed, while to *yere* someone is to steal from them. A *gaou*, on the other hand, is . . . someone incapable of discerning his surroundings, and therefore easily duped . . . Those who work are uncivilized *gaous*, targets waiting for a streetwise Ivorian to demonstrate [his] supposed cultural superiority" (Newell n.d.:5–6) The similarity with the universe of *coupé décalé*, in which easy money and ephemeral pleasures are vaunted, becomes quite apparent in Newell's description. It also makes clear that there were already elements of what I have described as the *coupé décalé* aesthetic that were part of Abidjanais street life and *zouglou* music but later were magnified in *coupé décalé*. The outcome of this attitude is not just a matter of hipness. Newell argues, "The stylistic convergence of Nouchi networks and contemporary youth militias [like the Young Patriots] seeking out *gaous* to oust from the country clearly points to the role these style hierarchies have played in shaping Ivorian identity and contemporary understanding of citizenship" (ibid.).

In this way we see how play can be "a solvent of morality" (Sontag 1966:290). By bracketing activity (fraud, hate speech, interethnic violence) as play (in this case in the distinction between *yere* and *gaou*), the actor claims license to do what he or she would condemn in another setting (e.g., robbing someone). This allows groups like the Young Patriots to recruit more broadly than they might otherwise. It is also important in explaining the question already posed by Konaté, namely how youths whose quotidian reality is profoundly cosmopolitan can slide into practices of violent xenophobia. The play frame makes it possible to claim that things are not really as they appear to be, and this slippage between the frame of play and the quotidian goes some way to explaining the paradox of urban cosmopolitanism and xenophobia. Many alternative explanations, including the fact that political elites with nefarious intentions might be "pulling strings" from behind the scenes, tend to treat young urban actors as if they were puppets.[24] The license granted by the play frame helps to explain both how *yere* youths justify committing robbery and theft against neighbors who work hard for little pay,[25] and how they justify beating up or terrorizing immigrants.

"LA DEUXIÈME GUERRE D'INDÉPENDENCE" AND THE RHETORIC OF REVOLUTION

> Je t'aime . . . Moi non plus
> SERGE GAINSBOURG

Some of the most striking instances of the razor-thin line between the humorous and the frightening in the sphere of enframed politics may be found in the rhetoric of the Young Patriots. Careening between virulent xenophobia, erudite historical analogy, and riotous humor, the public pronouncements of youth political figures show the different sides of the politics of play in Côte d'Ivoire. The rhetoric of the Patriots, of many Abidjan newspapers, and even of high-level political figures can be surprisingly inflammatory. Both scholars and activists have argued that this is simply the development of vulgar xenophobic discourse intended to foster a context in which mass violence is facilitated by demonizing and dehumanizing enemies (much as happened in Rwanda before and during the genocide there). In this section I try to show that this is a misreading. While taking very seriously the potentially violent outcomes of such rhetoric, I also want to insist that while much Ivorian political talk may be irresponsible and provocative, it is often launched in a kind of play frame in which actors like Blé Goudé appear to be carried away by their own rhetoric. This is tricky ground for analysis: the kinds of hateful speech I am analyzing represent true "deep play" in the sense that Clifford Geertz used the term, borrowed from Bentham. This is "play in which the stakes are so high that it is, from [Bentham's] utilitarian standpoint, irrational for men to engage in it at all . . . In genuine deep play, this is the case for both parties. They are both in over their heads" (Geertz 1973b:433). In other words, this is play that has long since ceased to be play in the usual sense of that term. For that very reason it is important to trace the genealogy of such actions back to the moment when they could still be regarded as play. Not only does this help to explain the rhetorical one-upmanship characteristic of the Ivorian conflict, it also shows how Ivorian politicians grant themselves deniability, claiming—plausibly, in the eyes of many Ivorians—that they did not truly mean what they said.

For instance, on October 2, 2006, Pascal Affi N'Guessan, president of Laurent Gbagbo's FPI party, and Gbagbo's prime minister between 2000 and 2003, spoke to a crowd in Côte d'Ivoire shortly before a meeting of heads of state of the fifteen-country Economic Community of West African States (ECOWAS).

> Prepare yourselves for the end of the week. ECOWAS is going to meet. What we are saying is for their benefit. When they make their decision, they had better not forget that they have thousands of compatriots here. Each one should think of his compatriots who are in Côte d'Ivoire before speaking. They should pause [*remuer la langue*] seven times before speaking. . . . Because if they talk in such a way as to bring fire and disorder here, we don't know what is going to happen. (Panapress 2006)

This passage alternated between two "bracketed" registers. In one, Affi N'Guessan made explicit threats that he later disavowed. When threatened with placement on the UN Security Council's assets freeze and travel ban list, he defended himself by saying that he really had not meant what he said. What Ivorian audiences understood as slight dramatic overstatement, he implied, had been misunderstood in the overly literal reading of the West African and other international diplomats. The latter section of the passage operates in a somewhat more veiled style. Ending with, "we don't know what is going to happen," it points to the agency of the zealous crowd, which the state cannot be expected to control. This discursive evasion of responsibility, which is common all over the world (Tambiah 1997), offers both political figures and participants license when agency is imputed to "the crowd."

Tracing the genealogy of this rhetoric also points out another crucial factor in Ivorian political speech: much of it borrows liberally from the French rhetoric of revolution. From the 1980s onward, the vocal opposition spearheaded by Laurent Gbagbo and other Ivorian intellectuals—many of them educated in France in the post–May 1968 student environment—also draws liberally from this tradition, which has surged forth periodically in France since 1789. Tracing this heritage shows how a French rhetoric of root-and-branch cataclysmic change has been appropriated and recast in some francophone countries. More interesting still, it shows how in Côte d'Ivoire it is not necessarily the generations that lived with colonization, or even with the heyday of Franco-Ivorian neocolonialism, who spearhead the rhetoric of purging the nation of its polluting French presence. Ivorian youth are the ones who went out in the street to throw stones at the French military base, to protect the *Présidence* from perceived attempts to storm it by French soldiers in 2004, and to terrorize French citizens into leaving the country that same year.

In an important sense, their revolutionary fervor was heightened by the fact that they had had less contact with a French community that had been rapidly disengaging from the country since the 1990s. If the decreasing presence of actual French bodies in Côte d'Ivoire cleared the way for a transformation from sweaty bodies and sunburned skin into the phantasmatic structure of more-or-less pure symbol, then the French revolutionary tradition served, paradoxically, as a model for resolving contradiction by "setting the clock back to zero" (Chauveau 2000).

If one wants to start with a clean slate, then what models are available for structuring one's speech, one's actions, in short one's communication with others? The French model of revolutionary leveling may not have been unprecedented, but it was exceptionally well articulated and packaged in such a way that it exerted tremendous influence on later moments of revolutionary negation the world over. The image of revolutionaries devouring their oppressors is one of the strongest metaphors available to express such erasure and the possibility of a new beginning. Although supplication may have dominated insurgent youths' claims for a place in a political and economic dispensation that seemed to have renounced them, the rhetoric of negation nonetheless emerged at times, drawing on French revolutionary precedents that are particularly familiar to the university educated elite.

The situation in Côte d'Ivoire, however, was never fully revolutionary. Although some members of the political class are strong ideologues, most Ivorians are far more practical in their ambitions—eating well, maintaining their families in good health and providing their children with good education, having some pocket money to enjoy the diversions of the city—and recognize the ways that a revolutionary upsetting of the order of things would imperil their own well-being. At the rhetorical level, Côte d'Ivoire's "second war of independence" borrowed heavily from the rhetoric of the history of the very country whose onerous yoke was said to be thrown off: the France of 1789, of 1848, of the Commune, and of May 1968. At a more affective level, the "family romance of Ivorian decolonization"[26] was so bitter in large part because it had been so long delayed. Amid this Franco-Ivorian mutual rejection we see less the leveling of revolution than the symbolic inversion of the carnivalesque. In this space the bitterness of postcolonial malaise (a malaise aggravated by poverty, pervasive violence, and xenophobia) is counterbalanced by play.

"IS THIS PLAY?" THE MEDIA AND THE EVENTS OF NOVEMBER 2004

> Intensity, passion, concentration, commitment: these are all part
> of the play mood. But this alone is not what makes play play.
> There is also the quality of acting out, of becoming another, of
> displaying a normally hidden part of yourself—and of becoming
> this other without worrying about consequences. Play implies
> getting away with it.
>
> RICHARD SCHECHNER (1985)

On November 4, 2004, in abrogation of all the agreements it had signed and several UN Security Council resolutions, the Gbagbo-led government in Abidjan began a series of bombardments of positions in the Forces

Nouvelles-held north. On the third day of these attacks (November 6), one of the government's Sukhoi jets dropped a bomb on a French barracks, killing nine French peacekeepers and an American. Within an hour, French jets based in Togo had flown over the political capital, Yamoussoukro, and the commercial capital, Abidjan, destroying or damaging most of the country's air force (two Soviet-era fighter jets and approximately one dozen Mi-24 attack and Mi-8 transport helicopters). That same night, Ivorians attempted to lay siege to the airport and the nearby French military base.

The next day, Ivorian youths began moving house to house, attacking expatriates, looting their property, beating many, and raping several French women. No expatriate was killed, but many were terrorized, and approximately 8,000 of the 12,000 French nationals resident in the country were evacuated, along with most other Europeans, North Africans, and North Americans. A large part of the Lebanese community left. In the following days, a standoff between French paratroopers and Ivorians gathered en masse outside the Hôtel Ivoire devolved into a massacre in which French soldiers killed several dozen Ivorians without any obvious provocation. In all, the Ivorian government listed sixty-four Ivorians killed by the French army in several clashes during this period.

Many aspects of this disastrous ten-day period are still the object of rancorous debate. Did the internationals (especially France) give the Gbagbo government an implicit green light to reconquer the North if it could? Was the bombardment of the French barracks an accident or a deliberate provocation? When a French tank started down the driveway to the presidential palace (next to the Hôtel Ivoire) was it an accidental wrong turn, or were the French about to remove President Gbagbo by force? Were the Ivorians at the Hôtel Ivoire shot by French troops or Ivorian gendarmes?

What is clear is that on the one hand there was disproportionate force used by the French soldiers on at least one occasion (at the Hôtel Ivoire) and there was organized and consistent incitement to violence coming from the Gbagbo government. This incitement specifically targeted Abidjanais youth, many of whom were already organized into the patriotic groups and militias described above. After the French counter-bombardment of November 6, Ivorian television was taken over by the Young Patriots, including Charles Blé Goudé, and transmitted messages such as the following in a continuous loop:

> It is night for the Ivorian revolution and for hope. The nation is in danger; the golden hour of glorious patriots is near.
>
> France has put a snake in the pocket of the Ivorian people.

Ivorians must offer their bodies up at the airport. Thus [the French] will [have to] kill us all before ousting Gbagbo.

If I find my Frenchman, I will eat him.

Thanks again to the magnificent patriots who shall march and write the beautiful history of Côte d'Ivoire with their blood.

Opposition newspaper offices were burned down and/or vandalized, and international radio broadcasts were discontinued on the FM band. None of the incitement or the preplanning of a "patriotic" rejoinder to the French attack excuses the killing of Ivorian civilians on November 9. We may still consider the ways that the rhetoric of revolution contributed to the situation's spinning out of control. In this regard, it is interesting to return to Bateson's essay on play, in which he makes the following comment in passing: "But this leads us to recognition of a more complex form of play; the game which is constructed not upon the premise 'This is play' but rather around the question 'Is this play?' And this type of interaction also has its ritual forms, e.g. in the hazing of initiation" (1973:182).

The violence of November 2004 overstepped what can be surmised as the limits rather strictly imposed in the past. While the taboo against killing expatriates was respected in this instance, the probable ban on the use of rape of expatriate women as a weapon was not. In this regard there was some dissonance between the various goals of the Ivorian government—maintaining a legitimate sense of moral outrage at French actions while using the opportunity presented to terrorize as many French citizens as possible into leaving. Moreover, the strength of the rhetoric also entailed a set of actions that were probably not desired by the Patriots. In this case, what may have started in the play frame spun badly, if not completely, out of control.

In the introduction to *African Guerillas*, Clapham (1998) argues that there are four broad types of insurgency in modern Africa. Independence insurgencies aim at throwing off the shackles of colonial domination, separatist insurgencies attempt to form a new state out of a region currently encompassed by another, revolutionary insurgencies aim to topple the sitting government with the objective of instituting a qualitatively different style of rule, and warlord insurgencies try to overthrow the government (or substitute for it within a given territory), although without revolutionary intent.

One of the most interesting aspects of the Ivorian conflict is that it has displayed elements of all of these types. The rhetoric of a "second war of independence" has been strong and many Ivorians have responded to the notion that Côte d'Ivoire's true decolonization was long overdue. The Forces Nouvelles' rebellion was partially separatist in nature, and over time they established many parallel structures in the country's North, including an education system, policing, and tax collection that operated autonomously from the Ivorian state. There were the beginnings of a youth "revolution" that might radically challenge the gerontocratic underpinnings of the Ivorian political class and the foreshortened opportunities for Ivorian youth. At the same time, the revolutionary firebrands of the FESCI like Blé Goudé and Soro found that there were significant rents that could be derived from the state of emergency characterizing a situation of "neither war nor peace."

Although all four of these tendencies coexist, often in the words and deeds of the same people, none of them seems to have been followed all the way to its conclusion. The anticolonial element of the conflict has remained an oscillation between rejection and reconciliation that I have described as *je t'aime, moi non plus*. The Forces Nouvelles frequently gestured at the possibility of secession, but always denied that that was what they were after. Revolution and pillaging coexisted, not so much mutually exclusive as tempering one another.

This halfway commitment could be read in an "Afro-pessimist" mode as a series of failures, as an instance of African lack. My own reading is in line with those of the other contributors to this book, as a characteristic approach of social and political actors who find themselves constrained on many sides. As Jackson (this volume) describes it, success in such circumstances requires "Hedging your bets and balancing your portfolio of societal debts and obligations." What I hope to have shown, at least in fleeting and partial fashion, is that such hedging brings together a political economy in which "trickster entrepreneurialism" (ibid.) flourishes. Hedging also conjures a sociology in which the networks facilitating political mobilization on university campuses transmogrify into protection rackets and into the violent extensions of political parties, then back to student politics. Finally, there are semiotic considerations, too, in which metacommunicative bracketing of violent political action as play can free a person or group to undertake acts they would otherwise condemn. This makes the use of violence as one tool in the repertoire of political actors in Côte d'Ivoire both unpredictable and potentially less devastating, as even intense violence framed as play tends to deescalate very quickly.

Even when violence is framed as play, and that play ensures both that actors "get away with it" and that it disappears as quickly as it appeared, its traces may not disappear so quickly. The intertwined worlds of *coupé décalé* and the Ivorian "patriotic" militias are by turns fascinating, diverting, and fun. They stand as a testament to young Ivorians' ability to carve out spaces of *jouissance* in the face of diminished opportunities and real precarity. Perhaps we can admire that fact while refusing to forget that such fun often comes at another's expense.

5.   Self-Sovereignty and Creativity in Ghanaian Public Culture

Jesse Weaver Shipley

In the streets and nightclubs of Accra, amid the political upheavals and economic crises of the 1980s, rap music emerged as the latest African dia-sporic[1] music to resonate with mostly elite youths. As local artists experi-mented with rapping, electronic beat making, and sampling, American rappers such as LL Cool J, Heavy D, Public Enemy, and later Tupac Shakur and the Notorious B.I.G. became popular heroes. While for some, African diaspora music provided a vision of black agency, others derided its bodily affect and clothing style as un-Ghanaian, even as a "foreign" imitation.[2] Groups such as Talking Drums and the producer Panji Anoff quickly began to infuse the genre with established styles of African performance and language usage, giving it local legitimacy. This music moved out of the schools and clubs onto a main public stage especially through the influ-ence of Reggie Rockstone Ossei. A Ghanaian rapper based in London, Rockstone returned to Ghana in 1994 and began rapping in the Twi lan-guage over heavy hip-hop beats and samples of Ghanaian highlife and Nigerian Afrobeat.[3] By the mid-1990s a new musical genre called *hiplife* emerged, combining older forms of highlife popular music, local language idioms, and proverbial oratory, with hip-hop sampling, scratching, and rap lyricism. Hiplife gained popularity through dance clubs, radio and televi-sion play, clothing styles, and the circulation of cassettes, videos, CDs, and magazines. Around the open-air drinking spots and nightclubs, markets, taxi stands, and compound houses of Accra, hip-hop and hiplife cloth-ing styles and bodily forms of expression reshaped urban speech culture and the mundane and spectacular narratives of nationhood and morality. This music was linked to the privatization of radio airwaves mandated in the 1992 constitution. New commercial radio stations in search of vibrant local programming played hiplife, popularizing the genre and opening new contexts for the political and moral concerns of the rising generation (cf. Schulz, this volume).

In this essay, I explore the mass-mediated circulation of Ghanaian hiplife music to show how Ghanaian publics reconfigure their relationship to state authority and dispersed individuated modes of consumption characteristic of Ghana's neoliberal state. I argue that hiplife provides parodic symbols through which youth creatively reshape public discourse. By inhabiting bodily and lyrical forms of expression young Ghanaians position themselves as legitimate and authoritative speaking subjects. Masculine aspects of public culture are emphasized through hiplife's moral metaphors, parodies, and irreverently critical bodily styles. Popular performance forms such as African hip-hop address questions of political and economic agency under neoliberalism for both performers and audiences. Ghanaian hiplife—and its connections to public notions of morality and consumption—appropriates the logic of market exchange, creating a flexible political-economic subject position both within and against the postcolonial state (see Ong 1999).

This ethnographic research shows that in urban Ghana popular circulation and mediation indexically link past forms of collective affiliation to individual creative expression. Hiplife relies on a dual logic where electronic technologies and dispersed affiliations elaborate upon older oral forms of Ghanaian proverbial speech culture (Lee 1997). African hip-hop and its mass-mediated circulation also enables consideration of the self-sovereign subject as a neoliberal consuming agent, appropriating the logic of the market to create a political-economic voice within and against the postcolonial state. Whereas centralized states demand subjects that are regulated through centralized institutions, neoliberalism fragments and locates discipline within subjects who self-regulate. This process of self-regulation "appears" as free expression. Popular musical circulation is likewise imagined as a form of free expression that produces subjects in relation to the morality of a dispersed, privatized state.

As John Comaroff (2002) reminds us, sovereignty—especially in the postcolony—is defined not only within the terms of the state but through the state's relationship to other more powerful states and transnational institutions of political and economic power. Citizens of postcolonial states increasingly confront the disjuncture between territorial and national belonging, state power or lack thereof, and possibilities for their own economic and cultural agency. In Achille Mbembe's examinations of the dramatic violence enacted upon and in the name of African political being, one of the central issues is the failed naturalization of the institutions and borders delineating the independent nation-state. For Mbembe the failures of postcolonial political sovereignty become the backdrop for a series of redemptive projects—from tricksters and the political grotesque to the self-writing African subject and the suicide bomber as the various hopes and tragedies of political being, legitimated violence, and artistic and political improvisation—within which creative actors rearticulate the relationship between subjectivities and economic and political power. Sovereignty and its bodily articulations, then, become crucial not only in considering state and nonstate violence, war, and terror but for examining cultural, practical, and subtly political forms through which neoliberal subjects and citizens purportedly confined and defined within specific states negotiate their positions through state and transnational imaginaries. Hiplife music reproduces gendered forms of power in the name of claiming new political self-sovereign subjects who claim the possibilities of self-expression and in the process internalize the contours of a liberal political subject. Transnationally articulated practices such as hip-hop allow African publics to consider how sovereignty and public authority, situated ostensibly in relation to a territorially-bounded polity, must be understood in terms of negotiating the ideological inside and outside of the borders of the state (Agamben 1998:24–29).

For both Mamdani (1996) and Mbembe (2003) African political subjectivity is shaped by the double failure of the state to fulfill its promise to foster, in Kwame Nkrumah's words, a new "African personality." According to Mamdani (1996:1–5) the postcolonial African state has moved between two unsuccessful polarities: first, relying on institutions of civil society to build political accountability and transparency, and second, attempting to identify and revive African traditional cultural-political forms. Mbembe (2003) has unpacked the ontological implications of this dual search for an institutional home for stability and truth. My task here is rather to explore how a youth musical movement produces political economic subjectivities that claim individuated self-expression and the performative context for affiliation within a dispersed community of Ghanaian liberalism. Hiplifers use ideas of creativity to posit themselves as viable political-economic actors despite their lack of recognition in the eyes of state institutions. In the process they internalize liberal forms of political authority embedded within ideas of "self-writing" (Mbembe 2003) and individuated being. This essay looks at the structurings of a self-sovereign liberal subject emergent within and against the state.

In the following pages I follow the trajectory of a song in its mediated circulation through urban Accra. I follow the political discussion sparked by "Vote for Me" on a *tro-tro* (mini-bus) heading toward Accra. Hiplife music moves across urban spaces in electronic and proverbial forms weaving together an evolving Ghanaian popular imagination. This genre is built upon a culture of circulation in which the terms of movement themselves produce subjects as mobile and flexible in relation to public life and its forms of purportedly static institutional power (Lee and LiPuma 2002).

EATING THE ELECTIONS AND POPULAR PARODY OF POLITICAL AGENCY

Vote for Me

Vote for me, I want chop president [2x]
Vote for me, I go make you vice president.
If I come power everything goin' be alright
Be you see what I dey talk e no be no lies
This one I know fit take, no controversial
Several times you suffer, no rescuer
Kenkey[4] price come down no more suffer
Appreciate educate school, form better plan
Come see different sense inside one man
No more promise and fail, no delay
I fit say I show you self you go proud

NATIVE FUNK LORDS (NFL)

In the months leading up to the 2000 presidential elections songs and radio call-in programs calling for peaceful elections, political change, and public accountability were a prominent new feature of the political landscape throughout the country. As Radio Gold Programme Manager B. B. Menson recalls, "the 2000 elections showed how much Accra had changed: we had so many stations on air that they became the main way people talked about politics. In the 1996 elections it had been mostly newspapers and state controlled media." The sudden prevalence of radio as a medium for political discourse followed from the privatization of the airwaves in the mid-1990s and the concomitant explosion of private stations. The 1992 Constitution of the Fourth Republic of Ghana marked increased privatization and decentralization of the state promoted through IMF and World Bank structural adjustment programs. The possibilities of private radio and media companies encouraged the return of Ghanaians who had left the country during difficult times in the 1980s or before. Many of the DJs and programming directors were young Ghanaians returning from Europe, the United States, and the Middle East with broadcasting and media experience and interest in hip-hop music in particular. These conditions gave hip-hop artists a national platform for their music. Furthermore, stations were eager to encourage new Ghanaian music so that the stations would have local appeal.

In Accra and throughout the country, radio became the main public forum for political and social commentary through call-in programs and music programming and the public debates these shows sparked. The multiple private stations provided dispersed nodes for the dissemination of ideas to the public. And in a relatively small but intense city such as Accra this sparked direct dialogues among people relatively unmediated by the state. Interview and call-in programs addressed public problems from flooding and power outages to accusations of political corruption and sexual indiscretions by local clergy. On occasion hundreds of people would gather at radio stations to have their opinions heard. Meanwhile, in emergencies radio stations were often called to request police intervention in a given part of the city, thereby expediting the arrival of help and ensuring the call for help was not lost in the dead spaces of government bureaucracy. Young musicians would also go to the stations in the hope of making a connection with one of the influential DJs. With the proliferation of mobile phones rapid public dialogues about the hot issues of the day centered on radio stations. It was not unheard of for a politician, sometimes even a cabinet minister, who was criticized on air to call the station from a mobile phone to make an immediate rebuttal.

On a hot afternoon in 2000 travelers wait at a bus stop to get a car into downtown Accra. The radio plays a Ghanaian hip-hop (or hiplife) song, "Vote for Me," by the Native Funk Lords (NFL) as I climb into a rusted fourteen-seater *tro-tro*. The engine rattles compete with the electronic beats and pidgin rap coming from the radio as we make our way from the outlying area of Adenta, past tire sellers and metal shipping containers converted into food stalls, and toward downtown Accra. The driver's mate leans to collect bus fares as he balances precariously on one foot; the other holds the van door closed. The morning rush is over and the torn plastic seats gain some relief from the constant pressure of overcrowded bodies; at the same time an intense midday heat has taken over. With a cool breeze blowing and the anticipation of progress into town comes a sense of casual intimacy in this mobile space. An important aspect of public life in Accra is banter about daily events, often provoked by the popular music of the day or the current events debated on radio news and call-in programs. The end of President Flight Lieutenant Jerry Rawlings' nineteen-year rule and the upcoming presidential elections in December 2000 bring both anxiety and excitement and people are increasingly willing to talk publicly about political differences, though often in comical or oblique ways.[5] A young man seated next to me chuckles as he listens to the humorous lyrics in pidgin English clearly aimed at the upcoming presidential elections. He says to no one in particular, "It's true, Ghanaians! We fool, oh." I ask him what he is talking about. He replies: "Look, we believe any promises politicians make. We never remember that these were the same things they have always said, until they actually get into power. Then they forget what they had been talking about and chop (eat) the money."[6]

Overhearing our conversation in the seats behind him, the driver joins in. In his mid-forties, he says that he supported the outgoing President Rawlings when he first came to power. Flight Lieutenant Jerry John Rawlings headed two coups, in 1979 and again in 1981. He came to power espousing moral discipline, critical of the corruption of African elites and Western economic exploitation. While calling for economic self-determination, in the face of currency fluctuations, drought, fuel shortages, and the sudden return of a million Ghanaians from Nigeria, the state was forced to accept IMF and World Bank loans in exchange for privatizing state enterprises and accepting Western ideas of democratic governance. Elected democratically in 1992 and 1996, Rawlings continued to call for state-based discipline and local control of resources though the policies of his government moved in the opposite direction. The state divested itself of interests in economic ventures, transportation, infrastructure, media and the culture industry, and so on. The tensions of this transition were played out across public life.

As we discuss the upcoming elections on the *tro-tro,* both the driver and the man next to me seem ambivalent about the two main political hopefuls, Rawlings's current vice president, John Atta Mills from the National Democratic Congress (NDC), and the opposition leader John A. Kufuor of the National Patriotic Party (NPP). Indeed, it seems that the political climate in Ghana is dominated by nostalgia—a reckoning with past hopes and failures—that tempers most working people's aspirations for the electoral process. After a silence as we stop at the University of Ghana, Legon, to let passengers on and off the driver reflects on the twenty years of political hopes and traumas that are just becoming part of the public reckoning with Rawlings' regime: "J.J. tried to change things. When he came, he tried to help we, the grassroots people. Junior Jesus, hmm. Now, Rawlings has grown fat . . . How? He can't fit into his military fatigues. Look at the price of petrol! He has been corrupted by being in power too long . . . Ghanaians need a change. Ghanaians, we are suffering . . . Vote for me, hmm!"

The politician's "fat" body is a synechdocal inversion of the national body. The populace who had supported the politician's rise to power on an anti-neocolonial platform does not benefit from state reform but is instead the victim of moral decay. In this suddenly intimate discussion on a public bus, the driver's personal lament and passengers' frustrations bespeak disillusionment, not simply with specific politicians but with the possibilities of the Ghanaian state itself as a viable political and economic collective and with the moral relationship of specific agents to it. All of this was inspired by a song on the radio, showing how the pragmatics of hiplife music in urban Ghana provokes and mediates state political discourse and ideas of individuated morality and consumption.

"Vote for Me" was one of several songs on the radio that addressed politics, though most were much less direct. With the chorus, "Vote for me/Make I chop president," it offers an ironic critique of Ghana's political process. The rhymes float over a clean electronic beat, but the song is unusual in that it is rapped in pidgin English rather than Akan as had become the fashion.[7] It describes all the beneficial things the singer will do if he is elected: provide cheap food, schooling, and hospital fees; kill all the mosquitoes; invite tourists and investors to Ghana; and arrange for free visas and easy flights. Recalling the promises of independence and pan-African unity, samples of Prime Minister Kwame Nkrumah's 1957 speech on the eve of Ghanaian independence and the jubilant shouts of the crowd on that night are mixed into the background. Nkrumah's haunting voice proclaims again and again, "Ghana . . . Ghana . . . Ghana is free forever . . . is free forever." Even the cassette cover recalls the moment of Ghana's independence. The three members of NFL stand on a platform surrounded by microphones, wearing traditional clothes from the North of Ghana and striking the same poses as in the famous images of Nkrumah and his ministers addressing the newly liberated nation at midnight on March 6, 1957. But the rappers also wear sunglasses, taking defiant hip-hop-oriented stances. This rich layering of familiar contemporary and historical symbols and the humorous and ironic tone of the delivery emphasize the discrepancy between the bold promises of charismatic politicians and the realities of daily life. The song reflects a common ambivalence at the time of both nostalgia and regret that Ghanaians carried to the election polls. These historical references indexically link past political and speech events to the current elections, providing a set of contexts for new conversations and political positions to emerge (Silverstein 1976; Bauman and Briggs 1990).

The song's central metaphor revolves around *chop*, a common pidgin term that means to eat or consume (Bayart 1993). It refers most directly to the consumption of food but is commonly used to refer explicitly or in parallel to the consumption of money or resources and the sexual consumption of women by men. Since English is the language of state politics, by using pidgin rather than formal English or another African language NFL positions the song close to the form of a political speech while emphasizing its subversive quality, in that pidgin is often associated with the uneducated and bawdy side of Ghanaian life. The rapper boasts about his imagined power to fulfill the nation's desires and relieve its social ills, humorously mocking the promises of immediate progress that politicians make when running for office. Eddie Blay, one of the members of NFL, recalls that "we made the song to be critical of the political process in Ghana and to show the hypocrisy of politicians who always say they will do things and then don't follow through. But we were also just having fun." As in many popular realms, humor can be the most potent form of critique, spreading rapidly and posing as something it is not.

Metaphors of eating have long been critical aspects of political debate in Ghana and across Africa and point to familiar public discussions of state excess and corruption as well as the historical impotence of postcolonial African politics in the face of foreign influence. Symbols of eating, bodily desire, and individual accumulation are central to the negotiation of personal moral action in the public sphere and thus to the nature of political authority. The explicit multivocality of the verb *chop* indicates how it links active processes of consuming with figurative ideas of self-transformation. This resonates with the process of voting, in that many Ghanaians saw this election as the one in which they were given a real choice. The uncertainty and excitement stirred up all sorts of stories about the possibilities and dangers of authority and success where many people had seen their political and economic circumstances spiral out of control. Putting voting and consuming (chopping) on a par with one another allowed for assessments of the actual transformative possibilities of the elections and the populace's role in them.

I want to return, briefly, to the conversation on the *tro-tro* heading into Accra. Initially the exchange had been partially directed toward me, with the possible intent of educating a foreigner about Ghana. However, it was also clearly meant for the ears of all in the car and was met with several nods of agreement. The comments I reproduce in the opening section of this chapter point to several key features of hiplife music and its incitement of political discourse. First, there is the use of "we," which speakers frequently used to define Ghana as a national community identifiable through the collective experience of political failure, economic trauma, and performative inaction in the face of (perceived) corruption—to use Fela Kuti's phrase, "shuffering and shmiling." The comments also point to the perceived relationship between the body of the leader and the body of the nation. Rawlings became the butt of jokes and was seen as being hypocritical as he got fatter and could no longer fit into his military uniform. As the economic crisis deepened he continued to talk about sacrifice and national unity. Having songs like this on the airwaves allowed Ghanaians to negotiate publicly new narratives of national political failure and trauma, using formal elements of humor and indirection to address the obligations and possibilities of an individual leader in the face of obvious and overwhelming structural inequalities.

The conversation continued sporadically after the song ended, before a series of advertisements for air conditioners and churches and the station-call for Radio Gold. As the car passed East Legon, with its luxurious homes and hotels, a woman in her thirties dressed as a young professional, who had said little up until then, chimed in with a final humorous commentary on the song. Speaking in pidgin and forcefully punctuating her words with her hands, she said:

> If I be president, I go keep the money well but I go chop small. If someone is president by all means he go chop the money. If I go out, I go use Benz car with air condition. I go flex. But if I go to work I go use abongo car. Chorolorry car! People go think say, I no get money but I go chop um small small. [If I was president, I would take care of the finances properly, but I would take a little bit of money on the side. I mean, anyone in that position is going to do the same thing. If I went out for an evening on the town, I would drive a Mercedes-Benz with air conditioning. I would show off. But when I went to work I would drive an old broken-down car so people would think that I don't have any money. But I would be stealing money on the side, which no one would know about.]

Several people laughed at her description, which masks more serious political commentary. By shifting the participant role structures (Goffman 1981), the woman humorously inhabits the role of president in a similar manner to the rapper in "Vote for Me." The disjunctures produced through this joke are heightened by the gendered difference. The masculine, consuming subject position is equated with political leadership through the action verb *to chop*. By linking her speech to the speech of the rapper as a fictional leader, the female speaker embodies a moral critique of political authority (Bakhtin 1986). She affirms that it is common sense for anyone in a position of power to take money while also acknowledging the moral imperative not to reveal it publicly. Her humor revolves around the same axis as the ironic tone of the song, that is, the disparity between public performance and private action. This discussion brings to mind Chinua Achebe's young teacher in *A Man of the People*, as he reflects on the morality of what politicians put in their mouths, and how West African societies negotiate the relationship between political power and individual consumption. Achebe's protagonist, referring to local villagers' celebration of a visiting government minister, reflects, "Tell them that this man had used his position to enrich himself and they would ask you—as my father did—if you thought that a sensible man would spit out the juicy morsel that good fortune placed in his mouth" (Achebe 1989 [1967]:2–3).

In "Vote for Me" the politician's blatantly impossible promises and his repeated insistence on the fact that he is not telling lies highlights the highly visible contradictions of the privatizing state and fears of the duplicitous nature of leadership:

If I come power everything goin' be alright.
Be you see what I dey talk e no be no lies.

Through reflexive denials of political rhetoric the rapper stresses the relationship between trickery and political performance. Politics is seen as a dangerous realm permeated with the seductive power of words, in which the language of collective moral obligation is only another form of entrepreneurial hustle. This reflexive uncertainty makes these kinds of stories "good to think with" for audiences.

The *tro-tro* discussion sparked by "Vote for Me" is indicative of the public role of hiplife music in the production of indirect, electronically mediated modes of political discourse as they revolve around the morality of entrepreneurial consumption. The history of Rawlings's regime was shaped by a struggle over the movement of goods and the control of consumer-oriented practices. After Rawlings came to power in 1979 one of his first actions was to raze Makola, the main market in Accra, and to subject those caught price-gouging or hoarding goods to public flogging.

After the capitulation of the socialist-oriented revolutionary government of the 1980s and, subsequently, the IMF and World Bank's backing of democratization in 1992, Ghana's political and economic path increasingly complied with the structures and outlines of liberal capital. International organizations espousing the virtues of the free market to alleviate Africa's political and economic ills called for privatization and decentralization, and Ghana complied in many arenas. The opening of state-monopoly radio and television airwaves to small-scale private competition in the early 1990s accompanied the return of many Ghanaians from abroad who had fled the economic slumps of the 1980s and the resurgence of African-American and Caribbean roots tourism. As I mentioned, many of these young professional Ghanaians had business and media experience, particularly with rising technologies such as portable video cameras and decks and electronic keyboards and samplers. Their return helped fuel the sudden birth of the Nigerian and Ghanaian video and film industry (Larkin 2004, Meyer 1998), as well as the growing interest in electronic music and hip-hop. And while the trappings of global modernity and tourist comfort are ever more visible in Accra, there is a growing lack of employment and increasing struggles over the privatization of basic resources like water and electricity, both of which acutely affect youth, many of whom have been displaced and spatio-economically ghettoized. In this context, popular culture appears in the guise of a neoliberal form of business practice promoting individual stardom, accumulation, and success over ethnic, familial, and national affiliations and older political hopes of a centralized, socialist, or pan-Africanist state.

The 1992 and 1996 elections in which Rawlings was elected the constitutionally backed president of the Fourth Republic of Ghana were relatively peaceful, though accusations of corruption and rigging were prevalent (Nugent 1995).[8] Rawlings's supporters saw him as betraying the ideals of anti-neocolonialism by acquiescing to IMF and World Bank demands for state liberalization—changes which appeared to benefit the wealthy. Meanwhile, his opponents criticized him for maintaining the trappings of military rule for too long and preventing the progress of free-market capital. The conundrums of transition could be articulated in the highly mobile phrase "Vote for Me." Under neoliberal reforms the government had given up control of much of the economic sector. However, it has meant the expansion and stabilization of state structures of democratic governance, the most fetishized of which—by both local and international political analysts—is the national electoral process. As the presidential elections approached, "Vote for Me" circulated in the same way as a proverb, provoking discussions and sparking debates on the relationship between individual action and the nature of power. It played a role within the popular imagination, humorously helping to bring into public discourse the traumatic failures of the state to achieve the promises of independence and pan-Africanism.

As I have argued elsewhere (Shipley 2003), in the early 1980s state populist spectacles and cultural nationalist displays and their centralized media coverage produced the legitimacy of Rawlings's populist leadership, while ironically facilitating Ghana's transition to neoliberal statehood. Public political ceremonies and state-sponsored performances were events through which national publics were produced and contested in the colonial, early independence, and early Rawlings years. One of the fascinating aspects of the rise of neoliberalism is that live state performances became increasingly common in efforts at shaping the national collectivity. In 2000, large rallies and political speeches were held by both parties in Accra, Kumasi, Sunyani, and other urban capitals, but they were not heavily attended, discussed, or widely covered in the press. Instead, at the end of the millennium popular cultural modalities and mass media had become more central to producing and contesting national imaginaries and individuated subjectivities. As Paul Nugent suggests in his study of political transformation in Ghana, "Rawlings had once cut an impressive figure as a home-grown revolutionary, whether it was haranguing urban crowds or pitching into manual work in rural areas . . . Whereas he had once poured scorn on 'mere elections,' he now occupied the office of elected President . . . he was a shadow of his populist self" (Nugent 1995:268).

Rawlings became less and less relevant as a public figure as the state's grip over the domain of cultural production loosened and mass media was privatized. Ghanaians looked more toward popular cultural figures and arbiters of style than political leaders to shape public discourses of morality and agency. In particular, transnational black imaginaries and signs of national foundation such as Nkrumah became reconfigured through an ironic popular idiom of racialized, national belonging rather than state-centered symbols or events. Hiplife, then, is the genre within which this imaginary emerges for performers, people involved in various aspects of the media and production industries, as well as dispersed audiences. Hiplife also conjures a liberal sovereignty that increasingly eludes state control.

Over the course of the 1990s, Accra increasingly developed as two parallel, overlapping geographies. This can be understood in relation to two incomplete and contradictory political projects: recent privatizing reforms overlaying an early independence nationalist-centered state. That is to say, in Habermas's sense, recent urban transformations of Accra point to the contested neocorporatist "societalization of the state" (Habermas 1996:432). Private banks, multistory glass buildings, the stock market, traffic lights, walled-off highway overpasses, government regulated markets, and transportation yards increasingly demarcate the means of mobility and uses of the landscape of Accra, encroaching on informal economic activity, transportation networks, and bustling crowds through which most West Africans experience the metropolis. Twisting and creative dirt lanes, open gutters, tightly packed mud-brick and wooden shacks, compound houses, tin roofs, families selling foodstuffs and clothing, dressmakers, tailor shops, barbers, car mechanics housed in kiosks, drinking spots, and chop bars that characterize the daily world of many people in Ghana's capital are more and more circumscribed by official businesses; walled compounds of rising middle-class houses, tourist hotels and networks; and the structural and ideological effects of the state's vocal acquiescence to privatization. New European cars are increasingly visible on the fashionable main streets of neighborhoods such as Osu, running alongside characteristically dilapidated private taxis and *tro-tros*. Public discussions seem of late to turn to considerations of the rapid increase in luxurious multistoried houses that are appearing in Accra and its suburbs. The National Patriotic Party (NPP) government of President J. A. Kufuor, which won the 2000 elections, has explicitly persisted in the liberalization initiated under the Rawlings regime. The growth of a bourgeois elite is a symptom of privatization that has placed social resources in the hands of those with connections to multinational corporate networks, increasingly redefining Accra as allied with the desires, hopes, and impediments of global capital. As in much of contemporary urban Africa, every luxury is available to the few with money, while the masses struggle to find jobs or even the basic resources of daily life. Poor neighborhoods such as Nima and Labadi and the ever-expanding suburbs are often referred to by young inhabitants in the language of ghettoization gleaned from hip-hop lyrics. Economic inequality is made visible daily as wooden shacks with pirated electric wires, shared outhouses, and hand-carried water stand in the shadow of houses with satellite television and central air conditioning protected by private security firms.

These starkly visible inequalities have bred only a fraction of the kinds of violent crimes and concomitant elite anxieties—in conflicts between increasingly isolated and disenfranchised youth, the state, and private security firms—that have become central to public life in comparable cites around the world like Johannesburg, Lagos, or São Paolo (Mbembe 2005:149). Rather, urban cultural styles mark especially male youths' "performative competence" and concomitant shifts in community identification and social mobility (Ferguson 1999:83, 95–96).[9] Hiplife provides performative styles that give youth new kinds of authority to reinvent subject positions within the imaginary of what Hart describes as entrepreneurial employment in the informal economy (Hart 1973).

For hiplife, as with political rallies and state spectacles, live performances are not primary sites of sociality, performative efficacy, or symbolic reference in and of themselves. The prevalence of unruliness at many live shows points to the fine line between humorous critique and civil unrest that characterizes youth culture in many places. Live performances become more important in the broader popular imagination as secondary references confirming the baptismal origins of the music in its continual mass-mediated circulation through dispersed, urban spaces (cf. Silverstein 1976). Concerts are primarily references to mass-mediated forms rather than the other way around. For Ghanaian hiplife audiences original authority emanates from the recorded song (on cassette, CD, or MP3) and its music video circulating on radio, television, and the Internet. Live renditions reference electronic originals, extending the authority of technology and media to real-time events. This is highlighted by the fact that in the 1990s and early 2000s live shows were, for the most part, lip-synched to studio recorded tracks with few deviations from or improvisations on the artist's widely known electronically mediated sonic and visual imaginaries. In fact, artists fear deviating because audiences explicitly come to hear the hit tracks and the advanced technology they represent.

"Vote for Me" is an example of an easily detachable, circulated piece of discourse, structurally predisposed to provoke oral and mass-meditated political, moral contestation in Ghanaian public life. In public debates ideas of moral personhood come to constitute popular opinion and shape political sovereignty and liberal personhood. Hiplife songs—like proverbs, Ananse trickster stories, and highlife songs—circulate by word of mouth. They are often explicitly described by musicians and listeners as "telling stories and using proverbs in ways that draw on the speech culture of Ghanaians, especially the Akan linguistic traditions."[10] In this sense, structures of formal speaking establish a proverbial phrase or nested set of proverbs which are then explicated and expanded upon in open-ended ways through a call and response storytelling form.[11] Morality and its public, performative negotiation set the terms through which political authority is contested. Public discourse around hiplife also creates spaces for the commingling of the pristine, the grotesque, and the absurd (Bakhtin 1986; Kapchan 1996). Actors become social critics through the changing role of media and democracy as they recall older forms of public circulation.

FROM POPULAR CULTURE TO URBAN PERFORMATIVITY

Hiplife as an emergent public performance genre brings together multiple traditions of public oratory, including proverbial speech, pastors' sermons, highlife lyricism, and Ananse storytelling. Young artists create a new type of critical public voice by manipulating how they reference and distance themselves from established genres and past speech acts. This form of public talk recalls Spitulnik's (1996) research showing how radio provokes public circulation of words that reflects changing national imaginaries in Zambia. It also suggests Kapchan's (1996:55) Bakhtinian argument that public oratory in the Moroccan marketplace is a genre "built upon the words of others," containing a "sediment of the past" in each new performance. The institutional power of the Ashanti kingdom from the seventeenth century has its political and juridical basis within its chief's palaces and courts. The centralized political authority and economic networks that emerged in this trade empire were coordinated in large part through the oral legal, diplomatic, and economic networks anchored in the formal speech of chiefs, elders, and the Okyeame, who operated as the chief's spokesperson, linguist, and interpreter. "A . . . chief cannot greet or be addressed directly, nor does he converse directly with interlocutors" (Verdon quoted in Yankah 1995:17). The Okyeame mediates all communication between chief and audience. Oral *mediation* and *indirection* are central features, then, of political negotiations between chiefs, the discussion of diplomatic strategy, or in the hearing of juridical cases. Typically the chief speaks to the Okyeame, who embellishes and elaborates the chief's statement (Verdon, in Yankah 1995:19).

An Okyeame's ability is measured in his skillful use of proverbial oratory and rich referential language to fill out the message of the chief. This mediation acts as surrogate speech to save face in communicative situations that are potentially disruptive or dangerous (Obeng 1999).[12] More generally in Akan societies, the largest linguistic and political community in Ghana, the craft of public speaking is highly valued. A speaker's ability to master proverbial speech (*bu me be*), metaphoric speech (*kasakwan*), rumor (*konkonsa*), indirection (also *konkonsa*), humor, and proper forms of social address are central to the production of authoritative social being.

From the 1940s through the 1980s, highlife popular music, especially as it was performed and circulated through concert party traveling theater troupes, was a crucial part of public political and moral discourse (Cole 2001). Cole (1997) has shown how this music and its movement across Ghana's physical landscape were central to the production of a collective sense of modern nationhood for Ghanaians emerging from colonial rule. Guitar bands used the latest technologies, incorporating current trends, music, and sayings from both at home and abroad. In the 1960s highlife bands began to incorporate soul and R&B music into their sound. For example, the Jaguar Jokers band covered James Brown's "I'm Black and I'm Proud," and Nana Kwame Ampadu of the African Brothers Band wore rhinestone-studded jumpsuits in the style of Wilson Pickett. Bands used generators to power electric guitars and amps on their tours of rural West Africa, bringing soul music's celebratory messages of black empowerment to the region (see also Collins 1994).

The multireferentality and aesthetic indirection characteristic of Akan speech culture defined how highlife tunes circulated in the middle of the twentieth century. One of the most popular highlife songs of all time was "Ebi Te Yie," recorded by Nana Kwame Ampadu and his African Brothers Band in 1967, though it maintained popularity through the 1970s. Nana Ampedu was known for both his showmanship and his masterful story-telling. "Ebi Te Yie's" popularity was due to the fact that it was structured as a proverbial morality tale about animals but circulated as an oblique critique of state corruption. It tells the tale of the antelope who is silenced by the lion every time he tries to speak at a forest meeting of animals. The antelope's lament is the song's hook. "Some of us are sitting well. Others are not sitting well at all." Because in Akan "te" can mean both "to sit" and "to live," many saw this as a criticism of corruption and lack of freedom of speech after the overthrow of Kwame Nkrumah's govern-ment in 1966.[13] Later the record was banned, making it more popular and controversial still (see K. Anyidoho 1983). Ampadu refused to say that the song was a direct political comment, averring that he was an entertainer telling stories about animals and that "people were free to make their own interpretations."[14]

Hiplife builds upon this established culture of circulation even as it uses different technologies of mediation to intersect with dispersed audiences (cf. Hirschkind 2006). Furthermore, rather than the centralized idea of nationhood, which was the focus of early independence Ghana, hiplife indexes subject positions indicative of the neoliberal focus on consumption and dispersal.

Studies of popular culture and religion have often implicitly used notions of genre as a way of delimiting the scope of research. I am interested in the intertextual aspects of hiplife and exploring the multiple practices and styles that go into the making of authoritative public genres and the media-tions and movements of symbols between popular and other public realms (Ferguson 1999). Hiplife lyrics, music, and bodily styles are pragmatic, mobile pieces of discourse that circulate through social space, connecting the purportedly separate social spheres of political and popular, state and pri-vate, elite and street (see also McGovern, this volume). Morality, desire, and consumption as expressed through this performance genre all form aspects of how politics are negotiated through civil institutions. The performative elements of this genre—as evoked in specific actor-centered events—focus on the production of authority and community identification, which are grounded in "emergent structures" of new contexts (Bauman and Briggs 1990:76). That is to say, the indexical elements of symbolic action call into being new relations between audiences and performers within changing political, economic, and social contexts. These speech communities are reshaped through the social circulation of hiplife music.

Birgit Meyer has argued that Ghanaian popular culture is central to electoral politics by inciting public debates on the "(im)morality of power" (Meyer 1998:15). She focuses on textual readings of films that focus on the intersection between Pentecostalism and the occult or traditional religion. Meyer demonstrates that the rise of the Ghanaian video-film industry is linked to liberalization and privatization and uses Christian-based morality tales to negotiate ideologies of tradition and modernity that often confound the state (Meyer 2004). Witchcraft and money become the terms of power through which moral value and political authority are negotiated. These films provide a moral language through which various kinds of talk publicly circulate. In examining the links among video-films, the recent rapid growth of Pentecostalism, and images of the supernatural, Meyer has taken seriously the political implications of West African popular culture and reinvigorated the work of earlier scholars who saw the continuities and disjunctures that make popular culture a field for reflexive negotiations of tradition and modernity, foreign and local, political power, and culture change (see Barber 1997, 1987).

Political discourse and its popular articulations are produced in the mediation and circulation of symbols and practices across informal urban spaces. As Lee and LiPuma argue, circulation "is a cultural process with its own forms of abstraction, evaluation, and constraint" (Lee and LiPuma 2002:192). These forms of expression are richly and explicitly intertextual engagements with changing forms of sovereign citizenship. Examining the pragmatic conditions through which certain texts get foregrounded as authoritative gives insight into how popular culture and political discourse come to appear as stable or shifting in the eyes of the public as well as many of its analysts.[15] Mass-mediated popular culture is linked to politics and religion precisely through the circulatory processes that produce and contest the boundaries between these social realms. The metapragmatic negotiation of boundaries—as ideologically rigid or permeable—separating political, popular, and religious speech genres and public spaces is a part of how moral authority is negotiated by Ghanaian publics. Social actors recontextualize musical texts and related bodily styles within their speech acts, gaining public authority in the ways they control the contexts and structures of an interaction (see Kapchan 1996:54–6). A performer's ability to produce an authoritative voice "is grounded at least in part in the knowledge, ability, and right to control the re-centering of valued texts" (Bauman and Briggs 1990:77). Hiplife is understood in local terms as an explicit marker of difference and newness and, therefore, its performative elements are foregrounded as sites for the reconfiguration of public authority.

As Meyer (2004) and Gifford (2004) have shown, popular culture and Pentecostalism are dialogically intertwined in both form and content with political transformation and the changing nature of the public sphere in Ghana. Indeed, as the hiplife superstar Obrafour's nickname Rap [O]sofo (Rap Preacher) suggests, hiplife music incorporates Christian morality but often in ways contradictory to the version espoused by established churches. And while many youth are involved in Pentecostal churches and its discourses of moral being, these same young men and women also inhabit a parallel social geography: the more risqué world of hiplife performances and rough audiences. I am particularly interested in how enduring structures of social circulation and authoritative speaking intersect with the agentive and disciplinary possibilities of new technologies and changing moral orders. Rather than focus on the explicitly diasporic, Pentecostal, or traditional aspects of public life, following hiplife music highlights how everyday experience in Accra is infused with the popular, religious, and political, particularly through perduring forms of humor, rumor, and styles of mediation.[16] As rappers, audiences, and local media folks alike have noted, in contemporary urban Ghana, rap lyricists take on the public role of pastors, oratory experts, and social critics, in some ways appropriating and in some ways competing with Christian and Islamic styles of public morality and political economic agency.[17]

Symbols of bodily consumption and their moral implications become the parallel poetic terrain upon which new forms of neoliberal publics are negotiated. Images and poetics relating to bodily fluids and fluidity, private desires and public indiscretions, become centrally meaningful in popular culture in Accra. Ideas of moral personhood expressed through tropes of the social permeability of the body and excessive bodily expression are often found in hiplife music and the types of talk it often inspires. The moral legitimacy of an individuated accumulating subject, then, is produced and contested in relation to notions of a sexual, consuming body and the value placed on seamless public performances of politicians as well as the musicians who comment upon them. Politics, then, is often enacted in a public sphere that is understood and contested in relation to a desiring body as it moves through public spaces and ideas of public political formations challenge the permeability and integrity of these bodies. This embodied public is in critical dialogue with state institutions and more formal realms of political engagement (Povinelli 2002:111–134; Warner 2002; Herzfeld 2005). Under this transnational liberal order, hiplife—as a popular cultural form—comes to signify a new type of public cultural space, allowing youth to configure themselves as masculinized agentive subjects moving through national, local, and transnational spaces while at the same time being newly confined by these forms of agency (see also Makhulu, this volume). While audiences consist of both men and women, the performative aspects of the music point to masculine subjects as agentive, relegating women to the realm of viewership and consumability.[18] Within this logic, practices of consumption—rather than objects of consumption or other forms of production—are presupposed to be productive of new social value and authority.

The circulation of hiplife music as it intersects with state politics across Accra's urban landscape demonstrates how privatized sectors of popular culture and circuits of oral communication operate in parallel to official and state sanctioned realms of politics and authority and give insight into the negotiation of public opinion in a neoliberal, democratic state such as Ghana.[19] Symbols of bodily desire and masculine ideals of the consumption of female sexuality, food, money, and value are salient in drawing the line between public and private acts and circumscribing the realm of political authority. A male actor's ability to manipulate this line and a musician's to comment on it performatively delineate the shifting boundaries of a critical subject. Making fun of excess bodily consumption also constitutes a critique of individual agency. In this critical voice a reflexive language emerges through which young Ghanaians build upon older speech conventions to engage with the personal and communal aspects of political power (Mbembe 2001).[20]

CONCLUSION: NORMALIZING THE EXCEPTION

Yenye die yebetumi mboa yen man
Oman boapa yo, katasihwe, niakikaho
Ama oman pinyin adwen ho
Weyi nye party sem
Mpanyin, brantie, nkolaa, mbaa
Bisa wo ho se wondi yee ti sen
Mfasuo ben na yebegya ekyire mba

[Do your best to help the nation
Bribery, evil doings and such
The president has thought that
This is not party politics
Elders, men, children, women
Ask yourself, access your character
What will be the legacy for the next generation?]
         OBRAFOUR [The Executioner], hiplife artist[21]

I am not arguing that the song "Vote for Me" in and of itself reshaped the election's outcome. Its movements are one small example of how popular culture draws both on older forms of speech circulation and global, racialized styles to reshape the way Ghanaian subjects talk about and understand the possibilities for choice and their position in relation to state authority. This is one among many hiplife songs that have a vibrant and limited circulatory life. Its trajectory follows established patterns of highlife and other popular cultural forms, though it has a political narrative particular to neoliberal transformation. It shows that public life is not dominated by grand political ceremonies. Increasingly as conditions of neoliberalism are normalized, dispersed semipublic realms are dominated by discourses of commercial taste and free expression. Yet "free expression" itself reinforces individuated subject positions required by the changing nature of the neoliberal state.

In 2000 hiplife music still had the outward appearance of newness and subversion. The freshness of deregulated radio also opened up public spaces for critical engagement. The music's edginess thrilled listeners as they waxed nostalgic for the glory days of highlife bands, debated the merits of hiplife, and whether or not hip-hop was "foreign," diasporic, or originated in Africa. In 2004 a song by Sidney the Hiplife Ninja entitled "Scenti No" (The Scent) also took on political connotations in the lead-up to the presidential elections. The song is nominally about bodily stench, but its chorus, "Scent no, scenti no, a gye be bia" [the scent, the scent is everywhere] became a proverb-like joke throughout Ghana as a metaphor for spreading state corruption. It was subsequently bought from the artist by President Kufuor's National Patriotic Party (NPP) for a campaign slogan. Here the state recognized the power of popular expression and public circulation. Unlike earlier state discomfort with critical voices, they appropriated the idea of free expression and parody, co-opting a song seen to be critical of its policies. Whereas in 2000 the youth voice seemed to play a fresh and ambiguous role in shaping the political process, a few years later hiplife's reflexive ideology of youth creativity and free expression had been appropriated by a marketized, liberal governmentality. In 2008 the hiplife artist Obuor put out a song titled "President" just before the election in which he described the types of responsibility he would take on if he was made president. Rather than offering parody or criticism of the state, the song sought to align hiplife and youth culture with good governance.

In 2008 I was a guest on the Friday night radio hip-hop show on Vibe FM in Accra. It is hosted by two hiplife pioneers, Kweku T, formerly of Talking Drums, and Eddie Blay, formerly of Native Funk Lords. They play Ghanaian hiplife and American hip-hop and invite new artists and others on to discuss music and current trends. I discussed my research on the music and the release of my recent film, *Living the Hiplife*, that chronicles its history. By this time the genre has become publicly acceptable, and songs from 2000 are seen as "old school." Blay explains this shift:

> Back in the day, it was new. No one knew where the music was going. We did it for fun and to make a statement . . . We made "Vote for Me" as a political statement to talk about corruption, to say we had a right to say what we wanted to say. Now it is more acceptable . . . It is more commercial. Some of the kids are making money, which is great, but there is not really enough money in the system to be really successful. Everyone is hustling, but the original message isn't there anymore . . . Did we lose the edge?

Free expression is seen as crucial to democratic governance and liberal economics. At the same time the commercial and political relegation of critical voices to the domain of the popular can be used to incorporate oppositional ways-of-being. The language of free expression is used to make criticism irrelevant by naming it as freedom.

This essay has argued that hiplife music indexically links multiple forms of performative agency embedded in national myths, transnational racial imaginaries, electronic technologies, and local genres of speaking and political discourse to create a new flexible public in which the appearance of free expression provides a new language of public discipline. Further, public spaces and face-to-face interactions are increasingly mediated by technologies of dispersal and indirection. Thus neoliberalism in Ghana recalls Agamben's proposition that "the state of exception comes more and more to the foreground as the fundamental political structure and ultimately begins to become the rule" (Agamben 1998:20). In this sense an African liberal subjectivity becomes viable only in the ways that it can normalize the exceptional, the illegal, that which transgresses the state morally and politically. The crossing of borders both literally and figuratively becomes a state of existence (Ferguson 2006; Ong 2006).

In the Ghanaian context, hiplife practices reflexively link individual creative potential to the changing ideas of political sovereignty. Hiplife valorizes the idea of public speaking while showing its impossibility. In parodying political hope "Vote for Me" confirms that speaking may feel free even if it is structured in ways that negate the possibilities of collective progress. All that is left is the potential to use ideologies of free expression for individual gain. Individuated bodily consumption becomes the terrain upon which Ghanaians think through public morality and the nature of the performativity of the political subject. This examination is significant for the study of media in that it shows that live, centralized events are often *not* the central authorizing events for subsequent mass-mediated movements of images and symbols. In these processes a Ghanaian urban public emerges that both aligns with older circulatory forms of storytelling and proverbial speech as well as new modes of electronic mass mediation. And in the performative movements between radio and television, public spaces and privatized media, transnational travel and local speech genres, hiplife music reshapes ideas of moral being and political authority.

6. "May God Let Me Share Paradise with My Fellow Believers"

Islam's "Female Face" and the Politics of Religious Devotion in Mali

Dorothea E. Schulz

In November 2003, with the fasting month of Ramadan in full swing, the director of one of Mali's two private Islamic radio stations in Bamako faced an unprecedented challenge. Since the radio's creation in 2002, its policy had been to call exclusively on male intellectuals and leading religious figures of Bamako to deliver sermons during the fasting month. Recently, however, that is to say a few weeks prior to that year's Ramadan, several delegates of the national Muslim women's association, UNAFEM,[1] had approached him to propose that in the blessed weeks to come special broadcast time should be set aside for them to speak on the radio station, address female listeners, and remind them of "women's central role as guardians of Islamic values." Without wishing to cause offense, the delegates added, they felt that the existing rule of excluding women from speaking on local and national radio needed to be revised because "in these times of moral disorientation," female teachers were more likely to convince the nation's women that they should work on the Islamic rejuvenation of self and society.

The director, scandalized at the mere thought of having women appear on his station, had initially declined any such idea. In an effort at diplomacy, he told them that their appearance on any kind of mass media outlet would jeopardize their good reputation and make them vulnerable to the accusation of seducing male listeners through the erotic tinges of their voices. After all, he added, a woman's public sermons were "forbidden in Islam," alluding to one particular *hadith* (report of the sayings of the Prophet Muhammad) that, according to some interpreters, questions the rightfulness of women's public preaching.

But the female delegates had not given up so easily. Soon after their encounter with the director, they rejoined their efforts by asking for the diplomatic intervention of an influential advocate, a member of the Ministry of Inner Affairs in charge of supervising the religious programming of the national radio and television station, ORTM.[2] In a conversation with the director, the official granted that programming decisions were of course entirely up to the latter. Yet, the official continued, paying justice to women's genuine vocation as teachers of Islamic values would certainly increase the radio station's appeal. By selecting "knowledgeable women with impeccable morals" to lecture to female listeners on a regular basis, the official continued, the director would follow a policy recently introduced by his ministry for national radio and bolster the director's claim that his radio station propagated an Islam truthful to its authentic sources yet also compatible with new developments.

The official's intervention on the UNAFEM delegates' behalf was to no avail; the director never complied with their request. The official's reasoning, however, as well as the initial exchange between the director and the delegates of the national Muslim women's association illustrate that controversies among Muslims over how to interpret "Islam's true teachings" are gaining in political poignancy. This development can be associated roughly with the era of neoliberal economic reform and post-authoritarian rule.

Since the introduction of multiparty democracy in 1991 ending the single-party rule of President Moussa Traoré, Mali has witnessed an upsurge of interest groups, which through associations claim recognition as structures of "civil society" and rely on the many new private media to publicize their aspirations.[3] Although the leaders of these groups have very different political agendas, they all share a keen interest in establishing ties to the new political and administrative elite, thereby seizing on the momentous opportunities opened up by the reconfiguration of the political system into another kind of single-party dominance since the early 1990s. Highly prominent among these actors are Muslim intellectuals and opinion leaders, many of them women, who publicly articulate an Islamic opposition to the continuation of the "culturally foreign" French model of secular politics, or *laïcité*. These men and women often play an enormous role in neighborhood politics where they offer material and institutional support in the name of Islamic charity. While they refer to the shared goal of "reestablishing true Islam" in Malian society, their objectives often prove to be diverse. They all establish a public presence that departs from earlier modes of public intervention. To a greater extent than before, they play a vocal part in controversies over governmental policy that address questions about the nation's foundational values and "common good," and thereby they draw on a globalizing legalistic discourse of citizenship rights and the rule of law.

What is remarkable about these advocates of Islamic moral renewal is the prominence of women among their ranks, both in terms of numbers and public visibility. From the scattered existence of a few groups in the early 1980s, women's mobilization has expanded into a dense network of urban-based neighborhood associations; these associations are the "alter ego" of the women's credit and savings associations that emerged in the 1980s in response to the often devastating effects of structural adjustment policies on urban households (see Makhulu, this volume, for a discussion of these associations in the South African context). Along with these developments, a rapidly proliferating infrastructure of Islamic proselytizing (such as mosques and schools) emerged, funded substantially by donors from the Arab-speaking world.

Most "Muslim women's groups" (singular, *silame musow ton*)[4] were founded by older, influential women who offer literacy classes in Arabic and knowledge in correct ritual practice. These leaders do not content themselves with instruction in immediate learning settings but seek to extend their "mission" or "call" (*da'wa* in Arabic) for moral renewal to a wider public. Some of them publicize their moral advice on "women's rights and duties in Islam" via audio recordings and on the local radio stations that have been mushrooming in urban areas, especially in Mali's southern triangle, since 1992 (Panos Institute 1993; Schulz 1999). Yet along with the new opportunities emerging for these women in a privatized media landscape, their greater public presence also generates new controversies over leadership and moral authority, not just between the government and its Muslim critics, but among different protagonists of Islamic renewal (Schulz 2008).

Although Muslim women's activities in public and semipublic arenas are not a novel phenomenon, their present interventions are distinctive insofar as women imbue them with a new significance by presenting them as essential to the moral reform of society.[5] Their public assertion that a woman's proper place is in the family may appear paradoxical, yet it reflects on these women's conception of the relevance of individual faith and ethics to public life.[6] They call themselves simply "Muslim women" (*silame musow*) and thereby set themselves apart from "the other women" (*muso tow*), who, they often maintain, are not "real Muslims" because they have not (yet) decided to "don the veil" (*ka musoro siri/ta*). This dress practice is associated by many people with "Arab Islam," a term that in local parlance refers to efforts to "purify" Islamic practice from unlawful innovation (*bid'a*), trends that are associated with *Salafiyya*-inspired reformist trends in Egypt and *Wahhabi* doctrine in Saudi Arabia.

Female Muslim leaders articulate a markedly conservative gender ideology and exhort their audiences to return to the original interpretations of Islam. Similar to male leaders, they present Islam as part of Mali's authentic traditions and thus gloss over the fact that broad segments of the population, particularly in the south, converted to Islam only during the colonial period.

The reasons for the appeal of Islam are not self-evident. Islam spread among broad strata of the population only during the colonial period and therefore never interlocked as thoroughly with modern institutions of governance as in some neighboring countries, most notably in Senegal and Nigeria.[7] To understand Islam's popularity, we need to understand in what ways the historical interaction between proponents of Islam on one side, and representatives of the state on the other, paved the way for Islam's current center-stage position in Malian politics. One could view the efflorescence of Islamic welfare institutions and of publicly enacted Muslim identities after 1991 as a sign of the empowerment of "civil society" and of the weakening of state control. However, the situation is more complicated and, I argue, reflects on some of the institutional reconfigurations prompted by neoliberal economic reform and, more recently, by political liberalization. Rather than consider Islam's present appeal as a threat to a secularist state, we should explore the invigoration of Muslim networks and of an Islamic moral idiom as indicative of recent rearticulations of the relationship between the state and actors and groups of "civil society" (see John L. Comaroff and Jean Comaroff 1999). As we will see, these rearticulations generate new spaces for enterprise and activism into which advocates of Islamic renewal insert themselves and that allow them to promote a particular political and religious subjectivity.

To understand the specific role that Muslim women assume in these emergent spaces, and the constraints and dilemmas they face in doing so, I will proceed by way of several analytical moves. One is to retrace the normative and institutional shifts that enabled Islam's present public prominence and its high appeal as a community-building idiom. I will also assess how Muslim activists' view of women's roles in the moral transformation of society contrasts with conventional understandings of legitimate realms of female and male practice. Third, I will examine in what ways Muslim activists reformulate conventional views of political subjectivity and collective responsibility.

To explore Muslim women's search for greater public presence by relating it to the vision of political subjectivity they seek to articulate shifts the analysis away from interpretations of women's involvement in Islamic movements as a patriarchal backlash against modernity. It also allows us to break with a view, still predominant in sociological and anthropological theorizing, that equates women's access to public arenas with their empowerment (see, for example, MacLeod 1991; Mirza 2002; Alidou 2005).

Informed by feminist critiques of Habermas's normative, implicitly gendered concept of the public,[8] several authors have recently explored the nature of women's engagements in postcolonial politics. In spite of their divergent theoretical perspectives, they all maintain that women's (nonverbal) forms of public participation call into question Habermas's rational-argumentative model. Navaro-Yashin (2002), for instance, in her study of contemporary Turkey, highlights the importance of commodification processes in shaping the conditions for politics under neoliberal conditions. She posits that Muslim women's consumption practices, such as their choice of modest apparel, constitutes a form of political intervention. Göle (1996, 2002) and Cinar (1998) similarly view Muslim women's visibility as a contribution to public controversy in Turkey; they identify women's "body politics" as the most characteristic features of the public space that "Islamist" groups carve out for themselves.[9] The nonargumentative, visual, and emotionally compelling nature of corporeal practices, these authors argue, allows Islamist women to challenge foundational liberal assumptions of secular state politics and thus commonsense understandings of political subjectivity.

The strength of this perspective on women's "politics of presence" lies in its departure from reductive interpretations of women's public prominence as a sign of greater political participation and "agency." It recognizes the significance of consumption practices to the public assertion and practice of identities and convictions, and thus it provides a counterpoint to Habermas's critique of consumer culture as heralding the demise of a critical argumentative public. However, the new interest in consumption illustrated by the above-mentioned studies also raises questions about the notion of the "political" with which these authors work. While I agree that anthropologists should distance themselves from universalistic and discourse-centered models of the public, there are also some pitfalls of overstretching the meanings of political praxis. I will query the assumption that (women's) "public presence" effected through acts of consumption has similar political weight as (men's) participation in public controversy. By situating my critique in the specificities of the contemporary neoliberal moment, I will tease out the particular constraints and limitations faced by Muslim women in Mali who chose consumption as a road toward public presence and political intervention.

ISLAMIC MORAL REFORM IN URBAN MALI: HISTORICAL ANTECEDENTS AND POLITICAL LOCATIONS

Recent attempts by Muslim activists to articulate norms of conduct in accordance with Islamic principles, and to make them binding for all Malians, are rooted in a longer process of interaction between actors and institutions of the state on one side and different groups of Muslims on the other. In this process, the state positioned itself in highly ambivalent ways vis-à-vis articulators and institutions of Islam and showed a high measure of inconsistency in its treatment of manifestations of "religion" in the public arena (Schulz 2006:212–14).

That the colonial and later postcolonial state consistently undermined the principle of *laïcité* that it claimed to establish is not in question (see Soares 2005). After all, as Casanova, Asad, and Bauberot remind us, the principle of secularism, understood as the state's full neutrality toward, and equal treatment of, its citizens' religious affiliations has been an ideal rather than a real-time achievement in Euro-American history or even in the postcolonial world (Casanova 1994; Bauberot 1998; Asad 2003; also see Chatterjee 1993; Bhargava 1998; Chakrabarty 2000). Rather, my point is that historically, Malian Muslims' evolving "discursive capacities" (Salvatore 1999) to formulate visions of public order and of personal conduct were shaped, yet never determined, by colonial administrators' efforts to control institutions and leading representatives of Islam. The resulting push-and-pull relationship between the latter and Mali's changing political elites continues to make its influence felt and forms the backdrop for the interventions by Muslim activists, both men and women.

The available, mostly oral, historical material leaves many questions open with respect to long-time continuities in women's religious practice.[10] It does suggest, however, that until the 1970s most women, especially those from nonelite backgrounds, gained only limited knowledge in religious and ritual matters.[11] The accessability of Islamic education to nonelite women afforded by Muslim women's groups (singular, *silame musow ton*) as much as their participation in public manifestations of Muslim virtue are developments of the last three decades.

Nowadays, most group members are younger (married) women from the urban lower and lower-middle classes. Their participation and the fact that some of their leaders disseminate their teachings on audiotapes and local radio indicate a broadening of access to religious knowledge, a process that, starting in the late 1930s, exacerbated ongoing struggles over religious authority and leadership (e.g. Kaba 1974; Brenner 2001; also see Eickelman 1992, 2000). Key to this process were male Muslim activists who, after graduating from higher institutions of Islamic learning in Saudi Arabia and Egypt, returned to the French Sudan and worked to counter the reach and rationale of the colonial state, for instance by reforming the traditional Qur'anic school system.[12] They provided a critical rejoinder to the discursive traditions formulated by influential religious lineages, many of whose practices and beliefs they denounced as distortions of the original teachings of Qur'an and Hadith (*bid'a*, unlawful innovation). Their activities contributed to the unsettling of the credentials and legitimacy of established religious authorities, even though the latter received strong support from the French colonial apparatus in its attempt to contain the influences of "radical" reformist tendencies in Saudi Arabia.[13]

Throughout the colonial period, views of proper religious practice and of the relevance of individual ethics to politics remained a highly contested terrain. Even if none of the reformist conceptions completely displaced earlier ones (Brenner 2001), they left an imprint on local ethical understandings and colonial politics in a period in which broad segments of the population gradually converted to Islam. Colonial Muslim controversy and activities thus laid the ground for a broader acceptance of Islam as a normative frame of reference for community constructions in postcolonial politics. Even if the influence of Muslim leaders and intellectuals was submerged periodically, such as under the first postindependence government of President Modibo Keïta (1960–68), it never fully vanished from the political landscape.[14]

Muslim interest groups gradually gained in influence after the coup d'état of 1968, which brought Colonel Moussa Traoré to power. Under his military regime and (after 1979) single-party rule, changes in the normative and institutional foundations of politics created the conditions for Islam's gradual emergence as a powerful moral idiom and as an alternative to official constructions of the common good. This development was the paradoxical outcome of Traoré's attempts to control established and newly emerging, powerful Muslim interest groups by granting them special privileges in spite of Mali's secular constitution.[15] The foundation of the national association of Muslims, AMUPI,[16] in the early 1980s consolidated state control over the religious establishment and its new opponents, the *arabisants*, that is, graduates from institutions of higher learning in the Arab-speaking world.[17] The organization allowed the government to monitor the funds that, starting in the late 1970s, flooded the country, under the orchestrated efforts of the Saudi government to extend the *da'wa* movement of proselytizing to Muslim sub-Saharan Africa (see, e.g., Mattes 1989; Schulze 1993:26ff.; also see Brenner 1993).

Echoing earlier initiatives, advocates of contemporary Islamic renewal aim to reform the moral and the social, and they highlight the importance of religious instruction and Arabic literacy (see Otayek 1993; Miran 1998; LeBlanc 1999; Loimeier 1997, 2003; Augis 2002; also see Schulze 1993; Hirschkind 2001a, 2001b; Mahmood 2005). Their activities benefit from the new opportunities for self-organization and expression introduced after President Traoré's fall from power in 1991.

President Konaré and his party, ADEMA,[18] elected in the country's first democratic elections in 1992, favored a stringent interpretation of Mali's secular constitution and ostracized the so-called *intégristes*, that is, Muslims who called for the introduction of "the *shari'a*." Yet neither President Konaré nor President Toumani Touré, who followed Konaré in the office in 2002, could risk antagonizing prominent Muslim leaders. Both presidents, in their efforts to control central domains of social and political life, have sought to accommodate and co-opt Muslim leaders whose mobilizing potential they fear and depend upon. This means that today, in the aftermath of neoliberal economic reform and political liberalization, Muslim leaders and state officials in Mali are caught in a web of mutual cooptation and dependency (Schulz 2006). Representatives of Muslim interest groups more than ever play an ambivalent role in state politics.

This dynamic is evident in the recently liberalized media landscape in which Muslims of various orientation and pedigree advance competing claims to religious leadership and interpretational authority. They cannot afford to bypass state institutions if they want to establish their position as a dominant one. Muslim leaders' struggle over access to state resources therefore secures state officials and institutions a key role in arbitrating intra-Muslim debate. In other words, contrary to the claims of Muslims who present themselves as defending "civil society against the state," recent democratization has not fundamentally reset the parameters of Muslim rivalry, even though the recent liberalization of the media market and the mushrooming of commercial radio stations complicate its effects.

Yet it is also evident that neoliberal economic reform and political liberalization have opened up new spaces for entrepreneurship into which key proponents of the renewal movement, as well as other Muslims, eagerly insert themselves. Key to their entrepreneurial activities is the expanding market for religious consumption. This market derives key impulses from its location in a transnational field of commercial enterprise that revolves around close ties to the Arab-speaking world, particularly Morocco, Libya, Egypt, and Saudi Arabia. Some of these transnational circuits of commercialization have intensified since the implementation of neoliberal economic reform in the mid-1980s, along with widening opportunities for cheap transport and travels to the sites of the Hejaz and other areas of the Muslim world.

The temporary boost in the national cotton production sector following its privatization in the early 1990s extended the infrastructure of Muslim piety to relatively prosperous rural areas. Growing numbers of farmers in the high-intensity cotton production areas of the south have benefited from a temporary rise in world cotton prices to convert economic prosperity into more lasting forms of personal salvation. Some finance the pilgrimage for elderly family members or embark on the hajj themselves; others set up a trade in religious commodities between Mali and North Africa or Saudi Arabia for their unemployed sons. Recent trends toward a neoliberal restructuring of the national economy allow these Malians to practice, experience, and display their conviction that economic success at once reflects and increases Divine blessing. Muslims, in their role as traders in and consumers of religious salvation, articulate the at once spiritual and economic meanings of prosperity that are deeply entrenched in West African Islamic discursive traditions (Cruise O'Brien 1971; Amselle 1985; Launay 1992).

Illustrative of these developments is the partial privatization of the organization of the hajj, formerly under tight control by the state, that triggered a mushrooming of hajj travel agencies run by businessmen with connections to Saudi Arabia. Their fierce competition over reputation and customers materializes in a range of marketing strategies, such as advertisements broadcast on national and local radio and television, and mounted on the four-wheel-drive cars in which these entrepreneurs circulate through Mali's urban and peri-urban arenas.

My argument here is not that under a neoliberal economic paradigm people's religious quest is "contaminated" by the rationale of profit maximization. Rather, Muslim leaders who extend their call for moral renewal to potential converts to "proper Islam" need to articulate aspirations and inspirations that extend beyond spiritual matters. Still, recent neoliberal economic reform and political liberalization do introduce certain changes in the material and institutional conditions under which Muslim piety may enter public arenas and challenge prevalent understandings of political subjectivity.

The moral endeavor of Muslim women is a case in point. Their attempts to extend their moral call to a wider constituency of believers are inflected by the new conditions of religious enterprise and by the expanding religious culture of religious devotion. And their moralizing impetus is fueled by their experiences of the contradictory demands and constraints that neoliberal economic reform has generated for many women in urban middle- and lower-middle-class households. After all, the mushrooming of Muslim women's groups since the early 1980s coincided with the fundamental restructuring of urban domestic economies under the effects of neoliberal economic policy.[19]

A sense of economic precariousness, of a material and emotional "permanent impermanence" affects families across the socioeconomic divide and transpires in the Bamanan neologism *k'i debruye,* from the French verb *se débrouiller* (to find makeshift solutions or fend for oneself; see Jackson, this volume). Women from the lower-middle and middle classes are often forced to assume greater financial responsibility for their families, a responsibility that reinforces the tension between women's economic significance and their limited decision-making power within the family. This tension is not only indicative of the new paradoxes generated within the broader neoliberal horizon, but it generates new contestations and (occasional) opportunities for autonomous action within the domestic realm (Schulz 2004).

Because Muslim women's groups attract those forced to make ends meet where the state fails to ensure basic social services, it is tempting to explain the groups as a resort to religion in times of economic hardship and thus as a product of neoliberal reform.[20] This interpretation resonates with a common explanation of women's involvement in revivalist movements. Yet it posits an inaccurate contrast between religious quest and economic motivation that disregards how historically, as in so many other areas of Muslim Africa, economic success was an important venue toward, and a sign of, a proper Muslim life (see, for example, Kaba 1974; Amselle 1977, 1985; Launay 1992). It also fails to elucidate the contrast that group members claim between conventional women's credit and savings associations and their own gatherings, which, they stress, are fired by a moral quest.[21]

At the same time, there are sound reasons to interpret Muslim women's groups as an outgrowth, or even the epitome, of the tension-ridden dynamics between various fields and sources of political power in African politics, dynamics reinforced by recent political and economic liberalization. The leaders of these groups are from economically privileged families with trade connections to the Arab-speaking world; many of them occupied leading positions under former President Traoré and, as their critics maintain, owe their enormous influence at the neighborhood level to their earlier political career. Some of these women seek recognition as representatives of "civil society" in controversies over policy making.[22] Yet, I will argue, their efforts to gain in formal political influence are seriously curtailed, not only by their various critics within the government and by some male Muslim activists, but also by specific modalities by which such women choose to render their "call" public.

CULTIVATING MORAL EXCELLENCE

In spite of some disagreement among different Muslim women's groups as to the "orthodoxy" of certain practices, such as the celebration of the Prophet's birthday (*mawlud*),[23] most members feel that these doctrinal and ritual differences should not undermine the collective nature of their joint endeavor.[24]

Women leaders understand their teachings as instruction in the practices through which a believer worships God (Arabic, *ibadat*).[25] Much of their advice reflects a tension between traditional gender morals and an emphasis on the responsibility of women for the moral renewal of society; this tension can be seen as a reflection of the new dilemmas many urban women face in the wake of limited income opportunities, a greater financial responsibility for family subsistence, and a persistent patriarchal gender ideology.

The female leaders admonish their followers to invite others "to embark on the path to God" (*ka alasira ta*)[26] and demand that a woman's dedication to her spiritual quest should manifest itself not merely in the performance of the obligations of worship, such as the five daily prayers, but in the cultivation of emotional capabilities essential to socially responsible conduct, among them *maloya* (modesty, "shame"), *sabati* (endurance, patience), and a capacity for self-control and submissiveness (*munyu*) toward husbands and seniors. Particularly striking are the leaders' emphasis on women's individual responsibility for "knowing about Islam," for "moving closer to God" (*k'i surun ala ma*), that is, for personal salvation and for societal renewal. This emphasis is significant in several respects. It illustrates changes in the significance of religious faith and observance since the colonial period,[27] from an element of family affiliation, professional specialization, or "ethnic" identity (Launay 1992), to a vision of Muslim faith as the result of personal conviction and a sense of collective responsibility.[28] Second, the emphasis on individual reasoning and conviction echoes the stress on individual agency and choice implied in neoliberal formulations of the citizen-consumer, and thus suggests a blending of different discursive parameters promulgated by state officials, politicians, and representatives of various interest groups (among them Muslim activists) in the current era of political liberalization.

Last, the emphasis placed by teachers on women's individual responsibility reveals that, although favoring a return to a traditional ordering of domestic relationships, they also reformulate the domains and forms of "proper" female action. Their stress on women's responsibility reflects on ambivalences and indeterminacies immanent to the ordering of gender relations,[29] yet also on the new contradictory demands for greater female responsibility and simultaneous submissiveness that emerged in the aftermath of neoliberal economic reform. In this sense, the teachings offered by female proponents of Islamic moral renewal articulate the paradoxical repercussions of recent intra-household economic reconfigurations for domestic authority structures. Those teachers, for instance, who argue that a woman's domestic role is determined by her bodily constitution pass over the fact that under current conditions the ideal of a fully dependent and submissive woman is not viable. And female leaders who exhort women to carry their role as guarantors of domestic stability into the public clearly depart from conventional gender stereotypes. All these leaders thus at once appeal to and reformulate "traditional" gender roles.[30] They articulate a vision of how "the personal (moral life) becomes political" that differs from that of leading female state officials and politicians who favor key notions of Western liberal feminism.

PRACTICING PIETY IN PUBLIC

Numerous Muslim women with whom I socialized pointed out, time and again, how important it was to extend their "call" to "other women" through personalized examples of pious transformation, of which the adoption of modest attire formed an essential part. In order to reach others and to convince them of the need to "revert" to proper Muslim practice, they explained to me, it was necessary to move certain elements of ritual observance (such as the afternoon prayer that usually concluded a Muslim women's learning session) to more visible places within a neighborhood. I argue that the emphasis my interlocutors and other Muslim women place on the embodied enactment of a pious disposition leaves them in a double bind. In certain ways, this double bind is indicative of the new forms—

and limitations—of political intervention that emerge for Muslim women out of recent, neoliberal reconfigurations of the relationship between the Malian state and its citizens.

Throughout the colonial era, ritual worship (*zeli*, from the Arabic *salat*) and participation in the Friday congregational worship were among the most important markers of Muslim identity in this area of West Africa (see, e.g., Launay 1992).[31] Women engaged in worship in a demarcated area of the mosque or within the courtyard, withdrawn from the scrutiny of onlookers. Those who today advocate an Islamic moral renewal of Malian society feel that *zeli*, in its embodiment of one's total submission to God's will, is emblematic of the moral order for which they labor.[32]

Following this line of reasoning, numerous Muslim women's neighborhood groups give greater visibility to their compliance with the obligations of worship. They jointly engage in *zeli* during their literacy classes inside the courtyard, thereby complying with the conventional prescriptions of worship. Yet they often shift the location of worship to a zone that is open to the scrutiny of neighbors and those who pass by. Their worship can also be easily viewed by men within the courtyard if the latter do not withdraw to a separate section. The consequence is not only a temporary inversion of the conventional separation of male and female arenas within the domestic sphere, but an unprecedented visible and audible presence of female Muslim piety at the center of city life.

The fact that Muslim women's visibility is widely commented upon in private press publications and in informal conversations shows the extent to which female piety leaves its mark on Malian public consciousness. Some of their fiercest critics come from the ranks of the state administration or are in other ways affiliated with the current political elite. Yet as the anecdote reported in the introduction shows, Muslim women's efforts to publicize their visions of moral order and of ritual as politically relevant practice is also contested by supporters of Islamic renewal, among them some key spokesmen of the movement. For instance, in the weeks following the exchange between UNAFEM women and the Islamic radio station's director, several preachers suggested in their radio sermons that a "dutiful Muslim woman" should not speak up in public, nor was it "a woman's business" to try to be heard on national radio. Their argument is highly significant. They exhort women to work as *signs* of virtue, yet they also seek to prevent them from engaging in public argument about it.

The attempts by these preachers and by other supporters of Islamic renewal to undermine the credibility of female Muslim leaders sheds light on the dilemma women face in times of political liberalization and given an ideology of participatory democracy. Influence at a national level needs to be achieved through institutions recognized and supported by the state, even if this state recognition simultaneously weakens the credibility such women seek for themselves.

EMBODYING A UNITARY MORAL QUEST

In contrast to their secularist critics who consider Muslim women's dress practices as signs of patriarchal oppression or of "Arab"—and thus foreign—Muslim identity, Muslim women view their "modest attire" as a register through which piety is achieved and practiced, not simply expressed. This view implies a conviction that the joint moral endeavor of "Muslim women," expressed in their choice of clothing, renders irrelevant status and income differences among them and unites them with equal-minded women in the Arab-speaking world. Yet, as I will show, Muslim women's highlighting of dress as a repertoire of *da'wa*, that is, of rendering personal piety politically relevant, confronts them with paradoxes that ultimately undermine their attempts to redefine the parameters of political subjectivity.

Dresses that are deemed "proper" by Muslim women include a range of different attires that index different positions in a hierarchy of age-dependent status, socioeconomic and professional standing, and also vis-à-vis interpretations of Islam that are inflected by reformist trends in Egypt and Saudi Arabia.[33] The majority of "ordinary" women wear a combination of items characteristic of mainstream female attire in urban middle- and lower-middle-class everyday life.[34] These are large and colorful robes (*dloki ba*, a full-length or half-length gown, or *grand dakar*, another full-length robe), wraparound skirts, and turbans, most often made of inexpensive imported or locally imprinted cotton.[35] What marks this outfit as "Islamic" is the additional colored or plain white scarf (*musòrò*) that Muslim women drape over their heads and shoulders, a dress practice to which they refer as "donning the veil" (*ka musòrò ta/siri*).[36] Because this additional scarf *may* serve as a prayer shawl (*kunabiri*), yet does not unequivocally indicate a Muslim identity,[37] it is often the particular cut and value of the accompanying robe, or its combination with yet other accessories, that indicate a woman's pious orientation.[38]

The second variant, in contrast, unequivocally communicates female Muslim piety. It consists of a loosely cut, white robe (*grand dakar*) and a white prayer shawl wrapped tightly around head, neck, and shoulders, often worn in addition to a turban. Similar to the first dress variant, it is not the wearing of an additional scarf per se that makes this dress "religious." Rather, it is the ubiquitous white color of the entire outfit that marks its owner's pious disposition. Whereas many leaders don all-white attire on a daily basis, their followers chose it only for special events, such as religious ceremonies, weddings, and other festivities.[39] White dress, a symbol of purity, links individual worshippers to a global community of believers (*umma*). It invokes a "sober" lifestyle, manifest in the refusal of Western consumer goods, and communicates central parameters of the present moral reform movement: a woman's quest for social qualities and religious virtue and her acceptance of the universal equality of all believers before God. Still, this dress is open to variation and the subtle assertion of accomplishment and wealth. As I often witnessed during learning-group meetings and religious ceremonies, women picked up with great alacrity and connoisseurship on subtle differences in quality, provenance, and ornamentation of this kind of attire, and commented on these indications of a woman's spending powers and social connectedness that allowed her to procure dress items through friends and relatives. Muslim women's white attire therefore allows them to simultaneously disclaim and establish differences in status and prestige.

Characteristic of the third dress variant is the borrowing of dress models, cut, ornamentation, and colors from a style that is locally identified with "Arab" fashion. *Jellaba*-style dresses (with a closed front section or with an embroidered frontispiece with buttons) are combined with full-length wrappers or large trousers. The high-prestige variant is often imported from Egypt, Morocco, Saudi Arabia, and Dubai.[40] Elaborate patterns made of golden or silver threads make these robes a precious investment and distinguish them from their low-cost variant, affordable for the majority of Muslim women. The latter, sewn by local tailors, is often made of relatively cheap material such as plain black fabric. Its embroidery imitates the ornamentation of more costly robes yet demands less input in labor and material. Whether imported or locally produced, this dress signals a woman's self-understanding as someone whose return to proper Sunni practice follows key tenets of reformist thought in Saudi Arabia and Egypt that, in spite of their heterogeneity, are lumped together in local parlance as "Arab Islam" (see LeBlanc 2000:454). This apparel signals a cosmopolitan orientation that appeals to younger women who decry the impropriety of Western-style dress cuts. This kind of "cosmopolitan" Muslim dress (and fashion) allows some Muslim women to resign from a consumerism they denounce and simultaneously to engage in morally more acceptable forms of consumption (Schulz 2007). This simultaneous renouncement and practice of (religious) consumption puts into relief the paradoxes emerging from the fact that women's daily practice of moral renewal is embedded in (and contributes to) an expanding culture of religious devotion and consumption. Muslim women may understand their apparel primarily as a means of pious self-making, yet their efforts to make their convictions known to other Muslims ultimately draws them into a broader public in which their dress is considered, and dismissed, as a symbol of either "oppression" or "religious identity politics."

The second paradox relates to Muslim women's perception that their "modest attire" marks the unitary nature of the movement, as well as the ethics of equality on which it is founded. As we have seen, sartorial practices facilitate the subtle assertion and reproduction of difference among women, and thus run counter to the emphasis on shared moral concerns.

Here again, we see that Muslim women's efforts to make personal piety a cornerstone of societal rejuvenation, and the particular forms of intervention with which they chose to do so, confront them with new dilemmas that ultimately restrict the efficacy of their attempts to participate in, and to redefine certain parameters of, political life.

Recent developments in the material, institutional, and economic conditions of public controversy in urban Mali shed light on the ways neoliberal economic reform and political liberalization have generated new spaces of action and (re)articulations between the state and particular interest groups within Malian society. Among other effects, these developments have facilitated changes in common understandings of the relevance of religion to daily life and politics.

Muslim women's claims that individual morality has important political implications, their distinct view of why and how the "personal is political," show that more is at stake than a growing permeation of an allegedly secular public within religious activism. Nor can the political complexities of this situation be adequately understood as a public display of signs of piety (Soares 2004). For one, Muslim piety is newly encoded and unfolds in the public imagination through often feminized signs and acts of religiosity. This new encoding brings with it new dilemmas and constraints for women who endorse Islamic moral renewal. Muslim women seek to redefine the forms and subject of political participation, and the meaning of politically relevant practice. They define it not just as a matter of critical, disembodied, reasoned argument, but as a particular, and ethically desirable, form of embodied practice. They present publicized forms of religious devotion as a focal point of moral practice and as a site constitutive, not merely representative, of moral community. By emphasizing the political relevance of publicly enacted worship, they challenge conventional understandings of ritual that seek to restrict its significance to the private realm.

However, while Muslim women's public interventions may challenge prevalent, secularist categories of the political, as well as commonsense assumptions about forms of intervention into secular politics, the ramifications of their public "participation" remain limited. This limitation is due precisely to the form of intervention they deem most relevant, that is, ritual performance. True, by highlighting women's central role as articulators of a morality that should be binding for the political community, Muslim women push the boundaries of common understandings of political subjectivity and of the criteria that validate participation in public controversy. At the same time, as the struggle over women's media appearances illustrated, the forms of public intervention for which they opt—or that they were granted by male representatives of the movement—has not allowed them to move significantly beyond playing an iconic role in the renewal movement. Within the dominant public discourse, in which many Muslim men participate and seek to be heard, "political" issues continue to be framed as something beyond religion, even if some Muslim women challenge this definition. Their ritual performances continue to be understood as politically "irrelevant." They are denied membership in a civil society which, at least implicitly, is defined as secular. Instead, they are associated with "religious factionalism" that should be kept outside of the domain of politics. Herein lays the double bind, which Muslim women, through their investment in the public performance of ritual, must negotiate. They push the limits of common assumptions about how to intervene adequately in the political domain. However, it is precisely their privileging of ritual as the politically most significant act that limits the recognition of their claims as a valid and valuable contribution to debates on the common good.

7. "Killer Bargains"

Global Networks of Senegalese Muslims and the Policing of Unofficial Economies in the War on Terror

Beth A. Buggenhagen

Like the smart bombs, laser-guided missiles and predator drones employed by our armed forces to hunt and kill *al Qaeda* in Afghanistan, the Patriot Act is just as vital to targeting the terrorists who would kill our people and destroy our freedom here at home.

JOHN ASHCROFT (U.S. Department of Justice 2004)

A WARRANT FOR A MAN NAMED GEORGE

Al Hajj Momar[1] faced a warrant for his arrest for street vending without a permit on the eve of Shaykh Amadou Bamba Day in 2003 in New York City. The annual event, organized by disciples of the Senegalese Sufi order Tariqa Murid, takes place in cities across the United States to celebrate the founding figure's peaceful resistance to French colonial rule. The significance of this day was not lost on its organizers, who faced a new fear ushered in by the events of September 11, 2001: that of increasing surveillance of their activities in the mosques and religious associations and on corners where they congregated as street vendors seeking to earn enough money to send remittances back home to Senegal. As Murid devotees prepared to commemorate Bamba, al Hajj Momar learned that being charged with a misdemeanor such as street vending without a permit was enough to land an undocumented immigrant in a deportation center under the auspices of the USA PATRIOT Act,[2] passed in 2001 to aid law enforcement authorities in the U.S.-led "war on terror." I learned of al Hajj Momar's startling encounter with the police when I telephoned him to ask for help to arrange a visit (*ziyara*) to Shaykh Mourtada Mbacke,[3] who traveled to European and American cities yearly to offer guidance to disciples living in predominantly non-Muslim lands. He described his astonishment when three men from the New York City Police Department (NYPD) threw open the unlocked door to his third-floor walkup and presented him with a warrant for the arrest of "al Hajj Momar." He said that he told the officers that their warrant was missing a last name. "Momar" he explained, was his first name, a common given name among Muslims, and not used as a surname, at least in Senegal. He produced his identity cards to prove that his last name was not "Momar," that he was a student, not a street vendor, and that he was in the United States legally. The officers confiscated his identity cards, indicating that they would only be returned to him after his appearance and arraignment the next morning. In describing his hearing to me later, al Hajj Momar said that when the judge called upon him he reiterated that the warrant was missing a last name and added, "it is like you had a warrant for a man named George so you went to the White House and arrested the President [George Bush]."[4]

I thought about al Hajj Momar's sense of humor during the arraignment as he told me about his encounter with the police and his long day in municipal court. I remembered that in the early 1990s acquaintances of his family, who trucked in the extralegal economy, had their Brooklyn apartment raided more than once by agents of the FBI who were searching for counterfeit copies of music cassettes and movie videos. The agents wrote "F-B-I" in large letters with a black permanent marker across the wall of the apartment. After a while, household members stopped trying to remove the letters and continued to stack media boxes underneath them. Perhaps they understood bureaucratic behavior better than I did, having long dealt with the whims of postcolonial West African states concerning the regulation of vending permits, market spaces, taxes, fees, and corruption.

Since Murid traders arrived in the United States in the 1970s, they employed similar tactics in dealing with the idiosyncrasies of municipal regulations and their arbitrary enforcement by local officials as they had in Senegal, especially concerning storing, remitting, and investing the proceeds of their trade (Stoller 2002). Yet hardened as they were to uneven and rapidly changing local regulations concerning street vending and federal immigration laws, Muridiyya said that they were troubled by this "war on terror." Even those who did not trade in the extralegal economy, like al Hajj Momar, were affected by the increasing scrutiny given to the activities of those who did, and everyone was connected to someone who engaged in extralegal activities to meet a host of social, moral, and financial obligations. Their concerns were not unfounded, as legislation passed after the events of 9/11—which articulated the attacks on the World Trade Center and the Pentagon not as a criminal act but as an act of war—contributed to the easy equation of crime with terror and, the inverse, terror with crime (cf. Comaroff and Comaroff 2004:4).

In addition, connections were drawn locally between immigration status, religious affiliation, and the propensity to engage in terrorist acts, and globally between extralegal economic networks, the supposed weakness of many postcolonial states, and Islam and terrorism (Kraxberger 2005:47). The attention paid to unregulated economic networks in Africa and elsewhere was not new; purportedly weak states have for some time been thought to be sites for the proliferation of criminal activities aided by new financial instruments and trade liberalization (see Comaroff and Comaroff 2004:3) and in some respects the blurring of the categories of illegal and illicit recalls an earlier U.S. "war," the war on drugs. But stories like al Hajj Momar's point to a critical distinction between the war on drugs and the new geopolitical narrative of the war on terror. In the latter, because the United States has considered itself to be at war, at home and abroad, illegal economic activities such as unregulated transfers of money and street vending can be framed as terrorist activities and as such, the subjects of regulation may be denied constitutional protections guaranteed to all persons regardless of citizenship status—including due process and protection from unwarranted search and seizure.

In the rhetoric of the war on terror nation-states have been cast as the primary guardians of security, largely through regulating their borders. Yet the ways in which Muridiyya have woven cargo and currency through official and unofficial spaces of the global economy has not undermined the Senegalese state (cf. Roitman 2005:18–19; Larkin 2004:297), making it more prone to criminal or terrorist activity. Rather than view the lack of regulation among some African countries as evidence of weak (Reno 2001), failed (Kraxberger 2005), or collapsed states (Zartman 1995), one might expand the definition of *security* to include community, social welfare, and economic networks (Kane 1997:47–48). Murid industry and piety have shored up this Muslim postcolony during conditions of protracted fiscal volatility in conjunction with economic liberalization.

Moreover, as states attempt to impose law and order, the legality of their actions is often questioned (Van Schendel and Abraham 2005:7; Das and Poole 2004; Roitman 2005). State practices could be viewed more productively as part of a continuum including legal, licit, illegal, illicit, and terrorist activity. For example, Van Schendel and Abraham suggest building "upon a distinction between what states consider to be legitimate ('legal') and what people involved in transnational networks consider to be legitimate ('licit')" (2005:4). Muridiyya, like many West Africans, have challenged the claims of regulatory authorities globally to define and delimit the slippery boundaries of licit, illicit, and, I would add, terrorist trade; that is, they have criticized what Janet Roitman has called the *intelligibility* of state regulation, and thus the "problem of legitimacy can only be addressed if the economy is apprehended as a political terrain" (2005:6).

Senegal, as elsewhere on the African continent, is thought to be peripheral to global capital due in part to setbacks in manufacturing and the decline of a world market for certain cash crops, yet it has realized greater integration through a lively trade in various forms, not only including goods deemed illicit and illegal such as drugs, small arms, and ivory, but also goods central to the livelihoods of many, including medications, cement, and cloth (Roitman 2005:16). If Murid *commerçants* have accumulated assets on the borderlines of official economies, as demarcated at various points in time by the Senegalese state and the United States in its global war on terror, Muridiyya have translated these global practices into the creation of the "spiritual metropolis" (Ross 1995) of Tuba, Senegal, the sacred capital of the Murid way. Murid circuits of wage labor and capital developed in the postcolonial period in response to changing conditions of agricultural production and fiscal volatility. In seeking to be "born of" the global, (Diouf 2000:682), Muridiyya drew on Tuba's eschatological significance as a gateway to paradise (Ross 1995) and directed new modes of accumulation toward constructing their autonomy from and centrality to the future of the Senegalese state. In endeavoring to direct the proceeds of their overseas trade to transportation, communication, electrification, public service projects, and ritual expenditures for family ceremonies, Muridiyya have sought to shape kinship and community despite the retraction of state patronage and social services under economic liberalization and privatization.

I never made it to visit Shaykh Mourtada in summer 2003. As I sat on the subway headed to Harlem for Shaykh Amadou Bamba Day in 2004, I thought about the arraignment of my interlocutor the previous year and Shaykh Mourtada's illness, which had made the 2004 commemoration subdued. As I sought to return to an aborted field project in which my interlocutors had become much more guarded and less likely to welcome the presence of Americans, especially those fluent in Wolof (for reasons I discuss below), I began to reconsider academic accounts of the remarkable creativity and tenacity of Muridiyya (Babou 2002; Carter 1997; Diouf 2000; Ebin 1992, 1993; Riccio 2004; Roberts 1996).

The 2005 commemoration, by which time Shaykh Mourtada had sadly passed, failed to elicit the same degree of exuberance I had noted at earlier events in Chicago in the late 1990s. And I had come to appreciate the ambivalence that my interlocutors themselves expressed toward economic liberalization in the post-9/11 world. After experiencing a dearth of employment opportunities in Senegal following economic liberalization (Cruise O'Brien 1988; Ebin 1992, 1993; Mbodj 1993) many Murid devotees embraced the liberalization of trade in 1997 (see also Callaghy and Ravenhill 1993). At the same time, they also spoke of their vulnerability to the global war on terror by virtue of their membership in the global Muslim community and the narrowing of possibilities for participation in global trade networks by stricter scrutiny of immigration and financial transfers in the United States and in Europe. Rather than heralding the possibilities of the global moment, I began to question the conditions that made it necessary for Senegalese men and women to search for livelihoods outside of Senegal and the consequences as more and more Senegalese youth embarked on unseaworthy vessels bound for Southern Europe (see the introduction to this volume), as the demonstrations of Arab and African youth shocked France and visas for the United States dried up. I also began to take seriously that as the arraignment of my key interlocutor had interrupted the fieldwork project that I intended to carry out, new security apparatuses haunted the globalized circuits of many postcolonial subjects worldwide.

If scholars have focused recently on the U.S.-led global war on terror, the attack on Afghanistan, and the war in Iraq in relation to the nature of U.S. power before and after 9/11 (Glick Schiller 2004; Hardt and Negri 2004; Kelly 2003; Mamdani 2004; Steinmetz 2003), fewer have considered the dynamics of the global war on terror on its home front. After 9/11, in addition to increasing its armed forces abroad, the U.S. also increased the presence of its armed forces internally (Bornstein 2005:52). It is important not to lose sight of the fact that "the 'war on terror' is a war on internal enemies—within nation states now policed under new stringent security acts" (Hansen and Stepputat 2005:1). To understand how the internal war on terror has intersected with Murid industry and piety, creating new tensions and new fears within this community in New York City, I focus here on the implementation of the USA PATRIOT Act by the state and its agents, the NYPD, the Department of Justice (DOJ), and the FBI. The initial implementation of the PATRIOT Act permitted the expansion of surveillance—including wiretapping and securing banking and library records, which were much debated domestically—contravening civil liberties, constitutional protections, and legally established human rights. The act reversed a century of court rulings in the United States granting non-permanent residents, as "persons," entitlement to civil rights and liberties guaranteed by the constitution (Murray 2004).

After 9/11, the United States, a state that had long been on the retreat in the realm of social welfare, pushed law and order as key priorities in the war on terror. The United States emphasized that the threat of terror created a need for a police presence that, when exercised, showed the "face and the force of the state" (Comaroff and Comaroff 2004:6). Yet many municipal police departments remained ill-funded for the task charged to them. Although everywhere in New York City police were more visible, the fact of their policing contributed little to combating terrorism (Bornstein 2005), even by their own admission (as I discuss below). My Murid interlocutors, including al Hajj Momar, often expressed that the tensions they experienced surrounding the forms of surveillance ushered in by the PATRIOT Act—the application of which was uneven, even illogical—could not be anticipated and thus could not be averted and resulted in a generalized sense of fear, expressed in ways ranging from a reluctance to don Muslim dress in public to an uneasy joking about the ways in which authorities employed Wolof interpreters to listen in to cell-phone conversations (hence the wariness of my interlocutors concerning non-Senegalese Wolof speakers). For this reason, I focus on the *performance* of security for a public audience largely through the rhetoric of the war on terror but also through new modes of regulation from street vending to money transfer to visa violations. It seems that in talking about the threat of terror, the United States deployed the figure of the migrant as one who existed outside of the state; "the other of the state is always a murky, secretive, and ubiquitous world of the traitor, the spy and the gangster" (Hansen and Stepputat 2005:31). As the United States muddled the boundaries of extralegal, illicit, and terrorist networks, how could rights and recognition be addressed in a global world "where legality and rights have been suspended for those declared 'illegal combatants' and incarcerated in Afghan prisons, Guantánamo Bay and other 'spaces of exception'" (2005:1)?

African states occupy a complicated position between neoliberal global capital and the war on terror; they provide critical resources like oil (Apter 2005; Ferguson 2005) and coltan, or tantalum ore (see Jackson 2002), and they traffic in a host of extralegal activities, including precious stones (De Boeck 1998), media piracy, and counterfeit goods. It is on this latter point that Murid practices became subject not only to local policing in New York City but also to the efforts of corporate interests, such as the Motion Picture Association of America, to stem the circulation of counterfeits worldwide under the pretext of stopping terrorism. In 2003 an Ohio news station ran a story linking the sale of fake designer goods to financing for terrorist operations and dubbed these sales "killer bargains." In 2007 a similar editorial appeared in the New York Times—"Terror's Purse Strings"—about handbags and their links to terror.[5] This slippage between unofficial, illicit, and terrorist networks that appeared in public discourse and among government and corporate spokespersons formed a critical part of the rhetoric and policing in the war on terror and its performance of security. Such language made possible the linking of criminal activities such as trafficking in grey market goods to the financing of "designated foreign terrorist organizations"[6] and lowered the threshold for search and seizure of those goods through the provisions of the PATRIOT Act.

MURID GLOBAL COMMERCIAL NETWORKS

During Shaykh Amadou Bamba Day in New York City in 2005 Murid disciples from European and American cities paraded from Central Park to 125th Street waving Senegalese and U.S. flags. Murid women dressed in matching dyed blue damask fabric adorned themselves in the cargo of translocal Murid trade—cloth and other decorative objects—their prosperity and piety encoded on their bodies. Upon reaching 125th Street, they congregated on the plaza of the Adam Clayton Powell Jr. State Office Building, where they listened to speeches given by a multinational group of local imams and municipal figures addressing the role of Muslims in New York City. In the evening, Murid disciples convened an interfaith conference at the United Nations concerning Bamba's message of peace. These public expressions of Murid contributions to American pluralism and to the promotion of a peaceful image of Islam globally were buttressed by a sustained concern to gain an audience with religious leaders at home, in Senegal. Through the performances of devotion, including visiting religious figures at the Murid center in Harlem, renewed vows of submission, and offerings of cash and cooked food, disciples parlayed their prosperity into recognition at home in Senegal.

Through these offerings (*addiya*) disciples constitute new social relations and possibilities. Through supplications to shaykhs (spiritual leaders) disciples enter the circuit of blessings (*baraka*) that are both spiritual and material, for through them followers gain access to eternal prosperity and to worldly wealth. Religious leaders convert their disciples' contributions into the "spiritual metropolis" (Ross 1995) of their sacred city of Tuba, Senegal—a feat of architectural and economic development that aims to realize the vision of the order's founding figure during his exile under French colonial rule. Although devotees have been engaged in the capitalist economy since the inception of the Murid way at the turn of the twentieth century through cash cropping, urban economies, and global trade networks, market value has not replaced other forms of value (cf. Akin and Robbins 1999; Carrier 1991; Zelizer 1994). Offerings, and the moral discourse framing them, are an essential aspect of Murid devotion to their spiritual masters and form part of a repertoire of possible economic practices that secures their vision of an Islamic modernity. Through the practice of offerings and their redistribution by the clergy, Muridiyya enclose wealth outside of what has historically been a volatile market (cf. Guyer 1999:237).

The high circulation of signs of wealth and well-being, including stores of cloth wealth, homebuilding, and cars, as well as mosques, clinics, and schools, were remarkable in the context of a declining postcolonial state. Yet despite this, at the close of the 1990s, Dakar was also in flux. Murid traders who had been based overseas returned home to participate in the capital city's emergent affluence, spurred by the investments of Chinese, Indian, and Gulf States in national infrastructure and natural resource extraction, specifically phosphates and iron ore. Grandiose homes, hotels, and casinos were under construction, walling off and privatizing previously public beachfronts. Behind the tables of trade wares that congested every sidewalk, intersection, and road in the capital, chocolatiers, patisseries, and nightclubs emerged for tastes that had been cultivated overseas. Yet many Dakarois were relegated to viewing these forms of wealth only on foot while they hawked wares, shined shoes, begged for alms, and pondered how inexplicable and unreachable the new affluence of Dakar had become. It was these forms of wealth, rather than rising poverty, that drove so many young men and a few women to endure a transatlantic voyage in wooden fishing vessels to the Canary Islands to participate in Barcelona's burgeoning construction industry between 2006 and 2008.

Although the Murid way was initially an agricultural movement, Muslims have long been associated with trade in West Africa (see, for example, Amselle 1971; Cohen 1971; Curtin 1975; Hopkins 1973; Meillassoux 1971; Stoller 2002). For many Muslims trade had "the stamp of divine authority" (Hunwick 1999:72). As much as it has been imbued with the language of salvation, the Koranic language of salvation is replete with economic metaphors; for example, worship and giving alms are referred to as a "profitable commerce (*tijara*)" (ibid.). It was not surprising then that by the 1970s Muridiyya had turned to trade in the urban areas to escape rural devastation and mounting debt. At first, Murid agricultural migrants were mere scavengers in the urban areas, recycling cleaned-up bits of string, bottles, and cans for sale in the market at the command (*ndiggal*) of Seriñ Abdoul Lahat Mbacke. Overtime, Muridiyya transformed the strategy of trading in the dry season to make ends meet in lean agricultural cycles into full-time urban settlement (Cruise O'Brien 1988; Diop 1981; Roberts 1996:87).

Although it might have seemed that urban disciples were in the process of becoming further entrenched in the world market through their trade, "they made a conscious effort to incorporate their unique temporality and rationality into world time by using their own vocabulary, grammar and worldview to understand the world and operate within it" (Diouf 2000:685). Urban male and female disciples congregated once a week in religious associations (*dahira*) during which they recited litanies, contributed cash offerings to the religious hierarchy, and invested in social projects. The *dahira* provided refuge as well as practical training in urban ways such as business skills for those lacking a French education (Babou 2002). The *dahira* could be a means of finding a business partner or securing the patronage of an established large trader with access to international markets who could advance credit and merchandise and enable one to avoid the financial and transactional costs associated with the formal banking sector (Thioub, Diop, and Boone 1998:79). Through these relationships Muridiyya avoided the favoritism toward owners, managers, and large depositors seen in the formal banking sector (Stiansen and Guyer 1999:5). Being able to rely on the social relations that were forged in religious associations for lodging, food, and protection from police was crucial for traders who often worked outside of the official economy beyond the parameters of state regulation or across state boundaries. The patronage of a senior member of the *dahira* also enabled Muridiyya to engage in financial transactions within the sphere of that which was morally sanctioned in Islam, thus avoiding *riba* (interest or increase), associated with formal sector economic transactions, and enabling adherence to Koranic injunctions against sacrificing religious practice for commercial gain in trade, gambling and speculation. Finally, such patronage relations enabled Muridiyya to follow recommendations that wealth should be used in the service of God, and that capital obtained through wrongdoing to others be avoided (Hunwick 1999:73–74).

Murid migrants to the city often became involved in so-called informal-sector transport and internal distribution networks since formal sector business was largely dominated by private French capital and state enterprise, while transport and real estate were controlled by Lebanese business people (Thioub, Diop, and Boone 1998:67). For those who did engage in the formal sector, they found that they could "work optimally when they had recourse to both kinds of systems, and therefore have a real interest in the maintenance of what the 'modern sector' may consider to be a 'traditional' form of moral authority and financial power" (Stiansen and Guyer 1999:5).

In the rural areas, a lively cross-border trade with Gambia in peanuts and contraband commodities emerged as peanut producers sought to escape the control of official marketing boards; much of this trade revolved around Tuba, which had maintained the status granted it by the colonial administration as an independent administrative district (Cruise O'Brien 1971; Kane 1997:61). As the informal sector and parallel trade circuits began to expand in the postcolonial period, the state made little effort to regulate these networks because they provided citizens with forms of employment and access to inexpensive consumer goods in the face of the inflation and global economic recession of the 1970s (Thioub, Diop, and Boone 1998:70). Between 1970 and 1981 the cost of living had tripled, urban unemployment affected more than 70 percent of the population, and inflation hovered at 30 percent (Mbodj 1991:124). Men and women sought employment in the informal sector where traders avoided payment of the "value added tax, merchants' registration fees, commercial profits tax, payroll tax and wage laws, customs duties and tariffs, and social security charges" (Thioub, Diop, and Boone 1998:70). Muridiyya succeeded in shifting from agriculture in the colonial period to trade in the second half of the twentieth century in part by becoming "part of the informal state structure (or more accurately, of the ensemble formed by the formal state and its informal shadow) via a web of informal concessions, carefully negotiated privileges—notably including impunity for economic offenses—and personal and political relationships" (Hibou 1999:89). As a consequence, traders operating in the thriving Marché Sandaga, the central market in Dakar, showed support for the ruling Partie Socialiste (PS) throughout the postcolonial period, contributing to its control of the presidency from independence until 2000.

As economic recession took hold in Senegal, due in part to the decline of agriculture and manufacturing but also to the state's inability to derive revenue from the thriving import trade in contraband (Thioub, Diop, and Boone 1998:71), the state implemented a series of reforms from 1985 to 1992 and again in 1995 mandated by the International Monetary Fund in exchange for loans from the World Bank. Structural adjustment programs addressed the stagnant economy and increasing external debt: they privatized state assets, removed trade barriers and constraints on financial flows, introduced fiscal discipline, reduced state involvement in the economy, ended agricultural subsidies, and in 1994 led to the devaluation of the CFA franc, the currency in Senegal and most other francophone countries in West Africa (Diouf 2004:270; Hesse 2004:4; Perry 1997:233). Further steps were taken by the government to reduce public expenditures, lower barriers on imports, and to privatize state enterprises such as peanut processing, water, electricity, and communications (Hesse 2004:4). The local impact of these reforms included an inflationary spiral—especially in the prices of tools, electricity, and fuel, as well as in imported rice and wheat, which were staples of the urban diet of rice, fish, and baguettes— that led to public protests and greater social and economic instability for Senegalese families (Creevey, Vengroff, and Gaye 1995:669). These new forms of impoverishment were matched by new forms of wealth as the gap between the rich and the poor increased over the decades as an unintended consequence of economic liberalization (ibid.:671). As the prospects of the state declined as international financial institutions sought to increase transparency and reduce graft by decreasing the amounts of development aid and loans that filtered through the state, government bureaucrats came to depend largely upon those who were doing well by working at the interstices of the formal and informal economy to survive.

In 1986, the Senegalese state's decision to rescind its policy of protecting Senegalese manufactured goods contributed to the emergence of the import-export and service sector and the expansion of Marché Sandaga, which came to be dominated by the Murid faithful (Diop 1981; Diouf 2000:692). Although trade liberalization in 1997 was designed to squeeze out parallel markets (where Murid activities, among others, thrived), liberalization in Senegal had the opposite effect, instead reinforcing the extralegal and unofficial economy (Hibou 1999:80). This can be partially explained by the way in which the Muridiyya successfully shifted between the formal and informal economies and in the intertwining of personal and commercial networks. Disciples made offerings of cash and merchant goods to their shaykhs not merely to gain an audience or to "count on their *marabouts* [shaykhs] to act as intermediaries with the Ministry of Finance or with customs authorities" (Bop 2005:1106). They also gave to their shaykhs to secure their commercial success, which was seen as a result of not only the commercial networks that *dahira* membership opened up to them, but also of the mystical power of the shaykhs themselves. Addiya offerings collected by local prayer circles provided assurances of salvation—of ultimately being in God's presence—in an uncertain moral and *fiscal* terrain. One might think of the kinds of *informality* employed by Murid traders less in terms of absence in the formal sector and more in terms of how "informality uses a proficiency in emergent formal institutions to elaborate new spaces of operation" (Simone 2004:24).

By the 1990s Tuba had become the second largest city in Senegal (Gueye 2001:107). Some have even gone so far as to suggest that Dakar became merely the earthly shadow of the otherworldly aspirations of Tuba (Bayart, Ellis and Hibou 1999:20). As the state became extraneous to Murid economic projects that were enveloped in translocal circuits of trade, many Murid followers saw the intertwining of religion and trade as the only possible means of shoring up the nation-state (Diouf 2000:691 n. 33). It is often argued that practices unregulated by the state, which often take place in the margins, contribute to "a weakening or shrinking of the forms of regulation and belonging that supposedly constitute the modern nation-state" (Das and Poole 2004:3). The very categories of official and unofficial and the assumption that the official could be equated with the legal and the unofficial with the illegal did not seem to apply to Senegal, as "illegal practices are also performed in the formal sector, while so-called informal economic networks operate with well-established hierarchies and are fully integrated into social life" (Bop 2005:1106). In fact, rather than undermining the state form, transnational citizens often challenge, renegotiate, and reconfigure their fiscal and political relations in light of their relationship to global capital (Ong 1999:214–15; Roitman 2005).

The president since 2000, Abdoulaye Wade, a Murid disciple himself, has more recently facilitated the international migration of Murid disciples. Wade was elected as the opposition candidate after twenty years of rule by the PS in part through his efforts to pursue the Senegalese business class and shop owners on 116th Street in Harlem who voted in the national election (Salzbrunn 2004:471). Following his electoral success Wade traveled to Tuba, where he renewed his vow of submission to the supreme leader of the Murid order to whom he attributed his electoral victory (Bop 2005:1105). Shortly thereafter market vendors circulated photographs depicting Wade kneeling on the floor with his legs tucked under his body in a position characteristic of a disciple submitting to his master seated above him on a couch. Many Senegalese read this gesture as the state bowing to the Murid hierarchy. But, as I argued above, though the symbiotic relationship between the state and the Sufi orders is the primary explanation given for Senegalese exceptionalism, the legitimacy of the state under Wade has come under recent attack in Senegal for dodging the demands, expectations, and even the most basic needs of citizens. Wade's presidency has come to be seen by many Senegalese as one more example of the criminalization of the state in Africa (Apter 2005; Bayart, Ellis and Hibou 1999; MacGaffey and Bazenguissa-Ganga 2000; Marchal 2004; Roitman 2005). In 2007, despite widespread dissatisfaction with declining economic conditions and political repression of the media in Senegal, Wade was elected to a second term. In part, his success had much to do with his courting of the Murid way through the granting of diplomatic visas and hajj trips to Mecca to the clergy and through the resolution of migrant land claims (Mbow 2008:162).

LAW AND ORDER IN NEW YORK CITY AND THE WAR ON TERROR

By the 1980s, Murid communities had grown in the United States, France, Belgium, and Italy (Diouf 2000). The numbers of Muridiyya in the United States grew after the passing of the U.S. Immigration Reform and Control Act of 1986 that regularized their status (Babou 2002:160) and the Immigration Act of 1990, which introduced the Diversity Immigrant Visa program that provided permanent resident visas to citizens of countries with low immigration rates to the United States (Beck 2008:200; also see Piot, this volume). It is hard not to notice the West African street vendors throughout Manhattan whose overloaded tables of purses, sunglasses, and cellular accessories have come to dominate the intersections of shopping and tourist districts.[7] Among them are tall young men who can be heard enticing passing women by whispering "Louis Vuitton" or offering to bring out logo-laden handbags upon request, or who sell the scores of DVDs and CDs lying on the ground on top of sacks that can be quickly drawn up as police approach. In New York City in 2003, it was estimated that there were 10,000 street vendors, even as only 850 general merchandise licenses were issued by the city.[8]

Although the street trader is the most visible face of a global trade network, many livelihoods are at stake in the buying and selling of merchant goods in the unofficial economy. These include the walking banks, who relieve the traders of their cash while they are on the street, guards who alert traders to police raids, transporters and distributors of wholesale goods, lenders and rotating credit unions that facilitate their savings and investment strategies, and the religious figures, the healers and the diviners, who guide them through an uncertain moral terrain—not to mention a complex economy of Senegalese restaurants, hair braiding salons, money transfer agencies, storage and shipping agents, and boutiques (which offer Senegalese music videos, movies, videography and photography services, tailoring, and Muslim paraphernalia including kaftans, cassettes, books, and prayer mats) (see also Stoller 2002). In one of the myriad shops lining 116th Street in Harlem, for example—the shops auspiciously named after major religious figures of the Murid order and bedecked with the religious iconography, including bumper stickers and other signage—one might find *bissap* (a variety of hibiscus), millet couscous, and *café Tuba*.

Moreover, Murid success rests in linking distribution points in Dakar with international wholesale centers, where New York City represents a single node in a larger global circuit (Diouf 2000:694; Ebin 1992:87). Those distribution points are underpinned by a web of financial agents that enable traders to store and remit the cash from overseas laborers, ranging from $15 to $30 billion a year (Sachs 2002; Babou 2002), of which Muridiyya contribute approximately $15–20 million (Babou 2002:168),[9] and on which the Senegalese state increasingly has come to rely. The inaccessibility of formal-sector banking in the United States and elsewhere, with its need for identity verification in the form of driver's licenses and Social Security numbers, fees, taxes, paperwork (especially for those who are illiterate), and discriminatory and exploitative business practices, led many small- and large-scale exporters to turn to the unregulated financial channels organized by Muridiyya. These channels often intertwined aspects of the official and the unofficial economy such as the unofficial banking system of Kara International Exchange that is organized around the principle of *hawala*, a system of monetary transfer built on honor, often through ties of kinship, alliance, and membership in Sufi organizations and their formal economic shipping transactions (Ebin 1992; Tall 2002).

A crucial aspect of financial liberalization in Senegal and elsewhere is that it "blurred the frontiers between what is and is not legal by facilitating the transfer of capital and property from the illegal to the legal sector and vice versa" (Hibou 1999:75). But the project of neoliberal global capital was interrupted after the events of 9/11 as U.S. President George W. Bush declared that the United States would follow the "money trail" to stem financing for "designated foreign terrorist organizations" by discriminating between the legal and the illegal in the chain of financial transactions that has come to characterize the greater integration fundamental to globalization. By dubbing the extralegal as *terrorist*, the United States threatened to unravel the immense effort that Muridiyya had put into weaving social and moral worlds at home through work abroad.

The disruption of international aid organizations and banking, and the naming of particular businesspersons as terrorists in the case of al Barakaat, the largest Somali money transfer operation (Marchal 2004: 142–3), alarmed Muslim African communities. Many Murid associations claimed nonprofit status, such as in the Murid Islamic Community of America Inc. (MICA), which was founded as a 501(c)3 tax-exempt organization (Salzbrunn 2004:479). Murid systems of Islamic finance relying on *hawala* became subject to attempts under the PATRIOT Act at new modes of regulation and surveillance of noncitizens as well as their bank accounts, driver's licenses, visits to the emergency room, and visa status. The act required money transfer agencies to be licensed, to automate, to report cash transfers to federal law enforcement authorities, and to request proof of identity from their customers so that they could be checked against a list of suspected money launderers and "designated foreign terrorist organizations" generated by the federal Office of Foreign Assets Control.[10] Likewise, those who transferred money had their information sent to the FBI (Sachs 2002), upsetting businesspersons who depended on saving and remitting their earnings to family for the viability of their trade networks, which were often family based. Immigration violations were selectively enforced, persons were detained longer than their violations warranted, and in some cases they even were deported, especially Muslim and Arab men required to submit to "special registration" (Bornstein 2005). Authorities approached West African imams asking them to surveil their worshippers and to report any incongruities, especially concerning those of Arab nationalities, among their congregation.

At the same time that scores of Senegalese men and women turned to selling counterfeit goods—purses, watches, DVDs, and CDs—as the tourism industry and employment associated with it declined after 9/11, local police and private agencies became engaged in controlling street vending and sales of counterfeit goods that were thought to finance terrorism (Fifield 2002). As the government, media, and corporations focused on the "dangers" of media piracy, few considered that this extralegal practice was also contributing to licit and legal projects (Coombe and Stoller 1994; Larkin 2004; Sassen 2002). As I previously mentioned, Muridiyya turned the proceeds of their global trade toward the reconstruction of moral forms of community in Senegal in the context of protracted economic volatility. Moreover, some aspects of the policing of unofficial networks through the rubric of the global war on terror were not new for Murid traders. Paul Stoller has detailed how throughout the 1980s and 1990s West African traders in general were removed from various locations in the city as part of efforts to control crime and clean up the city's image (2002:19).

Unlike municipal efforts to control crime, the implementation of the PATRIOT Act made possible the deportation or indefinite detention *without judicial oversight* of immigrants who committed misdemeanors, such as transferring money through unregulated networks (such as *hawala* transactions) and street vending without a legal permit. The passing of the PATRIOT Act in October 2001 augmented the surveillance and investigative power of law enforcement by facilitating information sharing with intelligence agencies and increased the penalties for engaging in or assisting terrorist acts or organizations. The act lowered the threshold of the 1978 Foreign Intelligence Surveillance Act (FISA) used to indict mafia figures and drug traffickers–that act allowed authorities to obtain information without a search and seizure warrant but did not allow that information to be used in a criminal proceeding since it would violate the Fourth Amendment. The PATRIOT Act allowed FBI agents to obtain search warrants without showing probable cause of criminal activity and then, nonetheless, to use that information in criminal procedures, an approach which *itself* blurs the boundaries between "licit," "illicit," and "terrorist." The United States could indefinitely detain and eventually deport suspected persons without judicial review, and such persons would have no opportunity to review the evidence against them in court. Though the PATRIOT Act was put in place to trace activities deemed to be terrorist, it built on much of the 1996 legislation that had already excluded permanent residents from the Constitution's equal-protection clause (Bassiouni 2004:2).

In practice, the PATRIOT Act allowed law enforcement and intelligence organizations to monitor religious and political associations without notice of doing so, even in the absence of evidence of criminal activity. Section 213 removed the requirement that law enforcement officials provide a person subject to a search warrant with contemporaneous notice of the search and permitted seizure of property and communications without prior notice. Moreover, Section 213 allowed this practice in the event that a person was suspected of any kind of activity that "constitutes evidence of a criminal offense in violation of the laws of the U.S.," not just under suspicion of terrorist activity, again creating a slippage between misdemeanors, like vending without a permit, and terrorist acts.

The PATRIOT Act also expanded the definition of "material support or resources" in the Anti-Terrorism and Effective Death Penalty Act of 1996 (ATEDPA) to include "expert advice or assistance," often referred to as the "material support bar," enabling the prosecution of those providing financial support, physical assets, or services to what the United States called a "designated foreign terrorist organization." Under the material support statute, the DOJ could prosecute those associated with a "designated foreign terrorist organization" who have yet to commit a crime (Lichtblau 2003). Additionally, according to Section 212 (a)(3)(B) of the

Immigration and Nationality Act, any person offering material support to a "designated foreign terrorist organization" could be charged with engaging in a terrorist activity. This section of the act was significant for two reasons: first, it potentially could equate donating money to a Muslim charity with supporting a terrorist; and second, it enabled the U.S. government and corporate interests to link the production, sale, and consumption of counterfeit and pirated goods with financing designated foreign terrorist organizations, a subject I will return to below (Millar 2002).

SECURITY FOR WHOM?

As the implementation of the PATRIOT Act made Murid trade more cumbersome by regulating financial transfers, visa violations, and donations to Muslim charities, its uneven enforcement continued to be exploited by Murid traders. This does not mean, however, that the fears of the loss of livelihood and of certain political liberties that Murid expressed have been unfounded—it is, after all, in the arbitrariness of punishment and the inability to predict it that fear lies. While the PATRIOT Act potentially provided new opportunities for policing, in operation its implementation was far more uneven—even contradictory (Bornstein 2005). In my interviews with the NYPD in the summer of 2004, I learned that the DOJ had tried to enlist local police to enforce federal civil immigration law by reporting visa violations to the Department of Homeland Security. In the course of their regular patrol duties officers were to check names of offenders in the National Crime Information Center database. This database contained not only the names of criminals but also the names of persons with outstanding orders of deportation, exclusion, and removal, and those who failed to follow the "special registration" for Arab and Muslim men. Yet Congress had specifically barred the police from engaging in civil immigration law enforcement (Bornstein 2005).

Given the existence of a joint NYPD and FBI counterterrorism task force, I thought that beat officers would see themselves on the front line of the war on terror. Yet many officers yearned to serve on Operation Hercules, in which heavily armed special interdiction forces of the NYPD have appeared in different places at different times, with no clear pattern, to throw potential "terrorists" off guard (Horowitz 2003 quoted in Bornstein 2005) or Operation Atlas, in which police have been paid overtime to patrol potential targets such as bridges and landmarks (Bornstein 2005). Instead, officers found themselves relegated to what they called the "peddler squad." In interviews with officers of the Fifth Precinct, encompassing Chinatown, Little Italy, and part of the Lower East Side, where many Murid merchants trade, officers expressed a disconnection between their daily activities and the war on terror. Members of the peddler squad said their mandate ought to be fighting terrorism; one officer gave an example of checking cargo containers at the port. Some expressed frustration with directives to clean up city streets and to pay attention to crime statistics, which were already so low that activities that would have been scoffed at a decade ago as "below one's rank" were now all that occupied high-ranking officers (Wilson 2004).

Officers looked puzzled when I asked if they viewed street vendors differently after 9/11. I was thinking of the media stories that linked grey market goods to terrorism financing and the implementation of New York state guidelines that linked Social Security numbers to driver's licenses (Bernstein 2004), making it impossible for traders in legal limbo (and thus not in possession of Social Security numbers) to obtain a driver's license so they could transport goods about town legally or to obtain a vending permit from the state (Richardson 2004). Peddler squad officers explained that a vendor unable to produce a driver's license would be issued a summons to appear in court with identification and reported to the Department of Homeland Security (DHS) under the PATRIOT Act. The burden of enforcing these new forms of bureaucratic discrimination fell on police officers and state office workers who were the least informed of federal immigration law and strapped for resources. Nonetheless, I had read reports that, according to one police officer, they made "a lot of arrests and seizures of counterfeit goods, Louis Vuitton, Gucci, Rolex, you name it . . . [and] one room in the precinct, used to store seized counterfeit items, is always full" (Amateau 2003). And I had learned that the Manhattan Borough Patrol Command, which coordinates the Fifth Precinct in its attempts to secure civil warrants for counterfeit goods, had teamed up with a law firm representing manufacturers of authentic goods to engage a private agency to investigate Chinatown shopkeepers secretly. Neither articulated a link to terrorism.

While the NYPD peddler squad had been unable to link counterfeit goods and terrorist financing, by 2003, when the "killer bargain" story emerged, the federal government had begun targeting marketers of counterfeit goods in its antiterrorism efforts. The United States was responding to a shift by al Qaeda and others away from using banks and unregulated wire services, which the United States had frozen to show "the world's resolve in putting a stranglehold on the financial lifeblood of terrorists" (Van Natta 2003). Al Qaeda and many other organizations engaged in the extralegal economy moved cash from hand to hand through the suitcase trade, where merchant goods were exchanged for cash, making it more difficult for authorities to trace transactions. The DOJ, responsible for carrying out renewed efforts to stem the flow of extralegal goods, was prompted by the Motion Picture Association of America (MPAA), Microsoft, and the Recording Industry Association of America (RIAA), all of whom intimated that profits were being funneled toward the activities of "designated foreign terrorist organizations" as state-sponsored funds for terrorism dissipated (Van Natta 2003). In March 2003 the House of Representatives Committee on the Judiciary, Subcommittee on Courts, the Internet, and Intellectual Property held a hearing on "International Copyright Piracy: A Growing Problem With Links To Organized Crime and Terrorism." Jack Valenti, President and Chief Executive Officer, MPAA, testified that movie piracy was "sucking the blood out of our business in the future" (U.S. House of Representatives 2003). Linking potential terrorist financing and intellectual property crime appealed to large corporations, in particular the RIAA, which has been fighting pirated copies and the production and trade of optical discs since sales began to drop in 2000 (Polgreen 2002). This connection empowered the Secret Service, which enforces copyright law, to crack down on counterfeit CD producers in New York and to disrupt their distribution network along the eastern seaboard (Polgreen 2002).

But how does piracy, even if linked to organized crime, constitute terrorist activity? Public figures often deployed the term to invite a slippage between misdemeanors, criminal activity, and terrorism. I suggested at the outset that those operating across official and unofficial economies have been painted as malicious figures as the state has attempted to secure its borders, and that this process is about the performance of security for a public audience. Van Natta, writing for the *New York Times,* used the idiom of "lifeblood," while Valenti of the MPAA referred to "blood sucking." In a speech given by the President George W. Bush to defend the PATRIOT Act in 2004, the categories of thievery and terrorist activity were confused: "see, with court approval, we have long used roving wire taps to lock up monsters—mobsters. Now we have a chance to lock up monsters, terrorist monsters" [*laughter and applause*] (Bush 2004). This kind of dehumanizing language, to which many on the margins of the corporate economy are subject, points to the contradictory position of the neoliberal nation-state, perceiving itself threatened by the very liberalization it has promoted. In fact, it seems that the nation-state, as LiPuma and Koelble have argued, "has never appeared more threatened" (or understood itself so to be?) by the financialization of capital (2004:99).

Though there was much public media attention given to the "killer bargain" of cheap counterfeit goods and terrorist financing, this connection did not seem to alter the practices of the NYPD with regard to street peddlers. This is an important illustration of the uneven implementation of PATRIOT Act legislation. In fact, the hype about policing following the events of 9/11 served only to fuel frustration among police officers that they were not making an impact in the global war on terror. Police officers had articulated a complex understanding of the "gray zones" of overlapping realms of legality and illegality, of formally regulated and unregulated fields of economic activity. As I noted, the government regularly updated its list of "designated foreign terrorist organizations," yet when Bush addressed the public, he often referred to the more general term "terrorist" in ways that invited a slippage between categories of illegal, illicit, and terrorist activity.

As I have argued, U.S. officials labored to link unregulated economic activities and security. For Muridiyya, unsurprisingly, "security" is conceived in a radically different fashion. For the many Murid traders in New York City, security involves not merely the legal quandaries of how to negotiate the complex legal bureaucracy of street peddling and immigration status but also how to negotiate the demands of discipleship and the rights and obligations of kinship and citizenship that compel them to find their futures elsewhere. Though we never made our *ziyara* to Shaykh Mourtada, my colleague al Hajj Momar got his day in court, during which he successfully protested the lack of coherence, transparency, and effectiveness of the PATRIOT Act and federal immigration reform. Though the state dragged him through the court system, this exercise of power was largely symbolic, giving the appearance of policing terrorism—a counterfeit counterterrorism. One is left to wonder: who is buying the "killer bargain?"

8. Border Practices

Charles Piot

The post–Cold War political and economic crisis in Togo has generated a wave of inventive pop-cultural and entrepreneurial practices. This essay explores one such practice—the rush of Togolese to sign up for the United States Diversity (Green Card) Lottery,[1] and their often ingenious attempts to work the system to their advantage.

The popularity of the visa lottery might be read as symptomatic of Togo's "abjection"—to borrow James Ferguson's (1999) phrase—from today's global economy (see also the introduction to this volume) and as an attempt, both desperate and inventive, by Togolese at inclusion. "The dictatorship has robbed us of our dreams," a lottery winner told me in summer 2006. "And now, with *le jeune* [the 'young one,' the son of the ex-dictator, Eyadéma] in power, it may be another four decades before we are able to dream again. Playing the visa lottery gives us hope that there may be a life beyond Togo and that we can live like the rest of the world."

But if global exclusion motivates participation in this popular phenomenon, a commitment to hope and invention—to "creativity amidst constraint" (see the introduction to this volume)—defines its practice. In focusing on the inventiveness as much as the constraint of the current conjuncture, I am as concerned with what this moment has "produced" (Foucault 1990; see also the introduction to this volume) as with what it has taken away or with what is lost. Put differently, I am interested in the ways in which the two faces of the current crisis—privation and invention—inform and feed off one another. In paying attention to peoples' inventiveness, I aim not to belittle the all-too-real hardships of the contemporary moment or to romanticize what it means to live under crisis but rather to acknowledge those worlds that Togolese inhabit in the only way they know how—by remaining persistently creative and creatively persistent, and by imagining, against all odds and despite enormous hard-ship, that today may be their day, and if not, surely tomorrow.

GAMBLING FUTURES

"Lotto visa," as it is referred to in Lomé, has become a major cultural event in Togo over the past ten years. According to a consular official I interviewed at the U.S. Embassy in August 2003, there were more green card lottery visa applications per capita in Togo that year than in any other African country, and Togo had ten times as many applications as Benin, the similarly-sized country next door—numbers that have held steady since.[2] An embassy employee told me in summer 2005 that he heard that one million Togolese (out of six million) played the visa lottery in 2004. This figure is certainly exaggerated, but the statement nevertheless captures something of the cultural cachet that this event holds for many Togolese today. Adding to local interest in this phenomenon—and the focus of this essay—is the fact that every lottery winner is permitted to bring a spouse and children (who may not have been listed when the winner applied), thus opening a space of considerable play, with many marrying others' spouses or siblings, or adopting their children in return for help in paying the embassy interview fee (U.S.$775 as of 2010) and a plane ticket to the United States (more than $1,000).

The involvement of Togolese in the green card lottery is a textbook illustration of the sort of "Atlantic African" economic practice that Jane Guyer (2004) suggests has characterized African economic history for centuries. In her 2004 book, *Marginal Gains: Monetary Transactions in Atlantic Africa*, Guyer argues that the domain of the economic in Africa has long been situated at the intersection of various crossroads and within a transcultural space between the local and that which lay beyond: the slave trade, the colonial, and, now, a differently globalized postcolonial. It has also straddled the material and the performative, the impersonal and personal, the formal and informal. Atlantic African economies are thus hybrid, improvisational border practices engaged in the ongoing negotia-tion and invention of registers of value and personal distinction, practices and negotiations that mediate (and are mediated by) an ongoing state of "crisis." Under conditions of perpetual turbulence, Guyer suggests, eco-nomic actors seek to gain by strategically accessing those multiple scales of value that are in play in such borderland spaces.[3] As with Atlantic African economic phenomena generally, lotto visa is an enormously inventive, entrepreneurial border practice, which has generated its own scales of value and pricing, and produced far-reaching networks of debt, rank, and clientage. These borrow from and innovate upon conventional scales of value, price, rank, and debt. Lotto visa is thus an example of the sort of "tactical" agency the editors of this volume suggest characterizes many actors across the African continent today—in which men and women make the best of possibilities made available to them and, when faced with contexts of protracted difficulty, innovate and improvise to create conditions of political, economic and cultural possibility (introduction).

Lotto visa is also a practice that bears the imprint of the post–Cold War neoliberal moment in West Africa, a moment that has fostered, among other things, cultures of duplicity and identity fabrication. The Nigerian "419" scam—the now-(in)famous practice of Internet fraud in which an overseas client is duped by the promise of sharing vast oil (or other) profits in return for sheltering money in a personal bank account, which is quickly emptied upon transfer of the account number (Apter 1999, 2005)—is one example of the sort of duping and identity fraud that has become ever more common in the current conjuncture. Closer to home, Togolese insist that counterfeits and fakes are so common today in the stores and on the streets of Lomé that one can never be sure whether an object one has purchased is "real" or not—a real or a fake Nokia phone, a real or an imitation piece of designer clothing, a new or a used car part. Lotto visa, too, is an act of conjuring, generating something of value (here, an identity, a proxy citizenship) out of nothing—conjuring that seems emblematic of the neoliberal moment more broadly, with its casinos and pyramid schemes and income-generating lotteries and stock market "futures": "casino capitalism," Comaroff and Comaroff (2000:295–298) call it, following Susan Strange (1997 [1986]).

In what follows, I explore the practices of the Togolese visa lottery largely through the experiences and narrations of a single lotto visa entrepreneur.[4] He is not only an impressive raconteur, with a keen eye for new practices and the latest invention, but has also himself been responsible for the introduction of key innovations in the larger system. He thus provides a privileged view of practices at once conventional and dynamic.[5]

A NOTE ON CONTEXT

The end of the Cold War affected this small nation as much as any other in West Africa. Surrounded throughout the early independence period (ca. 1960–90) by three countries with Soviet leanings, and occupying (during the early 1980s) an at-large seat on the United Nations Security Council,

Togo was of more than passing strategic interest to France and the United States. Not only were Togolese state coffers, and the pockets of the political elite, lined with money but the international community also turned a blind eye to President Gnassingbé Eyadéma's repressive state apparatus. With the collapse of the Soviet Union and the end of the Cold War, however, much of the money disappeared and Eyadéma's regime came under attack from below as well as above. Street protests in the early 1990s were accompanied by the cutting of United States and European Union aid to Togo, while the foreign embassies supported the political opposition in calling for Eyadéma's departure.

Even as Eyadéma remained in power throughout this period—through a mix of cunning, ruthlessness, and election fraud—the Togolese state nevertheless became a shadow of its former self. It was (and remains) a state that, to cite Achille Mbembe (1992, 2001), has been little more than a "simulacral regime," subsisting on "performance" and the staging of dramatic events—false coup attempts, hyperbolic celebrations of national holidays—as much as anything substantial. As one index of the state's withdrawal from the social field during the 1990s, the government bureaucracy stopped paying stipends to chiefs—a practice which had given it enormous local influence—and suspended support for social services like Affaires Sociales, the state's development agency which had offices in villages throughout the country and funneled significant amounts of money into rural development during the 1970s and 1980s. This withdrawal of state funds from the development field threw local communities back on themselves, ratcheting down the standard of living yet again and sending many close to the edge.

Adding privation to privation, in 1994 France devalued the CFA franc by 50 percent, and the IMF and World Bank imposed ever more stringent austerity and privatization measures. In response to the currency devaluation, the markets and the informal sector (on which most Togolese subsist) experienced a period of volatility and dramatic uncertainty. Market uncertainties were compounded by the influx of new, often cheaper, products—from East Asia, from Nigeria, and from new post-Fordist sites of production around the globe—products that often proved flawed and less durable, but sold anyway because of peoples' limited means. The disarray in value registers that characterized this period was manifest in rumors in both urban and rural markets that producers were now using illicit means to manufacture their products, products that were often considered "empty" or useless when consumed. As elsewhere in Africa (Ashforth 2001, 2005; Comaroff and Comaroff 1999, 2000; Moore and Sanders 2001), this was also a time of burgeoning occult economies, of the proliferation of magical means of capturing value and producing wealth.

Ironically, perhaps, this was a moment of hyper- (and increased) commodification, when every domain of social and religious life was seemingly up for sale and when the commodity form had seeped into the innermost cultural recesses. One example of the latter: Witchcraft imaginaries (in the area of northern Togo where I work) have undergone dramatic transformation since the late 1990s. Not only are witches today (unlike their 1980s and early 1990s counterparts) *allegedly* more abundant (though also more elusive, concealing their nighttime fires and frequently traveling in underground subways) but they are also said to have stopped consuming their victims, instead putting them up for sale and resale—classic Marxian commodity-into-money conversion[6]—in the markets of the night.

Togolese responded to the post–Cold War crisis in diverse ways. While a moment of extreme privation, it was also enormously productive in the Foucauldian (1990) sense, spawning a new round of extraordinarily inventive bricolage—of cycling and recycling, of dividing the seemingly indivisible, of surviving on nothing (cf. Jackson and the introduction to this volume)—and raised the art of the scam (the invention of false identities, the manufacture of papers and visas) to a new level. The current moment of privation has also produced a culture and imaginary of exile— and indeed, one might say, an entire nation in exile. Witness the northern town of Sokodé. This sprawling settlement of rusted tin roofs—the sleepy seat of bygone colonial power in Togo's hinterland—has since the late 1990s undergone a dramatic makeover. Today phone booths dot virtually every street corner and new Western Union stations go up every few months—conduits for information and money from the tens of thousands of Kotokoli who fled the country for Germany (and received political asylum there) after opposing President Eyadéma during the early 1990s. It is said of the Kotokoli that no Togolese group has as pure a collective fantasy as they, a dream that they will one day all live in Germany.

But fantasies of exile are by no means the province of the Kotokoli alone. One could say the same of residents of Lomé, where cybercafés sprout like mushrooms, filled night and day with people connecting to various elsewheres, and where playing the visa lottery has become a national pastime. It would not be exaggerating too much to say that everyone in Togo is trying to leave—by playing the lottery, by trying to get into European or American universities, by arranging fictitious marriages with foreigners, by joining churches that might take them abroad, by hoping to be signed on by a European soccer team, or by joining the fan club that accompanies the national soccer team overseas. Kodjo, a friend whose "wife" (someone he married expressly to obtain a visa) was selected in the green card lottery but failed the embassy interview—after having spent the better part of a year and all his resources preparing her—e-mailed me a week later to see whether I could help him get a medical visa to the United States to get a prosthetic arm (to replace an arm that had been deformed by polio in childhood). An acquaintance of his had received a visa for a hip replacement, and my informant imagined a parallel line of argument might work for him—a suggestion I found intriguing not only for the alacrity with which he developed a new exit strategy but also for his willingness to deploy his disability in pursuit of exile. But while many, like my informant, fail in their attempts to leave (while nevertheless spending all their time trying, thus enacting a sort of virtual exile), many others have succeeded. Thus, whereas in the mid-1990s expatriate remittances constituted only 10–20 percent of the Togolese GNP, today they are at least double that, with some estimates as high as 50 percent.

TOGO'S LOTTO VISA

The inventions of lotto visa culture are quite extraordinary and, in some ways, reconstitute kinship by other means. As I mentioned above, once an applicant has been selected (by the drawing in Williamsburg, KY), and before applicants go for the obligatory interview at the U.S. Embassy in Lomé, they often will attempt to add "dependents" to their dossiers. Sometimes these are legitimate relatives but usually aren't. (Indeed, they are often relatives of those already in the diaspora—who can better afford the quid-pro-quo payment of the visa winner's embassy interview fees and purchase of plane tickets to the States.) Since U.S. immigration rules only permit the visa winner to be accompanied by a spouse and children, the winner must then "marry" his sponsor's wife (or sister or cousin) and "adopt" any children before the interview and present proof that they are indeed their legitimate dependents. This in turn requires producing a file of documents—marriage papers, wedding photos, birth certificates. One somewhat atypical but nevertheless revealing example: an informant's wife recently arrived in the United States as the "wife" of a friend of her brother's. Three years ago, the brother and the friend both received political asylum (needless to say, under false pretenses) and entered into a "sister-exchange" arrangement, whereby each would "marry" the other's sister and pay her way to the States. As part of the agreement, my informant's wife's "husband" spent more than $2,500 returning to Togo to take wedding photos with his "betrothed"—for her to present at the embassy as proof that she was married to him. Moreover, the "husband" could not fly to Lomé itself—for fear that if U.S. authorities discovered he had been back in Togo it might jeopardize his asylum status. Instead, he flew to Accra, took a bus to the border—where they only check passports of non–West Africans—and crossed into Togo incognito and on foot.

Another area of play/invention: A lottery visa winner must either possess a high school diploma or have several years of job expertise in a profession that is on the U.S. Labor Department's job list. Thus, those without the "baccalaureate" who do not already fit the job profile are quickly "apprenticed" into the appropriate trades (and papers backdating the apprenticeship and subsequent work experience are manufactured). The U.S. consular official who was conducting interviews of lottery visa winners in summer 2003 told me that as soon as tailoring was put on the list, "everyone in Togo became a tailor!" And, in 2006, when *peintre en batiment* (house painter) was added to the list, the consul's office was flooded with the applications of those claiming to be painters.

A veritable cottage industry of lotto visa entrepreneurs has grown up around these practices—those who help others with the online visa registration, those who know who to bribe to get false marriage or adoption or job papers, those who arrange the shooting of wedding photographs, and especially those who serve as brokers between émigrés in the diaspora and people at home. Kodjo—who had inquired whether he might get a medical visa for an arm replacement after his "wife" failed her embassy interview—signed up more than 1,200 people for the lottery in fall 2005. He wrote to me just after the new online registration season had opened in October to say that he was leaving for northern Togo to enlist what he hoped would be several hundred applicants. In the north ("an untouched territory," as he referred to it), he visited local high schools, where he sought permission from the school principal to speak with those students in their last year, precisely because most in *terminale* are single (more easily enabling dependents to be added to the files of winners) and because they will qualify for the baccalaureate the following spring (ensuring an easier passage through the embassy interview). An innovation here in repertoire: Unlike other lotto visa entrepreneurs, Kodjo does not charge any of his enlistees to help them register—he takes their pictures and fills out the online forms for them, all free of charge—in return for "owning" their files. If they win, he will add "dependents" (and make money for doing so). He is quite levelheaded about all of this, saying that he simply plays the odds. "If only 1 percent of my applicants win, I can live for an entire year."

The embassy is of course fully aware of all of the gaming going on. Indeed, the U.S. ambassador went on television in 2006 to say that he assumed all those who came for the embassy interview were lying and fabricating identities, and that the burden was on the interviewee to prove they were not, and that the embassy had developed a set of tests in efforts to detect real from sham winners and, especially, real from false spouses. Thus, a common strategy is to interview spouses separately, asking about the habits and desires of the other: "What's your husband's favorite color? his favorite food? what did you eat yesterday and the day before that? what side of the bed do you sleep on?" The embassy also knows that as soon as they ask a particular question, it will circulate to those who are next in line for interviews. (Indeed, Kodjo showed me a file he keeps of all the questions asked of interviewees over the past several years, a file he shares with friends and clients who are prepping for the embassy interview.) Thus, a cat-and-mouse game has developed between embassy and street, the embassy trying to stay one step ahead by springing new questions and those about to go for interviews making sure they know as soon as new questions appear. In 2005, for instance, an interviewee's doctor's report— it is mandatory to have a physical exam and HIV/AIDS test before the interview—noted that there was a scar on one of his legs. The consular official conducting the interview asked his "wife" which leg, and, when she guessed incorrectly, they failed the interview. The next day, everyone on the street knew why they had failed—and had begun to explore the most intimate details of their visa-spouses' bodies. During an applicant's embassy interview in January 2006, the consular official challenged the woman she was interviewing by telling her that she didn't believe the man who had accompanied her was her husband and that she would give the applicant a visa while denying him one. Without hesitating, the woman responded that he was indeed her husband (though in fact he was not) and that if he was not granted a visa, she would refuse hers. This seemed proof enough for the consular official, and both were granted visas. Kodjo reacted by saying that it took this type of "courage" to pass the interview.

As one telling sign of the importance the visa lottery is assuming in the cultural life of Lomé today, I have heard repeatedly from Togolese that the (low-ranking) consular official who conducts the visa interviews at the embassy is far better known than the ambassador. "We don't even know who the ambassador is," a friend said. "But Mme. Johnson, we know her well. She's a celebrity here. We study her every move; after all, she's the one who will decide whether we have a life beyond Togo or not." The consular official in question told me that one day she was playing golf with the U.S. ambassador when a car stopped on a busy road nearby. The driver jumped out and ran across the golf course to greet her ("I have always wanted to meet you," he said), while entirely ignoring the ambassador. Before taking leave, he asked if Mme. Johnson knew yet when the next visa lottery enrollment period would begin.

Kodjo's history with the visa lottery—his evolution from applicant to entrepreneur—illustrates the often intimate connection between privation and invention that seems so emblematic of the contemporary moment and of actors across the continent who "attempt to renegotiate the terms of austerity," as the editors of this volume put it (introduction). It was his failure as a lottery participant that led to Kodjo's entry into and eventual success as an entrepreneur. After a friend he had helped apply was selected in the lottery, Kodjo spent a small fortune (and the better part of a year) "marrying" her, apprenticing her into a job on the Labor Department's job list, and prepping her for the embassy interview. When she failed the interview—overcome by nervousness, she became tongue-tied while answering the consul's questions—he sank into a deep depression. But he then realized that despite his failure, he had learned an enormous amount about how to put together a file and prepare for the interview. He began counseling others going through the interview process and met with striking success. Today, as one of the most accomplished visa lottery entrepreneurs in Lomé, Kodjo claims it was his initial failure that led to his subsequent success in the business.

BORDER ECONOMICS

I turn now to the economics of the visa lottery system, following Kodjo's business dealings, particularly his innovations and entrepreneurialism, and the ways in which he introduced practices uniquely his own but also informed by and in dialogue with those of the dozens of other lotto visa entrepreneurs operating in Lomé.

Kodjo's number of enlistees jumped dramatically between 2001 and 2005, from a few dozen, to several hundred, to 800, and eventually to 1,200. This sharp increase is both due to the fact that his reputation has grown with experience—he has now shepherded many successful dossiers through the maze of interviews and medical exams, through the local market in false papers and fictional identities, and through the complicated financing that must be put together to pay for interviews and exams and plane tickets (financing, that is, far beyond the means of most single Togolese)—and because, unlike other entrepreneurs, Kodjo waives the up-front fees that others charge (1,500 CFA = U.S.$3 as of 2010) for helping someone register. It is important to note that because registration is now filed online, and must include a digital photograph of the applicant, most Togolese who play seek the help of an Internet-savvy lotto visa entrepreneur.

Of course, Kodjo's success has also been dramatically enhanced by his pioneering forays into the north, into this "untouched territory." And here his ethnicity is a factor. Although Kodjo grew up in Lomé, and is in many ways more "southern" than "northern," he spent childhood summers in the Kabiyé north where his father was born (it is common practice for parents to send their children back to their natal villages during summer holidays in order "to teach them how to work"). Thus, it is through some of Kodjo's childhood connections, as well as those of his family, that he has been able to get his foot in the door of local schools (a summer playmate is now principal of one of the northern lycées), something that would be difficult for a non-Kabiyé. Noteworthy, too, is the effect of Kodjo's recruitment practices: Children in remote Togolese villages are now playing the lottery and dreaming of U.S. green cards—a fantasy recently made all the more real by the fact that one of Kodjo's northern enlistees was selected in last July's drawing.

In 2006, six of Kodjo's enlistees were selected in the Kentucky raffle. Because he signed them up free of charge, he "owned" each of their dossiers and was free to add "dependents" to them including a spouse (and sometimes children). It is these dependents, or more typically their brothers/spouses in the diaspora, who pay the cost of the embassy interview ($775 per person); the cost of the plane ticket to the States for the winner and dependent(s) (more than $1,000 each); the cost of apprenticing the winner into a trade; the cost of obtaining marriage papers, wedding photographs, and new identity papers (and sometimes passports); and the cost of having Kodjo broker the entire affair. However, he insists that the winners, not the dependents, pay for the $200 medical examination that applicants must undergo before the embassy interview. Kodjo's reasoning here is that there must be some additional incentive for the winner to perform at peak level during the interview, and having him spend his own money beforehand is the best way to ensure that.

If a particular entrepreneur doesn't want to do the work of shepherding a dossier through the bureaucratic maze of forms, fees, and photographs, he can sell the dossier to another entrepreneur or directly to a sponsor. One such case I was told about in summer 2006 had a price tag of $3,000, though it only fetched $1,500 in the end, and this just for access to the winner's dossier. The price was high, I was told, because the person already had his "bac" (baccalaureate) and was seen as a sure winner. Indeed, there are categories or ranks of winners, "high risk" to "certain winners," which affect pricing outcomes.

This market in visas has brought new risks as well. Apparently for the first time, in 2007 an entrepreneur began counterfeiting winners' letters for his clients—on counterfeit State Department stationery—and then selling the "winners'" dossiers to Togolese in the diaspora. After receiving his transaction fees, the entrepreneur vanished, leaving those he had victimized to slowly realize (in the end, confirmed by e-mail communication with the processing center in Kentucky) that they had been had. But notice the fraud within a fraud—a recursiveness, so to speak—that this new practice represents, and the distinctions that emerge for players around the category of "fraud" itself. Thus, Kodjo and others found this particular incident completely reprehensible—a type of "inauthentic" fraud—in contrast with those practices, those more authentic fakes, with which they were engaged (in helping Togolese achieve a better life abroad). Notice, too, the way in which such a practice generates new procedures and safeguards in lotto visa culture. Kodjo is now consulted by other entrepreneurs' clients who seek to verify the authenticity of the State Department letter announcing their selection. In summer 2008, he discovered two counterfeits—noting small misspellings and incongruities in the "official" letter—and was handsomely rewarded by those near-dupes he had saved from certain and disastrous debt.

This system is also the source of many stories of monumental, even tragic, loss. I know some who, without friends or relatives in the diaspora to help them with the cost of the embassy interview, raised their own money locally—by selling land or a family home, or by borrowing from family members what amounts for many Togolese to a lifetime's savings—only to fail the interview. Indeed, in fall 2006, after a particularly difficult interview season during which only a few were granted visas—on one day alone, only three out of forty applicants were successful—several hundred lottery winners staged a protest in a local park, demanding that the embassy return the interview fee to those who were denied visas. The embassy capitulated in part, and now returns the fee for a denied winner's spouse (though never the interview fee for the actual winner). Still not satisfied, these same protestors began a daily sit-in at the entrance to the U.S. Embassy in April 2008, a sit-in that lasted five months, until early October when the embassy asked Togolese security forces to remove the protestors.

Price structures within this popular economy are the result of an on-going dialectic between conventionalized practices and innovation. Practices among entrepreneurs become standardized, only to be partially unsettled by improvising individuals like Kodjo who waived the entry fee for applicants and who began requiring winners to cover some of the costs of pre-interview expenses. But such improvisations quickly circulate and affect the practices of other entrepreneurs, before becoming standardized and before new innovations in turn unsettle them once again. These are pricing mechanisms generated "from below," not only beyond the purview of the state but also only partially driven by principles of supply and demand. When the winner with the baccalaureate's dossier value fell from $3,000 to $1,500, this outcome was the result of negotiation between those in the diaspora (with their varying means to pay such an entrance fee) and the needs of entrepreneurs in Lomé (needs driven by familial and network commitments as much as by any prior standardized pricing scale).

All told, the financing for one of these cases costs between $5,000 and $10,000 (depending on the initial cost of access, and the number of dependents added to a dossier). With roughly 1,500 Togolese going for embassy interviews each year (out of 3,000 winners),[7] up to $15 million is spent annually on this system—not an insignificant sum for a small West African country in the midst of a prolonged economic crisis. Indeed, this system might be read as a partial solution to Togo's development impasse, for it serves as a remittance magnet, drawing millions of dollars annually from the diaspora back home. Moreover, it has a significant spillover effect, redistributing monies along networks of kin and friends and supporting entire cottage industries in document fabrication, photography, as well as those apprenticing winners into trades, doctors administering the medical exams, and the visa lottery entrepreneurs themselves.

But this popular economy also informs, and is informed by, other practices of the informal sector in which it is implicated. Lomé today is nothing if not a crowded intersection of hundreds of informal economic ventures. Everyone, it seems, is hustling and jostling for position within the limited means of this post–Cold War economic moment. Moreover, the players in many of these groups overlap, with information about pricing, credit, and debt (and the latest innovations) circulating among them. For example, Kodjo also sells used German cars with a group of friends who work at Lomé's port, while another of his friends who helps obtain false documents for his enlistees is involved in the export of "exotic" animals (pythons and iguanas) to Germany, Japan, and the United States. Money and credit, too, move between these circles, with a busted deal here drawing on potential

future earnings there (cf. Makhulu, this volume). I have spent hours trying to follow the baroque and bewildering movements of money and debt
from venture to venture and party to party and always come away feeling
I have never fully gotten to the bottom of the logic of exchange and debt
being transacted.

DESIRING THE GLOBAL

What sort of popular practice is this: a remittance system? a system of
redistribution? a citizenship-for-sale scheme? Or merely a clever set of
income-generating devices for Kodjo and others like him? Certainly it is
all of these. But I think visa lottery is more, as well. For it draws on all the
resources and imaginaries of the moment, those of the post–Cold War conjuncture—of its felt crisis, of the eviscerated-though-still-dictatorial state,
of social death and the emptiness of citizenship under such conditions, of
a sprawling transnational diaspora and the desires and longings it creates,
of informationalism and its new technologies—in their way producing
a generative fantasy about exile and citizenship and global membership
(Ferguson 1999, 2002, 2006).

Togolese, like others across the continent, are acutely aware of their
position in the world today, of their "abjection" or expulsion from (or
persistent noninclusion within) European modernity—a modernity they
see every night on the TV screen but cannot touch, a modernity they hear
spoken of but may never inhabit. In the same way that Ferguson reads
mimicry of the modern and emulation of European style among Zambians
as a type of global plea, as an attempt to stake a claim to the "rights of full
membership in a wider society" (Ferguson 2002:555), I see the same desire
in Togolese participation in the visa lottery. Lotto visa is nothing if not a
passionate plea to establish rights to inclusion in global society.

This desire for global citizenship is what motivated lottery winners
who were denied visas to sit in at the U.S. Embassy in Lomé throughout
spring and summer 2008. Despite the serendipity of the selection process,
those who were chosen had an abiding sense of entitlement. "We were
picked for visas, then denied them on arbitrary grounds, and we are here
to claim what is rightfully ours," the organizer of the sit-in said when I
met him in June 2008. Behind him, the group of 300 strong, all dressed
in red ("to show our wounds"), united in prayer to the Holy Spirit, one
of their thrice-daily pleas for divine intercession. With a persistence that
strained credibility—they appeared at the U.S. Embassy every day for five
months, from eight o'clock in the morning to five in the evening, through

blistering sun and driving rain, until they were forcibly removed in early October by Togolese security forces—they pleaded for global access.

But why do so many more apply from Togo than from neighboring countries like Benin and Burkina Faso? Certainly, as many to whom I put the question suggested, Togolese enthusiasm for the lottery is due to the ongoing political and economic crisis in their country, a crisis exacerbated by the continuation of Eyadéma's dictatorship beyond the end of the Cold War. This political climate, combined with the economic privation brought on by structural adjustment and the withdrawal of EU funding, has created a near-universal desire to leave for what they imagine are greener pastures in Europe and the United States. Moreover, things are worse in Togo, they add, than in Benin and Burkina Faso, precisely because of the ongoing dictatorship (as opposed to the more open, and frankly unexpected, electoral outcomes that have characterized those two countries' recent political histories). When Kodjo returned from a trip to Burkina Faso to see whether his Togolese clients could attend an embassy interview there rather than in Lomé (where the failure rate skyrocketed in 2006), he reported that life in Ouagadougou was infinitely better. "The roads are all paved, the street lights work, and when it rains the water runs off in an orderly manner into large cement ditches beside the road. Lomé is years behind." This testament to Burkinabé modernity is equally a testament to the variations in material conditions *among* neoliberal regimes (see the introduction to this volume), in this particular case, among three neighboring countries in which the neoliberal dispensation has been experienced in significantly different ways.

While political-economic factors may thus condition a Togolese longing for exile, and explain the higher incidence of visa lottery participants than in neighboring countries, such factors cannot fully account for the extraordinary popularity of, or the specific practices entailed in, the Togolese lottery phenomenon. The visa lottery also needs to be understood as a cultural practice, which as elsewhere (Baudrillard 1996) has taken on a life of its own and has come to produce its own excess. "These things start small and spread through the streets and, when successful, get taken up by others," Kodjo said. "Then they grow and grow, and, if some are successful, others follow. And, you know, each country has its own thing. With Nigerians it is 419; with Togolese it is the visa lottery."

This phenomenon, like entrepreneurialism throughout West Africa, also needs to be thought in terms of the "performative" (Guyer 2004). As an event that generates stories and discourses about itself, that feeds collective fantasies, and that produces reputations and markers of distinction, it is as much cultural performance as economic practice. Moreover, its dramatic growth and popularity among Togolese depends on the multi-talents of entrepreneurs (or performers) like Kodjo. Not only must he be Internet savvy and have impeccable interpersonal skills—for example, counseling people how to treat one another as "spouses," calming those who may be out of money because they failed the medical exam or the embassy interview. Kodjo must also be able to broker deals with people all over Lomé and draw on networks throughout the diaspora. He also has to know the ins and outs of the lottery system and U.S. immigration law.

A bizarre case presented itself in summer 2005, in which a Togolese national in Minneapolis, who had sponsored one of Kodjo's winners in return for the latter's marriage to his wife and adoption of his son, sued the winner for child support. In point of fact, the Minneapolis-based man had remarried his wife after she arrived in the States but had never re-adopted his son, and he felt the winner, who remained the son's legal father, should help pay to support him. Because he had brokered the original deal between the two men, Kodjo was contacted in Lomé, by both sides, to help resolve the dispute. He proceeded to take a crash course in Minnesota family law and then weighed in as mediator. He was outraged at the hubris of the sponsor bringing the suit, and the case was finally resolved, and the child support claim withdrawn, when the winner threatened to go public with the illegalities in obtaining visas for both wife and child. "All in a day's work," Kodjo concluded with a wry smile.

Notes

CHAPTER 1. MAKHULU, BUGGENHAGEN, AND JACKSON, INTRODUCTION

1. According to FRONTEX, an EU agency based in Warsaw created as an independent body to coordinate cooperation between member states in the field of border security, the top three points of origin for the Canary Island migrants were Senegal, Gambia, and Ivory Coast (FRONTEX 2007).

2. In 2006 more than 31,000 West Africans landed in the Canary Islands, six times the number of men and women who landed there in 2005. It is estimated that about 6,000 persons died en route in 2006. See "Canaries Migrant Death Toll Soars," *BBC News*, December 28, 2006; available at http://news.bbc.co.uk.

3. For a related discussion of the Canary Islands migration, and of the dilemma of doing well in difficult times, see Fullwiley (forthcoming).

4. Even as Western nation-states struggled to parse a distinction between legal and illegal migration, and Spain ramped up efforts to repatriate the new arrivals, young West African men, and the few plucky women among them, confounded the authorities by declaring "Barça ou barzakh!" (Barcelona or death). In Muslim thought *barzakh* is a temporary stage following death prior to resurrection where the soul is separated from the body. See "Emigration clandestine: Barça ou 'barzakh' (Barcelone ou l'enfer), le leitmotiv des partants de Thiaroye-sur-Mer," *Le Soleil*, April 7, 2007; available at http://www.lesoleil.sn.

5. See *Le Figaro*, August 5, 1999, 8.

6. A process that has, tragically, again intensified, with conflict once again raging in the eastern DRC in late 2008, more than a million people displaced in North Kivu province alone, and the DRC's neighbors in the region tempted once more by the politics (and economics) of intervention.

7. This relationship with the world is long-standing, of course. Although Europeans see African migration as an urgent and recent occurrence in places like Malta and the Canary Islands, for West Africans such mobility has been

an ongoing rite of passage expressed differently in different historical periods. In terms of voluntary migration, African Muslims have long crossed the Mediterranean for the hajj pilgrimage, as well as for work and to attend centers of Islamic learning; across the continent young men often have migrated seasonally to garner cash in the urban colonial economy for bride-wealth; others took advantage of the right to travel to Europe and the United States in the 1960s for university degrees and to engage in wage labor in the context of the postwar labor shortage that befell Europe; and more recently, still others have sought to participate in the global market in cheap labor through sojourns to the Canaries and elsewhere. Here we underline that African economies have for the most part always been extroverted.

8. Immanuel Wallerstein, "The Depression: A Long-Term View," commentary no. 243, October 15, 2008; see http://www.binghamton.edu/fbc/243en.htm.

9. Neoliberalism's timeline is also debatable. Reagan and Thatcher are more or less synonymous with the rise of the "New World Order" in the early 1980s, further their strong support of "free" markets, a cornerstone of neoliberalism, is pretty much assumed. In the Third World, particularly sub-Saharan Africa, structural adjustment policies were central to the transnational reorganization of relations between states and capital, also beginning in the 1980s and also clearly indissociable from neoliberalism. However, some suggest we ought to reach back further, to connect classic liberalism to neoliberalism, or in Tim Mitchell's recent work on "carbon democracy," to look back on that long twentieth-century struggle to secure oil as a site of the renegotiation of the political. He has argued that flows of oil and international finance together tell us something about democratic stability, or at the very least that conjuncture of specific economic and political principles. Again, to this end, the timeline for neoliberalism might be pushed back (see Mitchell n.d.).

10. African conflicts have been depicted in Huntingtonian terms as a clash of civilizations, reducible to the pathological work of culture and ethnicity.

11. The recent economic crisis has raised questions about the stability of the southern European economies; Spain's construction business has been particularly hard hit. Carter Dougherty, "Economy in Europe Contracted in Second Quarter," *New York Times*, August 14, 2008.

12. The United Nations Development Programme ranks Malawi 166th of 177 countries on the Human Development Index (HDI) (see UNDP 2006). In addition, Malawi ranks 171st in life expectancy, 106th in adult literacy; and 171st in GDP per capita (just behind Tanzania and ahead of Sierra Leone). Thus, when the American pop singer Madonna called for Westerners to address what she saw as a "state of emergency" in Malawi and other sub-Saharan countries, this in the aftermath of her controversial adoption of a young Malawian boy, she may well have been right, at least in one sense (see Thomas 2006). UNDP indicators suggest that life is not without its challenges for ordinary Malawians. And while most other regions in the world have improved their HDI scores in the past two or more decades, countries in sub-Saharan African have not—largely owing to economic stagnation and the impact of the HIV/AIDS

epidemic. Yet, these are difficulties of an enduring nature—less a "state of emergency," a Darfur, so to speak, than a slow burn.

CHAPTER 2. MAKHULU, THE SEARCH FOR ECONOMIC SOVEREIGNTY

ACKNOWLEDGMENTS: Research for this essay and the broader project from which it is drawn, *The Geography of Freedom: Revolution and the South African City*, has benefited from the generosity of a great number of institutions and the fellowships and grants they have extended to me. These include the Shelby Cullom Davis Center for Historical Studies Fellowship, Princeton University (2006–7); the Duke University Arts and Sciences Committee on Faculty Research Travel Grant, Duke University (summer 2006); the Princeton University, Cotsen Post-Doctoral Fellowship, Princeton Society of Fellows in the Liberal Arts (2003–5); and the Princeton University Committee on Research in the Humanities and Social Sciences Travel Grant, Princeton University (January 2005). My sincere thanks go to those who graciously received me in their homes year after year and without whom I could not have conducted research. I would also like to acknowledge the attentions of generous and meticulous colleagues, among them: Patrick Bond, Beth Buggenhagen, Gabriella Coleman, Jean Comaroff, John L. Comaroff, Mary Harper, Stephen Jackson, and Hylton White, as well as students and colleagues at the Shelby Cullom Davis Center for Historical Studies, Princeton University, and Duke University. An earlier draft of this essay was presented in the Davis Seminar, Princeton University, and the Cultural Anthropology Colloquium Series, Duke University. All errors and omissions are mine.

1. Here, "debt" covers a whole range of things, including store credit, credit-card debt, informal loans, even loan sharking, in other words, monies owed in both formal and informal sectors.

2. RDP homes were first built in the two or so years following the country's first democratic elections in 1994 and were intended to address South Africa's history of spatial engineering, migrant labor, and housing deficit. As a project of national reconstruction the state offered subsidies to cover the costs of "starter" or "core" homes. But as neoliberalization progressed and this welfarist agenda sat uncomfortably with new efforts at deregulation and privatization, the scheme became more and more compromised: core structures shrank in square footage, while the actual cost of construction rose as a function of outsourcing and an indication of the expanding market basis of public welfare. Today RDP homes are often referred to as "matchboxes," echoing old apartheid policies, and are generally grossly inadequate for the needs of families, extended and otherwise.

3. See the Ward 35 demographic profile, derived from 2001 census data, at http://www.capetown.gov.za/en/stats/2001census/Documents/2006%20Ward 035.htm.

4. Much changed in political life in 2008: Thabo Mbeki was forced to resign

the presidency in September and was succeeded temporarily by Kgalema Mot-lanthe, the ANC's deputy president, ahead of general elections in 2009. Per-haps even more dramatically, an ANC splinter organization officially named the Congress of the People (COPE), formed in November under the leadership of "Terror" Lekota (the former defence minister), and threatened to contest 41 seats in 5 provinces in the 2009 elections. Since that time, Jacob Zuma, a highly controversial populist figure—a Zulu traditionalist and polygamist who was exonerated of charges of graft and rape—has ascended to the presidency.

5. On the dollar-a-day calculation of poverty, see Reddy 2004.

6. For Arendt there existed a logical continuity between forms of surplus labor and surplus populations—populations conceived as subjects for elimina-tion. In this sense, Arendt anticipated Foucault's genealogy of the biopolitical state, even while the concept was never more than implicit in her own work.

7. While the current national unemployment rate hovers at 28 percent and 2001 census data disaggregated for Ward 35 indicate that 48 percent of people between the ages of 15 and 65 are employed, the South African government has opted for a "narrow" definition of unemployment. This definition covers those seeking jobs, rather than all those of working age who would otherwise choose to be employed. Such definitional artifice notwithstanding, the fact that almost 52 percent of working-age people in Ward 35 are unemployed speaks precisely of the unevenness in unemployment rates across the country and to the concentration of joblessness within informal settlements and the rural areas. See http://www.statssa.gov.za/ for 1996 and 2001 Census Data, and http://www.capetown.gov.za/en/stats/2001census/Documents/2006%20Ward 035.htm for disaggregated Ward 35 data.

8. See http://www.oecd.org/dataoecd/48/38/1826412.pdf. Another way to think about uneven access to employment is to consider income inequality in terms of consumer spending. In South Africa the total consumer expendi-ture of the bottom 62 percent of South Africans is currently slightly less than that of the top 5.7 percent (totaling over R172 billion), what Patrick Bond has argued can only be considered accumulation by dispossession (personal com-munication). See Hilton Shone, "Poor Make Rich Pickings," *Sunday Business Times*, January 30, 2005.

9. In 2006 the South African rand was valued at approximately R7 to the U.S. dollar. It subsequently depreciated and was valued at R9.75 to the dollar by the end of 2008.

10. See Collins, Murdoch, Rutherford, and Ruthven 2009; also see "The Financial Diaries," http://www.financialdiaries.com/financial.htm.

11. See http://www.standardbank.co.za/SBIC/Frontdoor_03_02/0,2361, 3447_19033_0,00.html. Note that a so-called Standard Bank "Society Scheme" is geared to *umgalelos* and encourages group savings.

12. Julius Makoni, personal communication.

13. A parallel might be drawn between such forms of abnegation and the cultivation of religious asceticism as a means of self-realization through denial (my sincere thanks to Stephen Jackson for this insight).

14. See Christina Scott, "Finance-South Africa: Rare Insights into Poor People's Bank," *Inter Press Service News Agency*, Sunday, January 7, 2007, available at http://www.ipsnews.net.

15. I am not suggesting that the poor do not consume. As Wal-Mart and other low-end chains clearly show, poor people are a tremendous source of profit, largely owing to the volume of sales rather than the price of goods. Instead, the mechanisms of "belt-tightening" to which many respondents referred suggested, on the one hand, patterns of delayed consumption (waiting until December to make large purchases, and so on), but, on the other, great care in distinguishing between basic needs and desire. To be sure, these are not universal in any way, but at every turn households necessarily negotiated a fine line between the two. Moreover, we cannot assume such economic behaviors to be motivated by a sense of utility. Consider Helen Meintjes's (2001) work on Soweto housewives and the uses to which so-called luxury appliances are put (or not) in the running of households, and what conceptions of useful and highly valued labor are at stake in decisions about washing clothes by hand while owning a washing machine, for example.

16. Again, note the state-mandated introduction of low-minimum-balance Mzansi accounts across the South African banking system. At the same time, while promoting banking for the poor advocates stopped short of regulating banks when it came to fees and other penalties.

17. Fluctuations in daily takings were related to the times during the month when pensioners received social grants (R800 per month) and mothers with dependants collected child grants (approximately R180 per child).

18. Pyramid and Ponzi schemes occur at all economic levels. In December 2008, possibly the largest Ponzi scheme in history hit the headlines worldwide, making the name Bernard Madoff infamous in the annals of financial criminality. See Diana B. Henriques and Zachery Kouwe, "Prominent Trader Accused of Defrauding Clients," *The New York Times*, December 11, 2008; http://www.nytimes.com/2008/12/12/business/12scheme.html.

19. This relationship to lending at high risk of default and of diversifying risk by playing both a high- and low-risk game—through involvement in the scheme as well as loan sharking—parallels in many respects the attitudes of banks and investors who seek to rearrange and diversify risk at every opportunity (Alex d'Aspremont, Princeton University, personal communication).

20. There is some discussion of changing the rules pertaining to the age at which children are cut off from access to child grants. Most recently policy makers have suggested raising the age limit to eighteen (from fourteen), since most eighteen-year-olds and/or school-leavers are more-or-less unemployable and generally remain in a relationship of dependency with parents and extended family.

21. One such example would be the emergence of free enterprise zones, which sit "outside" the borders of nation-states and effectively conceal or displace sites of production.

22. To be fair, Luxemburg's ideas foreshadowed the madness of current

lending and brokerage practices when she wrote of the antics of the French and British engaged in the construction of the Suez Canal. "These operations of capital," she argued, "at first sight, seem[ed] to reach the height of madness. One loan followed hard on the other, the interest on old loans was defrayed by new loans, and capital borrowed from the British and French paid for the large order placed with British and French industrial capital" (Luxemburg 2003:414).

23. See the World Health Organization's Country Survey for South Africa, http://www.who.int/countries/zaf/en/.

24. Crime is indisputably a factor, but the present discourse about crime lacks historicity, such that current anxieties overlook continuities with the past and a long and varied relationship with violence in the society as a whole (Comaroff and Comaroff 2006).

CHAPTER 3. JACKSON, "IT SEEMS TO BE GOING"

ACKNOWLEDGMENTS: This essay has its origins in papers presented to the Princeton Conference "After Afro-Pessimism: Fashioning African Futures" in April 2005, and the 2005–6 "University Seminar on Studies in Contemporary Africa" at Columbia University in February 2006. It has benefited significantly from constructive criticism offered by colleagues in both of these, as well as from detailed thinking-through with my co-editors in this volume, Anne-Maria Makhulu and Beth Buggenhagen.

1. War in the Kivus actually began as early as 1992, with widespread, provincial-level conflict known as the "Guerre Inter-Ethnique." This was followed by the 1994–96 knock-on effects of Rwanda's Genocide, and then the 1996–97 "AFDL war," which, beginning violently in the Kivus, eventually overthrew Mobutu Sese Seko and brought Laurent-Désiré Kabila to power. In August 1998, Rwanda and Uganda, both disaffected Kabila allies, together with elements of the Congolese Rwandophone community, formed the RCD and launched a long-running, violent, but ultimately unsuccessful attempt to overthrow Kabila.

2. An enticing further reference suggests itself. As in many cultures, in the DRC the Western term *development* is translated in various local languages through variants on the verb "to go" (*maendeleo* in Kiswahili is connected to *kuende*, to go, for example—*Duterimbere*, the Kinyarwanda name of a prominent Rwandan NGO, means approximately "let's go forward together," and so on). With equivalent teleology, therefore, *ça semble aller* tempts the translation "things seem to be developing."

3. A Dutch term, borrowed in French, originally meaning the mass said yearly on the anniversary of the foundation of a church in honor of its patron saint, but now more generally evoking a fair of some kind.

4. De Boeck is writing of the tail end of the *Mobutiste* period in Zaire, but his diagnosis remains cruelly accurate.

5. Wyatt MacGaffey similarly underlines an "admirably postmodern" instrumentalization of flexibility in clan-ethnic identities amongst the BaKongo even in the precolonial period (MacGaffey 1998).

6. A prescription said to have been provided by Mobutu in a political speech in the 1970s.

7. "Ça sera difficile: Le Congolais vit dans l'air; il n'a pas une position fixte"—as in English, *une position* carries connotations of a location, an opinion, and/or a job.

8. Underlining its economic and cultural centrality, Pepe Kalle, one of Zaire's biggest music stars, celebrated this instinct in his 1985 hit "Article 15, Beta Libanga."

9. Much has been written about *Système D*'s cultural importance. Through it, cunning becomes accentuated as a social value and the pursuit of lifestyle and status as an aesthetic (Bayart 1993; Bayart, Ellis, and Hibou 1999; Mbembe 2001; Werbner 1996; De Boeck 1999), frequently a transnational one (Mac-Gaffey and Bazenguissa-Ganga 2000; White 2000). Analysts have envisioned *Système D* as a space of new politico-cultural as well as economic possibility, one in which "people are taking matters into their own hands" (MacGaffey 1991) and where the quest for status, superiority, self-identity, and "savoir-vivre" (De Boeck 1999) could radically rework long-standing cultural tropes of resourcefulness and guile.

10. Congolese street vendors who sell petrol or diesel from jerricans by the side of the road.

11. One impact of the pervasiveness of *Système D* has been to render the terminology of "informality" all but irrelevant. De Boeck mordantly asks of Congo/Zaire "What is the use of distinguishing between formal and informal or parallel economies when the informal has become the common and the formal has almost disappeared?" (De Boeck 1996). See also Roitman 1990 for a detailed argument concerning the epistemological problems attached to the formal-informal distinction in Africa more generally.

12. A then senior RCD official in an interview with the author, February 1999, Goma.

13. Now a General in the unified Congolese army, the FARDC.

14. Beyond the obvious contemporary parallels (in, say, the Lords Resistance Army in northern Uganda or the Parama insurgency in Mozambique), the Mayi-Mayi phenomenon recalls the 1912 Nyabingi uprising in northern Rwanda (DesForges 1986) and the 1905 Maji-Maji rebellion in Tanzania (Iliffe 1967), a point not lost on some Mayi-Mayi propagandists (Jackson 2003b).

15. For a popular account that is as entertaining as it is informative, see Wrong 2002.

16. Compare, for example, the following two characterizations: "It might be said that contemporary African history began in state collapse, in the famous events associated with the collapse of the colonial state in the Congo (now Zaire)" (Zartman 1995); and "The Democratic Republic of the Congo . . . was not just a failed state in 2002; it was the epitome of the failed state. . . . By any of the conventional yardsticks—declining institutional performance, military indiscipline, harassment of civilians, inability to collect taxes, and governmental spending on public services, notably health and education—Zaire in the

early 1990s stood at the top of the list of Africa's failed states" (Lemarchand 2003:38).

17. See Rotberg 2003:5–9. For another litany, see former UN Security-General Boutros Boutros-Ghali's take: symptoms of state collapse include "the collapse of state institutions, especially the police and judiciary, with resulting paralysis of governance, a breakdown of law and order, and general banditry and chaos. Not only are the functions of government suspended, but its assets are destroyed or looted and experienced officials are killed or flee the country" (cited in Thürer 1999:731).

18. And compare this symptomology with the careful analytical position on Congo/Zaire mapped out by Hebert Weiss: "What is the line between very badly managed and collapsed? According to Zartman, collapse involves the regime falling and 'bring[ing] down with it the power that it has concentrated in its hands,' and the consequent creation of a 'vacuum'. At least up to the time of writing, these are not conditions that prevail in Zaire" (Weiss 1995:158).

19. Which, I cannot resist sniping, seems to depict the D.R. Congo in its pajamas, slumped over a glass of water and two Aspirin, moaning quietly to itself as it nurses the "hangover" induced by one World Bank loan too many.

20. I add this etymology not in order to buy into notions of cultural evolution. Rather, I intend to accentuate the idea that involution involves inventive recycling and reworking, but not necessarily innovation. This suggests, of course, a further twist on *ça semble aller*, glossing it as "things only seem to be developing, but are, instead, involving [i.e., involuting]."

CHAPTER 4. MCGOVERN, THIS IS PLAY

1. See Shipley (this volume) for a parallel discussion of metapragmatic speech in music.

2. In the video for the song, singer DJ Zidane and his band members (in orange jumpsuits) are manhandled by beautiful women in camouflage trousers and tight tank tops who alternate between "menacing" the singer with a Rottweiler and gyrating to the irresistible rhythms along with the band. Clearly these are Zidane's accompanying female dancers, pressed into double (and ironic) service as part of the sexualized eye candy of most *coupé décalé* videos and as players in the mise-en-scène of the prison scenario.

3. From the mid-1960s, Marxists have questioned the foundations of the so-called miracle (Amin 1967; Campbell 1978).

4. The literature on African cities is burgeoning and is one of the most vibrant facets of contemporary Africanist scholarship; see, for example, De Boeck and Plissart 2004; Mbembe and Nuttall 2004; Simone 1997; and Simone and Abouhani 2005.

5. There is considerable debate about what constitutes "youth" in Africa. I opt here for a commonsense demographic definition, which allows us to include people well into their thirties who, because of lack of money or prospects, have frequently not yet married and started families.

6. FESCI's first president, Martial Ahipeaud, was imprisoned by the Houphouët-Boigny government, as Soro and Blé Goudé were by Bédié's government. A photo of Blé Goudé, shackled to a hospital bed during his incarceration in 1999, was on the cover of one of the reggae star Alpha Blondy's albums.

7. See, for instance, the cartoon of President Gbagbo standing before demonstrating "Patriots," expressing surprise that the Patriots seem to be more interested in money than their country's welfare, in *Le Patriote* 2484, January 19, 2008.

8. For a glossary of Nouchi terms, see http://www.nouchi.com.

9. See http://www.nouchi.com.

10. *Gazeur*, or stylish reveler, comes from the Nouchi *gazer*, or to have a good time. The figure of the *gazeur*, like that of the Congolese *sapeur*, is linked to dressing well, dancing, and the overarching aesthetics of stylish fun that falls under the term (used in both contexts) of *ambiancer*.

11. See Konaté 2002:788. In French as in English, the term *given* expresses the double sense of a "datum" and of something granted.

12. See the lyrics from "Premier Gaou" cited above, in which the wily ex-girlfriend plans to *couper* the now-successful singer.

13. For more on *feymen*, see Malaquais 2001. On 419 scams, see Smith 2007.

14. In this lexicon, the everyday work of ordinary people does not earn the name *travailler*, but rather the pejorative *djossi*, as quoted in the lyrics of "Guantanamo" above.

15. The video shows scenes of the couple walking down the Rue Princesse choosing a chicken to be braised in a *maquis* (outdoor bar) and looking at the poster for a Nigerian film they are about to see. It even includes a video within the video staged in the classic 1990s low-budget African music video style, with the four singers standing in downtown Abidjan, signaling their modernity by performing in front of a modern office building.

16. Saga's given name was Stéphane Doukouré (he died in 2006). "Douk" came from his family name and "Saga" from "Sagacité."

17. An interesting bridge between the original "Premier Gaou" video and "Sagacité" and other *coupé décalé* videos is a remake of "Premier Gaou," in which the entire video takes place at a chic nightclub with a multiracial clientele. It could be in Abidjan or Paris, but gone are the rustic images of the protagonists eating street food and barefoot children dancing in a courtyard.

18. The best known of these is probably Erickson le Zulu, a son of Zairois parents who grew up in Abidjan. Not all Zairois/Congolese came to Abidjan to seek European visas, or as musicians. As one of the continent's most cosmopolitan cities, it has long-standing communities from most francophone African countries. The particular Congo-Ivorian *brassage* to which I refer here was, however, emphasized to me by two DJs who work throughout the continent, one of whom is Abidjanais with a Congolese mother, during a discussion in Conakry, October 4, 2008.

19. See Human Rights Watch 2008.

20. I discuss Ivorian ethical evaluation of politics elsewhere (see McGovern 2009).

21. It is worth remembering that the main rebel group in the north originally called itself the Patriotic Movement of Côte d'Ivoire.

22. But see also Simmel 1971 and Habermas on what he calls "dramaturgical action" (1984). A tantalizing parallel also exists between "play" as I am using it in this essay and Susan Sontag's formulation of camp, which she calls "a solvent of morality. It neutralizes moral indignation, sponsors playfulness" (1966:290).

23. These so-called *cours communes* are set up as a series of one- or two-room apartments surrounding a large open courtyard where children play, women cook for their families, and people gather to talk or perhaps watch a television that is brought into the open space for the occasion. Such accommodation is inexpensive, provides an immediate social network for those who have just arrived in the city, and allows parents to keep small children out of the street. Most such courtyards are ethnically heterogeneous.

24. My insistence that they are not puppets does not deny that other factors are indeed relevant; it merely underlines that such explanations are insufficient.

25. For more on the "moral economy of theft" in Abidjan, see Newell 2006.

26. The term is bowdlerized from the title of Lynn Hunt's 1993 work *The Family Romance of the French Revolution*.

CHAPTER 5. SHIPLEY, GHANAIAN PUBLIC CULTURE

ACKNOWLEDGMENTS: This research was conducted with funding from Fulbright-IIE, the Wenner Gren Foundation, and Bard College. I owe a great debt of gratitude to John Comaroff, Jean Comaroff, Beth Povinelli, Tabetha Ewing, Laura Kunreuther, Anne-Maria Makhulu, Brad Weiss, Adeline Masquelier, Misty Bastian, and Diana Brown for critical readings and comments on this work. Portions of this paper were presented in talks at Bard College, Duke University, the University of California, Irvine, Indiana University, New York University, and the Contemporary Anthropology Conference—I must thank those present for their invaluable insight and patience. I also thank Kelvin Asare-Williams, Delali Noviewoo, Ruti Talmor, and Ghana Boy for invaluable research assistance and support, and Kwesi Brown for the translations of song lyrics. This research would not have been possible without the insight, support, and creativity of Reggie Rockstone and Sidney. I must also thank John Collins, Dhoruba Bin Wahad, the Mobile Boys, Paa Kwesi Holdbrook Smith, Goodies, Panji Anoff, the National Theatre of Ghana, and Metro TV. Small portions of this chapter were previously published in my essay "Aesthetic of the Entrepreneur: Afro-Cosmopolitan Rap and Moral Circulation in Accra, Ghana," *Anthropological Quarterly* 82:3(2009), and reused here with permission. For more information on hiplife music and culture, interested readers may consult my Web site, http://www.livingthehiplife.com.

1. Since the early twentieth century, vaudeville, jazz, rhythm and blues, reggae, and gospel have influenced and combined with local performance traditions in the making and remaking of popular West African musical forms.

2. Tricia Rose and others have argued that American hip-hop has "an [ambivalent] 'focus on consumption,' offer[ing] an alternative means of attaining status for urban African-American and Latino youth who face unemployment, racism, and marginalization in a post-industrial economy" (Tricia Rose in Maira 2000:333). For African youth, hip hop presents performative authority in terms of ambivalence towards individuated success and cosmopolitanism. In the neoliberal moment, then, local and global racial politics are often articulated in terms of individual accumulation and consumption rather than collective political movements. I address these issues at length in other writing.

3. Interview with Panji Anoff, Accra, Ghana, December 2004.

4. A staple food made from mashed cassava or yam and sold on the streets wrapped in corn husks or banana leaves.

5. Another way new freedoms of expression and movement were manifest was through a marked increase in seemingly diverse forms of public violence, from armed robbery to rioting at entertainment events before and after the 2000 elections (Shipley 2003). These violent incidents were often seen as an extreme response by Ghanaians to years in which forums for public expression were absent. As one radio commentator said, "Some people think that individual freedom means they can do and take whatever they want" (Radio Universe, February 10, 2000).

6. Kwesi Boateng, private correspondence, November 2000.

7. The question of language choice and code switching is a major part of the development of the musical genre. Older popular highlife music was dominated by Akan and Ga with some pidgin. Native Funk Lords were one of the first hip-hop/hiplife groups in the early 1990s to experiment with African languages and rap. The use of pidgin was more prevalent during that period in the development of the music. As hiplife evolved, by 1999 most popular songs, while they might include pidgin and English, were primarily sung and rapped in Akan, Ga, Ewe, or other African languages.

8. Indeed, the opposition boycotted the 1996 parliamentary elections, leading to an overwhelming majority for the NDC.

9. Elsewhere (Shipley n.d.) I focus more explicitly on clothing style and bodily affect in hiplife, especially in the making of the genre during the 1990s. Weiss (2002) has addressed hip-hop styles in Tanzania as markers of fantasies of modernity for urban youth. For descriptions of the political implications of style see especially Hebdige 1996 and Comaroff 1985.

10. Formal interview with Esi Sutherland Addy, Accra, Ghana, December 2004.

11. Elsewhere (Shipley n.d.) I address more directly the musical aspects of hiplife music and its multiple instrumental, vocal, and technological influences. Collins (1994) and Chernoff (1979) show that popular West African

highlife and Afrobeat music can draw on the communicative styles of talking drums to musically communicate proverbial messages.

12. Metalanguage about the use of speech and bodily control are also central aspects of public authority. Political discourse often revolves around discussing how the power of language is mobilized. Yankah (1995) shows how language is understood to be efficacious. A chief's curse is "believed capable of causing madness" (Yankah 1995:19). Conversely, the chief is put in danger through the power of direct words, insults, or profane acts which the Okyeame buffers him against (ibid.).

13. Personal interview with Bob Vanns, Arts Cenre, Accra, January 1998.

14. Personal interview with Nana Ampadu, Accra, November 2000.

15. See Bauman's (1995) discussions on performance and the production of tradition through performance (traditionalization).

16. K. Anyidoho (1983) and A. Anyidoho (1994) have written about the moral, critical, and aesthetic roles of oral poetry in various contemporary and traditional Ghanaian societies.

17. As Jean Comaroff (1985) demonstrates, African Christian movements and their ritual, performative, or poetic force need to be examined not simply in terms of public visibility or demographic rise increase but in the contexts of the history of colonialism, political power, and cultural formations.

18. Elsewhere I discuss the gendered aspects of hiplife music (Shipley n.d.). Many songs focus on the consumption of female sexuality by men as both a condition and sign of their economic success. I show how this music reinforces older hierarchies of gendered public speaking.

19. Hiplife practices provide both forms of agency and forms of discipline. Hiplife operates at the junctures of local theories of language use, state authority, and transnational networks of capital and black diasporic imaginaries. Here liberal agency articulates through sensual bodily experience and its metaphoric portrayal. Youth engage in popular practices purportedly in contrast to, but rather in dialogue with, state political authority and its various forms of nationalist performative displays and technologies. Popular culture, then, presents a set of disciplinary practices that articulate its actors with broader forms of transnational power, outside of state control (Ong 1999, 2006). Though the neoliberal state continues to demarcate how power is enacted, naturalized, and contested and how popular culture and ideas of free expression operate (Comaroff 2002).

20. In the context of the postcolony, metaphors of performance have become prevalent ways to interpret the contingencies of politics and daily life, though often with multiple implications. At the root of Mbembe's (2001) work—from his more grounded analyses of vulgarity, the reversals of power, and performance in Cameroon to his more recent synthetic efforts to describe an ontology of the creative and politically redemptive African subject—there is a surprisingly similarity to a romanticized Kantian subject: unified, self-actualizing, and implicitly dependent on the state and its civil protections for its sense of becoming. However, he brings into dialogue the hopes and disappointments of collective political opposition and individual creative action that

is central to daily survival in the contemporary world, in order to argue for the inchoate force of the self-producing individual.

21. Translated by Kwesi Brown with additional assistance from the author.

CHAPTER 6. SCHULZ, RELIGIOUS DEVOTION IN MALI

1. Union Nationale des Femmes Musulmanes du Mali.

2. Office de la Radio et Télévision du Mali.

3. Alpha Konaré and his party, ADEMA, won the first democratic elections in 1992 and were reelected in 1997. In June 2002 Colonel Toumani Touré, the leader of the military putsch of 1991, was elected president.

4. Unless indicated otherwise, all local terms are rendered in Bamanakan, the lingua franca of southern Mali.

5. Muslim activists generally refer to this quest as an attempt to "move closer to God" (ka magrè ala la). Only those literate in Arabic (occasionally) use the Arabic term da'wa to refer to their "invitation" of others to join the moral reform movement.

6. Because the public proclamation of their renewed faith is central to these women's self-understanding, I will refer to them as "women activists" or simply as "Muslim women."

7. In Senegal and Nigeria, Muslim authorities owed their crucial positions of political brokerage in the colonial system to the political standing their lineages had held prior to colonial occupation. In Mali, in contrast, the political influence of religious lineages was limited to some urban areas, among them Segu, Nioro du Sahel, Kayes, Djenne, and Timbuktu.

8. For a critique of Habermas's normative, gender, and class-specific conception of the public, see Fraser 1992; and Landes 1995; also see Smart 1992; Bloch 1995; and Davidoff 1998.

9. According to Göle (2002), women shape political processes by publicly displaying their Muslim faith, and by engaging in corporeal practices that go against the Western-modeled, modernist, and liberal division (separation) between individual pious self-making and secular public issues.

10. The existing historical and ethnographic documentation tends to focus on women affiliated with Sufi orders and thereby reflects the "Sufi bias" typical of scholarship on Islam in West Africa (see Triaud 1986a; Boyd and Last 1985; Boyd 1989; Sule and Starrat 1991; Reveyrand-Coulon 1993; Asma'u 1997; also see Constantin 1987; Dunbar 2000). The excellent research on female Murid activities conducted by Coulon (1988) and Rosander (1997, 1998, and 2003) is representative of this tendency. It offers invaluable insights into the significant support of Sufi leaders by female acolytes. But the question remains how representative the activities of women who are organized around the "holy clan" of individual brotherhoods are for the mass of Muslim women whose affiliation with a brotherhood is loose at best. It is therefore difficult to ascertain to what extent female Muslim activists' understandings of religious subjectivity present a rupture with earlier practices.

11. This observation is based on my own oral historical research on female religious practice in the period between 1920 and 1950 and on Sanankoua 1991.

12. The representatives of this reformist thought were labeled "Wahhabi" by colonial administrators, and still by many people today, although they understand themselves simply as "Sunnis" (or Ahl al-Sunna, Arabic, "the people of the Sunna"), that is, those who follow the regulations and doings of the prophet Mohammad.

13. For sustained analyses of these dynamics, see Amselle 1977, 1985; Kaba 1974; Harrison 1988; Triaud 1997; Launay and Soares 1999; Brenner 2001; and Soares 2005.

14. President Keïta's secularist policy sought to neutralize the influence of Muslim leaders on local politics and, in keeping with the French principle of *laïcité,* treated Islam as private conviction.

15. For example, a greater share of broadcasting time was reserved for Muslim religious programs than for those of Christians.

16. Association Malienne pour l'Unité et le Progrès de l'Islam.

17. The *arabisants* soon occupied leading posts in the state bureaucracy, thereby entering into open competition with representatives of the Sufi orders and the older generation of "Sunni" merchants.

18. Alliance pour la Démocratie au Mali.

19. In contrast to Côte d'Ivoire and Senegal, where many activist groups are geared toward adolescents of different economic and educational background (see, e.g., Miran 1998; LeBlanc 1999; Augis 2002), in Mali groups for married women predominate, and comparatively few groups address the urban youth (Sanankoua 1991; cf. Hock 1998). The Malian associations in Mali thus resemble Islamic associations in Niger that similarly mobilize primarily adult women (Alidou 2005; also see Glew 1996).

20. By cutting across kinship and ethnic divisions (see LeBlanc 2000; Launay and Miran 2000), the groups diverge from urban networks that emerged in the colonial period and were organized along neighborhood or ethnic ties (see, e.g., Meillassoux 1968).

21. Their view is shared by many urbanites, even by those who look upon "Muslim women" with scorn. They find Muslim women's groups more credible than the credit and saving associations (*tontines*) created in response to the structural adjustment programs of the 1980s.

22. These controversies are, ultimately, about whether political and social life should be reformed according to "Islamic principles" (however diversely defined), or whether Islam should be treated as private faith (Schulz 2003).

23. From the Arabic *mawlid al-nabi.*

24. The fact that most female participants in the moral reform movement do not define their moral quest by denouncing (what are generally referred to as) "traditional" readings of Islam and their representatives, the lineages of Sufi leaders and other religious specialists, opens up an interesting contrast to neighboring countries such as Senegal and Niger. Here, supporters of Islamic moral renewal seem to emphasize their distance from practices

and beliefs associated with local traditions of Islam (Masquelier 1999; Augis 2002). Although similar attitudes have been reported for earlier generations of Muslim activists in Mali (Amselle 1985), these are not prominent among "Muslim women." The relationship of the latter to local traditional Islam and to "reformist" influences from Egypt and Saudi Arabia are so diverse that it would be problematic to characterize them in terms of an opposition to Sufi-related religious traditions.

25. *Ibadat*, in the narrower sense of the term, refers to the prescribed activities of worship, in particular to those representing the "five pillars" of a believer's enactment of faith. In a broader sense, *ibadat* encompasses a variety of daily mundane and ritual acts, all of which should express a believer's "submission" (the literal meaning of Islam) to God's will (Bowen 1989:600).

26. *Alasira* is commonly translated into French as "religion." Although the metaphor resonates with the Sufi notion of "path," I never witnessed a teacher or follower explicitly establishing this connection.

27. For the different importance that teachers and followers attribute to a believer's attitude, as opposed to the application of rules of proper conduct, see Schulz 2004.

28. In this new conceptualization of Muslim faith, influences from earlier intellectual trends in Saudi Arabia merge with Salafi-Sunni revivalist tendencies in contemporary Egypt (see Triaud 1986b; Mahmood 2005).

29. Male-female relations are characterized by ambiguous patterns of dependency and influence. These patterns, and gender-specific standards of conduct, are shaped by status and age-specific notions of "respect," "honor," and "shame," all of which pertain to a broader discursive system that defines age and rank difference and other forms of social inequality (Schulz 2001). Although men and women are associated with distinct spheres of social activity and moral responsibility, domestic politics are messier than this neat mapping of gender roles suggests. The notion of *taafefanga* ("wrap power") is at the heart of equivocal constructions of female powers because it presents a woman's sexual and procreative capacities as the source of her influence within and outside the family. In current public debate, recurrent references to *taafefanga* reflect men's and women's ambivalent feelings toward developments that render the ideal of female acquiescence to male family authority impracticable.

30. Muslim women and men often advance differential and contending constructions of the ways in which women should make personal ethics relevant to communal life. While most men and some women limit women's leading role to pious conduct and ritual performance, there are a few Muslim women who struggle to participate in debates on proper (female) Muslimhood. Their competing views of female moral and political responsibility bring forth tensions within the Islamic revivalist camp, which, among other dimensions, result from the different extents to which Muslim activists integrate the political aspirations of Western-oriented intellectuals and feminists.

31. In southern Mali, where most people only converted to Islam during the colonial period, the practice of *zeli* allowed people (and colonial administra-

tors) to establish a three-tiered classification, distinguishing between those who belonged to families of religious specialists and were "instructed" or were "scribes" (*kalimutigi*, from *kalimu*, "feather," and *tigi*, "owner"). This group was contrasted to regular Muslims, that is, "those who pray" (*minw bè zeli kè*), and to pagans. Members of religious lineages expressed their affiliation with a particular Sufi order through additional prayers and the recitation of special litanies and verses from the Qur'an.

32. For an instructive parallel to modernist conceptions of proper Muslim practice formulated by Acehnese leaders in Indonesia, see Bowen 1989:600–604. In contrast to the strongly communal character of congregational worship, *zeli* has conventionally been understood as worship that establishes a direct communication with God. Numerous Malian Muslims also seek the assistance of religious specialists to engage in another form of individual communication with God, the petitionary prayer (*du'a*). The common acceptance of mediators who, *qua* their special spiritual powers (*baraka*), are suited best to increase the efficiency of petitionary prayer, shows traces of West African Sufi-related notions of spiritual authority.

33. Most Muslim women mix designs and accessories, so the different varieties presented in the following discussion should be considered ideal types rather than neatly distinguishable styles.

34. Most women in town have a least one set of better quality "city" clothes, which they don whenever they go out. While at home, they dress in everyday clothes, which are often worn or bleached out. As LeBlanc (2000:448) observes with respect to female dress fashion in Bouaké, Côte d'Ivoire, this distinction indicates an emphasis on the public "display function" of dress.

35. The headscarf (wrapped as a turban around the head so as to cover a woman's hair) and a skirt that covers the legs below the knee are the most important indications of a woman's marital status and of more advanced age. Some young unmarried women wear this kind of gown too. These are often women who are about to get married, but among them there are also a growing number of single mothers who have been unable to find husbands. These women "stretch the limits" of dress as a marker of female (married) status to accommodate a position of postponed womanhood.

36. Comparatively few women wear black scarves that cover the face except for the eyes. These women are usually from families with close ties to the Arab-speaking world. Their apparel is often considered (by members of the reform movement and its critics) as a sign of "radicalism" and of a culturally foreign, Arab influence.

37. Many women who travel in a bus or ride a motorcycle combine their various local or Western-style robes with a headscarf wrapped around head and neck, to protect themselves from dust and exhaust.

38. Prior to the 1980s, the draping of an additional scarf over the head and shoulders indicated a woman's respectability and advanced age. Nowadays, in contrast, as a consequence of a broad movement towards Islamic moral reform, the symbolic significance of a tightly wrapped headscarf has changed but

remains an issue of controversy. People who are critical of Muslim activists tend to associate a closely wrapped prayer shawl with lower-class status, analphabetism, the conservative outlook of "old" women, and intellectual rigidity. To those who look more favorably upon Muslim women's moral cause, wearing a closely wrapped prayer shawl expresses a claim to a special status, a status no longer based on age but on morality.

39. Until the 1980s, a woman adopted plain white apparel to announce her status as "Hadja," that is, having completed the pilgrimage to Mecca. Over the past fifteen years, however, the significance of white dress has broadened.

40. Depending on the degree of ornamentation and the quality of the fabric, the costs range between 12,000 and 150,000 CFA francs (FCFA; 1,000 FCFA = ca. U.S.$0.75 at the time of research).

CHAPTER 7. BUGGENHAGEN, "KILLER BARGAINS"

ACKNOWLEDGMENTS: The research in New York was supported by an NEH Summer Stipend (2005) and in Senegal by the Wenner-Gren Foundation (1999–2000). An earlier draft of this paper was presented at the American Anthropological Association annual meeting in 2004 as part of a panel organized by Charles Piot and Misty Bastian, "Citizenship in Exile," and at the University of Chicago African Studies Workshop conference "Struggling with the State" in May 2004, and in June 2004 at the UCLA Summer Institute on Migration.

1. All names and identifying data have been changed.

2. The USA PATRIOT act stands for "Uniting and Strengthening America by Providing Appropriate Tools Required to Intercept and Obstruct Terrorism Act." It was enacted by Congress and signed by President Bush on October 26, 2001. The 342-page document may be viewed online at http://www.epic.org/privacy/terrorism/hr3162.pdf. There is no definition of the terms "terrorist" or "terrorism" in the act itself.

3. Mourtada Mbacke is now deceased.

4. Luckily, al Hajj Momar's papers were returned to him that day, as a result of his having shown up in court.

5. Dana Thomas, "Terror's Purse Strings," *New York Times* A23, August 30, 2007. See "Are You Funding Terrorism?" February 3, 2003; http://www.whiotv.com/news/1952345/detail.html.

6. For a definitional list of the term "designated foreign terrorist organization," see the U.S. Department of State fact sheet, "Secretary of State Designates Foreign Terrorist Organizations (FTO's)." Available at http://www.state.gov.

7. The 2000 U.S. census shows that 2,136 Senegalese live in New York City. In 1997 Diouf-Kamara (1997) estimated that there were about 8,000 Senegalese living in the United States.

8. See "State Officials Approve Street Vendor Bill," March 1, 2004; available at http://www.lowermanhattan.info/news/downtown/week_in_review_88294.aspx.

9. In 1999 the International Organization for Migration gathered statistics concerning official remittances to Senegal, excluding unofficial transfers outside of state regulation, and put the overall figure at $92 million (International Organization for Migration 2003).

10. See New York State Consolidated Laws, Banking Article XIII-B: Transmitters of Money, Section 641(2)c, licensing requirements.

CHAPTER 8. PIOT, BORDER PRACTICES

1. This is the global lottery system that annually awards up to 50,000 permanent U.S. residency visas to those from countries with low rates of immigration to the United States, especially those in the global South. Applicants apply online and are randomly selected by lottery (in Williamsburg, KY), before submitting themselves to a lengthy process of medical exams and embassy interviews in their home countries. If they successfully jump through all these hoops, they receive a green card and, five years later, a U.S. passport.

2. For instance, in the 2005 Diversity Visa Lottery (DV-2005), 2,857 Togolese were selected while only 233 Béninois were chosen—numbers that clearly reflect the size of the applicant pool. In the same year, 53 were chosen from Niger, 76 from Burkina Faso, 321 from Côte d'Ivoire, 1,540 from Cameroon, 3,618 from Kenya, and 3,974 from Ghana. In DV-2006, 2,138 Togolese were selected, while 328 were chosen from Benin, 164 from Burkina Faso, 374 from Côte d'Ivoire, 1,639 from Cameroon, 2,867 from Kenya, and 3,880 from Ghana. In DV-2007, 1,592 Togolese were chosen, and 218 were selected from Benin, 95 from Burkina Faso, 308 from Côte d'Ivoire, 1461 from Cameroon, 2,337 from Kenya, and 3,088 from Ghana. These data are available at http://travel .state.gov by searching on the term "visa bulletin" and relevant abbreviation, e.g., "DV-2005." The lottery drawing takes place six to eight months after the completion of online registration in early December, with the embassy interview following up to sixteen months after the drawing. Thus, those in the DV-2007 pool applied in fall 2005, were chosen by lottery in late spring 2006, and went for the embassy interview in 2007.

3. The visa lottery system might also be seen, in Jean-François Bayart's terms, as an example of "extraversion." Thus, Bayart (1989) suggests that African political actors have long embraced, appropriated, internalized, hybridized, and resignified what lies beyond the local (the colonial, the European, the modern, the global), recycling and putting such outsides to use for their own political ends.

4. By "entrepreneur" I mean someone who helps others apply for the lottery and then helps winners prepare their dossiers for departure.

5. I also draw on conversations and interviews I have had with dozens of Togolese lottery applicants and winners on both sides of the Atlantic, as well as with three consular officials at the U.S. Embassy in Lomé who are responsible for interviewing winners before they are granted visas. Given the sensitive

semi- and extralegal nature of the material presented, I have used pseudonyms throughout the text to protect the anonymity of all individuals.

6. In volume 1 of *Capital*, Marx (1990 [1867]) distinguishes an economy based on "use-value" from one based on "exchange-value" and the commodity form. Whereas the aim of economic exchange in the former is the conversion of one use-value into another, either directly through barter (C-C) or indirectly through currency-mediated exchange (C-M-C)—selling in order to buy, and buying in order to consume—economic exchange in the latter aims to convert use-values into exchange-values (M-C-M)—buying in order to sell—and, in its purest form, the conversion of money into more money (M-M'). While the economy of the witch in the area of northern Togo where I have worked has long been organized around the idiom of consumption—witches kill and "consume" their victims in night markets—its logic has recently shifted to one based more on exchange and the acquisition of money. Witches' victims are no longer consumed but are rather sold and resold to acquire money. This echoes the logic of expanded commodity exchange under advanced capitalism.

7. The low incidence of winners who actually go for the embassy interview—only 1,500 out of 3,000—is largely due to the high cost of the interview fee, the medical exam, and the plane ticket. If a winner is unable to draw on family or friends in the diaspora for help, it is unlikely they will be able to afford these finances alone. In addition, those winners who fail the medical exam, because they have AIDS or some other very serious medical condition, are barred from obtaining visas altogether.

References Cited

Achebe, Chinua
    1989   *A Man of the People: A Novel.* New York: Anchor Books [1967].
Agamben, Giorgio
    1998   *Homo Sacer: Sovereign Power and Bare Life.* Stanford, CA: Stanford University Press.
    2005   *State of Exception.* Chicago: University of Chicago Press.
Agence France-Presse
    2002   "Une Dissidence de la rébellion veut une vice-présidence à Kinshasa." Brussels, August 31.
Akin, David, and Joel Robbins
    1999   *Money and Modernity: State and Local Currencies in Melanesia.* Pittsburgh, PA: University of Pittsburgh Press.
Akindes, Simon
    2002   "Playing It 'Loud and Straight': Reggae, Zouglou, Mapouka, and Youth Insubordination in Côte d'Ivoire." In *Playing with Identities in Contemporary Music in Africa*, M. Palmberg, ed. Uppsala: Nordiska Afrikainstitutet.
Alidou, Ousseina
    2005   *Engaging Modernity: Muslim Women and the Politics of Agency in Postcolonial Niger.* Madison, WI: University of Wisconsin Press.
Amateau, Albert
    2003   "Police Commander Takes Over Chinatown Precinct." *Downtown Express* [New York] 16(19):7–13.
Amin, Samir
    1967   *Le Développement du capitalisme en Côte d'Ivoire.* Paris: Editions de Minuit.
    1976   *Unequal Development: An Essay on the Social Formations of Peripheral Capitalism.* New York: Monthly Review Press.

Amselle, Jean-Loup

1971   "Parenté et commerce chez les Kookoro." In *Development of Indigenous Trade and Markets in West Africa,* Claude Meillassoux, ed. London: Oxford University Press.

1977   *Les Négociants de la Savane.* Paris: Editions Anthropos.

1985   "Le Wahhabisme à Bamako (1945–1985)." *Canadian Journal of African Studies* 19(2):345–57.

Anyidoho, Akosua

1994   "Tradition and Innovation in Nnwonkoro, an Akan Female Verbal Genre." *Research in African Literatures* 25(3):141–59.

Anyidoho, Kofi

1983   "Oral Poetics and Traditions of Verbal Art in Africa." Ph.D. diss., University of Texas, Austin.

Appadurai, Arjun

1999   "Dead Certainty: Ethnic Violence in the Era of Globalization." In *Globalization and Identity: Dialectics of Flow and Closure,* Birgit Meyer and Peter Geschiere, eds. Oxford: Blackwell Publishers.

Apter, Andrew

1999   "IBB=419: Nigerian Democracy and the Politics of Illusion." In *Civil Society and the Political Imagination in Africa: Critical Perspectives,* John L. Comaroff and Jean Comaroff, eds. Chicago: University of Chicago Press.

2005   *The Pan-African Nation: Oil and the Spectacle of Culture in Nigeria.* Chicago: University of Chicago Press.

Arendt, Hannah

1994   *The Origins of Totalitarianism.* New York: Harvest Book, Harcourt, Inc. [1951].

Arrighi, Giovanni

1994   *The Long Twentieth Century: Money, Power, and the Origins of Our Times.* New York: Verso.

2002   "The African Crisis: World Systematic and Regional Aspects." *New Left Review* 15:5–36. Available at http://newleftreview. org/A2387.

Asad, Talal

2003   *Formations of the Secular: Christianity, Islam, Modernity.* Stanford, CA: Stanford University Press.

Ashforth, Adam

2001   *Madumo: A Man Bewitched.* Chicago: University of Chicago Press.

2005   *Witchcraft, Violence, and Democracy in South Africa.* Chicago: University of Chicago Press.

Asma'u, Nana

1997   *Collected Works of Nana Asma'u, Daughter of Usman dan Fodio*, Jean Boyd and Beverly Mack, eds. East Lansing: Michigan State University Press.

Augis, Erin

2002   "Dakar's Sunnite Women: The Politics of Person." Ph.D. diss., University of Chicago.

Babou, Cheikh Anta

2002   "Brotherhood Solidarity, Education and Migration: The Role of the Dahiras among the Murid Muslim Community of New York." *African Affairs* 101:151–70.

Bakary, Tessy

1997   "Political Polarization over Governance in Côte d'Ivoire." In *Governance as Conflict Management: Politics and Violence in West Africa*, I. William Zartman, ed. Washington, DC: Brookings Institution Press.

Bakhtin, M. M.

1986   *Speech Genres and Other Late Essays.* Austin: University of Texas Press.

Banégas, Richard

2006   "Côte D'Ivoire: Patriotism, Ethnonationalism and Other African Modes of Self-Writing." *African Affairs* 105(421):535–52.

Barber, Karin

1987   "Popular Arts in Africa." *African Studies Review* 30(3):1–78.

1997   "Preliminary Notes on Audiences in Africa." *Africa* 67(3):347–62.

Bassiouni, M. Cherif

2004   "Don't Tread on Me: Is the War on Terror Really a War on Rights?" In *Civil Rights in Peril*, Elaine C. Hagopian, ed. Chicago: Haymarket Books and Pluto Press.

Bateson, Gregory

1972   "A Theory of Play and Fantasy." In *Steps to an Ecology of Mind*. New York: Ballantine Books.

Bauberot, Jean

1998   "The Two Thresholds of Laicization." In *Secularism and Its Critics*, R. Bhargava, ed. New York: Oxford University Press.

Baudrillard, Jean

1996   *The System of Objects.* London: Verso.

1998   *The Consumer Society: Myths and Structures.* London: Sage

Bauman, Richard, and Charles Briggs

1990   "Poetics and Performance as Critical Perspectives on Language and Social Life." *Annual Review of Anthropology* 19:59–88.

Bayart, Jean-François

1989   *L'Etat en Afrique: La Politique du ventre.* Paris: Fayard.

1993   *The State in Africa: The Politics of the Belly.* Translated by
            Mary Harper, Christopher Harrison, and Elizabeth Harrison.
            London: Longman. [Translation of Bayart 1989.]

2000   "Africa in the World: A History of Extraversion." *African
            Affairs* 99(395):217–67.

Bayart, Jean-Francois, Stephen Ellis, and Béatrice Hibou

1999   *The Criminalization of the State in Africa.* Oxford: James
            Currey.

Beck, Linda

2008   *Brokering Democracy in Africa: The Rise of a Clientelist
            Democracy in Senegal.* New York: Palgrave.

Benjamin, Walter

1999   *The Arcades Project.* Trans. Howard Eiland and Kevin
            McLaughlin. Cambridge, MA: Belknap Press of Harvard
            University Press.

Bernstein, Michael André

1992   *Bitter Carnival: Ressentiment and the Abject Hero.* Prince-
            ton, NJ: Princeton University Press.

Bernstein, Nina

2004   "Immigrants Face Loss of Licenses in ID Crackdown." *New
            York Times,* August 19, B1.

Bernstein, Peter L.

2005   *Capital Ideas: The Improbable Origins of Modern Wall
            Street.* New York: John Wiley & Sons.

Bhargava, Rajeev, ed.

1998   *Secularism and Its Critics.* New York: Oxford University
            Press.

Bilton, Richard

2006   "Migrants Flock to Tenerife." *BBC News,* September 15,
            digital video. Available at http://www.bbc.co.uk.

Bloch, Ruth

1995   "The Gendered Meaning of Virtue in Revolutionary America."
            In *Rethinking the Political: Gender, Resistance, and the
            State,* Barbara Laslett, Johanna Brenner, and Yesim Arat, eds.
            Chicago: University of Chicago Press.

Blunt, Robert

2004   "'Satan Is an Imitator': Kenya's Recent Cosmology of Corrup-
            tion." In *Producing African Futures: Ritual and Reproduction
            in a Neoliberal Age,* Brad Weiss, ed. Leiden: Brill.

Bond, Patrick

2000   *Cities of Gold, Townships of Coal: Essays on South Africa's
            New Urban Crisis.* Lawrenceville, NJ: Africa World Press.

2006a   *Looting Africa: The Economics of Exploitation.* London: Zed
            Books.

2006b   "Reconciliation and Economic Reaction: Flaws in South
Africa's Elite Transition." *Journal of International Affairs*
60(1):141–56.

Bop, Codou

2005   "Roles and the Position of Women in Sufi Brotherhoods in
Senegal." *Journal of the American Academy of Religion*
73(4):1099–1119.

Bornstein, Avram

2005   "Antiterrorist Policing in New York City after 9/11: Comparing
Perspectives on a Complex Process." *Human Organization*
64(1):52–61.

Bowen, John

1989   "Salat in Indonesia: The Social Meaning of an Islamic Ritual."
Man 24(4):600–619.

Boyd, Jean

1989   *The Caliph's Sister: Nana Asma'u (1793–1865), Teacher, Poet,
and Islamic Leader.* London: Cass.

Boyd, Jean, and Murray Last

1985   "The Role of Women as 'Agents Religieux' in Sokoto."
Canadian Journal of African Studies 19(2):283–300.

Brenner, Louis

1993   "Constructing Muslim Identities in Mali." In *Muslim Identity
and Social Change in Subsaharan Africa,* Louis Brenner, ed.
Bloomington: Indiana University Press, 59–78.

2001   *Controlling Knowledge: Religion, Power, and Schooling
in a West African Muslim Society.* Bloomington: Indiana
University Press.

Burawoy, Michael, Pavel Krotov, and Tatyana Lytkina

2000   "Involution and Destitution in Capitalist Russia." *Ethnography*
1(1):43–65.

Bush, George W.

2004   Remarks by the President on the USA PATRIOT Act. Hershey
Lodge and Convention Center, Hershey, PA, April 19.

Callaghy, Thomas M.

1984   *The State-Society Struggle: Zaire in Comparative Perspective.* New York: Columbia University Press.

Callaghy, Thomas M., and John Ravenhill (Dennis Michael), eds

1993   *Hemmed In: Responses to Africa's Economic Decline.* New
York: Columbia University Press.

Campbell, Bonnie

1978   "The Ivory Coast." In *West African States: Failure and
Promise,* John Dunn, ed. Cambridge: Cambridge University
Press.

Carrier, J.
1991   "Gifts, Commodities and Social Relations: A Maussian View
            of Exchange." *Social Analysis* 6(1):119–36.
Carter, Donald Martin
1997   *States of Grace: Senegalese in Italy and the New European
            Immigration.* Minneapolis: University of Minnesota Press.
Casanova, José
1994   *Public Religions in the Modern World.* Chicago: University
            of Chicago Press.
Castells, Manuel
1996   *The Rise of the Network Society.* Cambridge, MA: Blackwell.
Ceuppens, Bambi, and Peter Geschiere
2005   "Autochthony: Local or Global? New Modes in the Struggle
            over Citizenship and Belonging in Africa and Europe."
            Annual Review of Anthropology 34:385–407.
Chakrabarty, Dipesh
2000   *Provincializing Europe: Postcolonial Thought and Historical
            Difference.* Princeton, NJ: Princeton University Press.
Chaskalson, Matthew, Karen Jochelson, and Jeremy Seekings
1987   "Rent Boycotts, the State, and the Transformation of the
            Urban Political Economy in South Africa." *Review of African
            Political Economy* 40:47–64.
Chatterjee, Partha
1993   *The Nation and Its Fragments: Colonial and Postcolonial
            Histories.* Princeton, NJ: Princeton University Press.
Chauveau, Jean-Pierre
2000   "La Question foncière en Côte d'Ivoire et le coup d'état; Ou,
            Comment remettre à zéro le compteur de l'histoire." Unpub-
            lished manuscript.
Chernoff, John
1979   *African Rhythm and African Sensibility: Aesthetics and
            Social Action in African Musical Idioms.* Chicago: University
            of Chicago Press.
Cinar, Alev
1998   "Bodies, Places and Time: Islamic Visibilities in the Public
            Sphere and the Contestants of Secular Modernity in Turkey."
            Ph.D. diss., University of Pennsylvania.
Clapham, Christopher
1998   Introduction to *African Guerillas,* C. Clapham, ed. Oxford:
            James Currey.
Coghlan, Benjamin, Richard J. Brennan, Pascal Ngoy, et al.
2006   "Mortality in the Democratic Republic of Congo: A Nation-
            wide Survey." *The Lancet* 367:44–51.

Cohen, Abner

1971   "Cultural Strategies in the Organization of Trading Diasporas."
              In *The Development of Indigenous Trade and Markets in West
              Africa*, Claude Meillassoux, ed. London: Oxford University
              Press.

Cole, Catherine M.

1997   "'This Is Actually a Good Interpretation of Modern Civilisa-
              tion:' Popular Theatre and the Social Imaginary in Ghana,
              1946–66." *Africa* 67(3):363–388.

2001   *Ghana's Concert Party Theatre*. Bloomington: Indiana
              University Press.

Collins, Daryl, Jonathan Morduch, Stuart Rutherford, and Orlando Ruthven

2009   *Portfolios of the Poor*. Princeton, NJ: Princeton University
              Press.

Collins, John

1994   *Highlife Time*. Accra: Anansesem Publications Limited.

Comaroff, Jean

1985   *Body of Power, Spirit of Resistance: The Culture and History
              of a South African People*. Chicago: University of Chicago
              Press.

Comaroff, Jean, and John L. Comaroff

1999a   "Occult Economies and the Violence of Abstraction: Notes
              from the South African Postcolony." *American Ethnologist*
              26(2):279–303.

1999b   "Alien-Nation: Zombies, Immigrants, and Millennial Capital-
              ism." *South Atlantic Quarterly* 101(4):779–805.

2000   "Millennial Capitalism: First Thoughts on a Second Coming."
              Public Culture 12(2):291–343.

2004   "Criminal Obsessions, after Foucault: Postcoloniality, Policing,
              and the Metaphysics of Disorder." *Critical Inquiry* 30(4):
              800–824.

2006   "Figuring Crime: Quantifacts and the Production of the Un/
              Real." *Public Culture* 18(1):209–46.

Comaroff, John L.

2002   "Governmentality, Materiality, Legality, Modernity: On the
              Colonial State in Africa." In *African Modernities: Entangled
              Meanings in Current Debate*, Jan-Georg Deutsch, Peter
              Probst, and Heike Schmidt, eds. Portsmouth, NH: Heinemann.

Comaroff, John L., and Jean Comaroff

1997   *Of Revelation and Revolution, Volume 2: The Dialectics of
              Modernity on a South African Frontier*. Chicago: University
              of Chicago Press.

1999   *Civil Society and the Political Imagination in Africa: Critical
              Perspectives*. Chicago: University of Chicago Press.

Constantin, François
1987   "Condition féminine et dynamique confrérique en Afrique
            orientale." *Islam et Sociétés au Sud du Sahara* 1:58–69.
Coombe, Rosemary, and Paul Stoller
1994   "X Marks the Spot: The Ambiguities of African Trading in
            the Commerce of the Black Public Sphere." *Public Culture*
            7:249–74.
Coulon, Christian
1988   "Women, Islam, and Baraka." In *Charisma and Brotherhood
            in African Islam*, Donal B. Cruise O'Brien and Christian
            Coulon, eds. Oxford: Clarendon Press.
Creevey, Lucy, Richard Vengroff, and Ibrahima Gaye
1995   "Devaluation of the CFA Franc in Senegal: The Reaction
            of Small Business." *Journal of Modern African Studies*
            33(4):669–83.
Cruise O'Brien, Donal B.
1971   *The Mourides of Senegal: The Political and Economic Orga-
            nization of an Islamic Brotherhood*. Oxford: Clarendon Press.
1988   "Charisma Comes to Town: Mouride Urbanization, 1945–86."
            In *Charisma and Brotherhood in African Islam*, Donal B.
            Cruise O'Brien and Christian Coulon, eds. Oxford: Clarendon
            Press.
Curtin, Philip D.
1975   *Economic Change in Pre-Colonial Africa: Senegambia in
            the Era of the Slave Trade*. Madison: University of Wisconsin
            Press.
Das, Satyajit
2006   *Traders, Guns and Money: Knowns and Unknowns in the
            Dazzling World of Derivatives*. New York: Financial Times
            Prentice Hall.
Das, Veena, and Deborah Poole, eds.
2004   *Anthropology in the Margins of the State*. Santa Fe, NM:
            School of American Research.
Davidoff, Leonore
1998   "Regarding Some 'Old Husbands' Tales': Public and Private in
            Feminist History." In *Feminism, the Public and the Private*,
            J. Landes, ed. Oxford and New York: Oxford University Press.
Davis, Mike
2006   *Planet of Slums*. New York: Verso.
De Boeck, Filip
1996   "Postcolonialism, Power and Identity: Local and Global
            Perspectives from Zaire." In *Postcolonial Identities in Africa*,
            Richard Werbner and Terence Ranger, eds. London: Zed Books.
1998   "Domesticating Diamonds and Dollars: Identity, Expenditure
            and Sharing in Southwestern Zaire (1984–1997)." *Development
            and Change* 29(4):777–810.

1999 "Domesticating Diamonds and Dollars: Identity, Expenditure and Sharing in Southwestern Zaire (1984–1997)." In *Globalization and Identity: Dialectics of Flow and Closure*, Birgit Meyer and Peter Geschiere, eds. Oxford: Blackwell Publishers.

De Boeck, Filip, and M.-F. Plissart
2004 *Kinshasa: Tales of the Invisible City*. Ghent: Ludion.

de Certeau, Michel
1984 *The Practice of Everyday Life*. Berkeley and Los Angeles: University of California Press.

Derrida, Jacques
1994 *Specters of Marx: The State of the Debt, the Work of Mourning, and the New International*. New York: Routledge.

Desai, Ashwin, and Richard Pithouse
2004 "'What Stank in the Past is the Present's Perfume': Dispossession, Resistance, and Repression in Mandela Park." *The South Atlantic Quarterly* 103(4):841–75.

DesForges, Alison
1986 "The Drum Is Greater Than the Shout: The 1912 Rebellion in Northern Rwanda." In *Banditry, Rebellion and Social Protest in Africa*, Donald Crummey, ed. London: James Currey.

de Soto, Hernando
2000 *The Mystery of Capital: Why Capitalism Triumphs in the West and Fails Everywhere Else*. New York: Basic Books.

Diop, Momar Coumba
1981 "Fonctions et activités des dahira Mourides urbains (Sénégal)." *Cahiers d'études africaines* 20(1–3):79–91.

Diouf, Mamadou
2000 "The Senegalese Murid Trade Diaspora and the Making of a Vernacular Cosmopolitanism." *Public Culture* 12(3):679–702.

Diouf, Sylviane
2004 "The West African Paradox." In *Muslims' Place in the American Public Square*, Z. Bukhari, S. Nyang, M. Ahmad, and J. Esposito, eds. Lanham, MD: AltaMira Press.

Diouf-Kamara, Sylviane
1997 "Senegalese In New York: A Model Minority?" *Black Renaissance* 1(2):92.

Dreyfus, Hubert L.
1991 *Being-in-the-World: A Commentary on Heidegger's* Being and Time, *Division I*. Cambridge, MA: MIT Press.

Duffield, Mark
1998 "Aid Policy and Post-Modern Conflict: A Critical Review." Occasional paper, School of Public Policy, department of International Development, University of Birmingham.

Dunbar, Roberta Ann

2000   "Muslim Women in African History." In *The History of Islam in Africa*, N. Levtzion and R. Pouwels, eds. Athens: Ohio University Press.

Duyvendak, Jan Willem

1995   "From Revolution to Involution: The Disappearance of the Gay Movement in France." *Journal of Homosexuality* 29(4):369–85.

Ebin, Victoria

1992   "A la recherche de nouveaux poissons: Stratégies commerciales mourides en temps de crise." *Politique africaine* 45:86–99.

1993   "Les Commerçants mourides à Marseille et à New York." In *Grand commerçants d'Afrique de l'Ouest*, Emmanuel Grégoire and Pascal Labazée, eds. Paris: Karthala-ORSTOM.

Economist

2006   "The Dark Side of Debt: Why It Matters That Markets Are Going Private." *The Economist*, September 23, 11.

Eickelman, Dale

1992   "Mass Higher Education and the Religious Imagination in Contemporary Arab Societies." *American Ethnologist* 19(4):643–55.

2000   "Islam and the Languages of Modernity." *Daedalus* 129(1):119–38.

Ferguson, James

1999   *Expectations of Modernity: Myths and Meanings of Urban Life on the Zambian Copperbelt.* Berkeley and Los Angeles: University of California Press.

2002   "Of Mimicry and Membership: Africans and the 'New World Society.'" *Cultural Anthropology* 17(4):551–69.

2005   "Seeing Like an Oil Company: Space, Security, and Global Capital in Neoliberal Africa." *American Anthropologist* 107(3):377–82.

2006   *Global Shadows: Africa in the Neoliberal World Order.* Durham, NC: Duke University Press.

Fifield, Adam

2002   "The Knockoff Squad." *New York Times*, June 23.

Flynn, Daniel

2007   "Senegal Sees 'Atlantic Dubai' New Beachside Capital." *Reuters Africa*, ay 31. Available at http://www.reuters.com.

Foucault, Michel

1990   *The History of Sexuality, Volume I: An Introduction.* New York: Vintage Books [1978].

Frank, Andre Gunder

1981   *Crisis in the Third World.* New York: Holmes & Meier Publishers.

Fraser, Nancy
1992   "Rethinking the Public Sphere: A Contribution to the Critique
              of Actually Existing Democracy." In *Habermas and the Public
              Sphere*, Craig Calhoun, ed. Cambridge, MA: MIT Press.
Frick McKean, Philip
1989   "Towards a Theoretical Analysis of Tourism: Economic Dual-
              ism and Cultural Involution in Bali." In *Hosts and Guests:
              The Anthropology of Tourism*, Valene L. Smith, ed. Philadel-
              phia: University of Pennsylvania Press.
FRONTEX
2007   HERA III Operation. APRIL 13. http://www.frontex.europa.eu/
              newsroom/news_releases/art21.html.
Fukuyama, Francis
1992   *The End of History and the Last Man*. New York: Free
              Press.
Fullwiley, Duana
Forth-   *The Enculturated Gene: Sickle Cell Health Politics and Bio-
coming   logical Difference in West Africa*. Princeton, NJ: Princeton
              University Press.
Geertz, Clifford
1963   *Agricultural Involution: the Processes of Ecological Change
              in Indonesia*. Berkeley: University of California Press.
1973a   "Thick Description." In *The Interpretation of Cultures*. New
              York: Basic Books.
1973b   "Deep Play: Notes on the Balinese Cockfight." In *The Inter-
              pretation of Cultures*. New York: Basic Books.
1984   "Culture and Social Change: the Indonesian Case." *Man* 19(4):
              511–32.
Geschiere, Peter, and Stephen Jackson
2006   "Autochthony and the Crisis of Citizenship: Democratization,
              Decentralization, and the Politics of Belonging." *African
              Studies Review* 49(2):1–14.
Gifford, Paul
2004   *Ghana's New Christianity: Pentecostalism in a Globalizing
              African Economy*. Bloomington: Indiana University Press.
Glew, Robert
1996   "Islamic Associations in Niger." *Islam and Sociétés au Sud du
              Sahara* 10:187–204.
Glick Schiller, Nina
2004   "Is Freedom Now 'Another Word for Nothing Left to Lose'?
              An Introduction to the Debate about Freedom and Democracy
              in the Age of Neoliberalism." *Identities: Global Studies in
              Culture and Power* 11:89–92.

Godfrey, Hannah
2006   "On a Voyage of Peril to the Mirage of Europe." *The Observer*, November 19. Available at http://www.guardian.co.uk.

Goffman, Erving
1967   "Where the Action Is." In *Interaction Ritual: Essays on Face-to-Face Behavior*. New York: Pantheon Books.
1981   *Forms of Talk*. Philadelphia: University of Pennsylvania Press.

Göle, Nilüfer
1996   *The Forbidden Modern: Civilization and Veiling*. Ann Arbor: University of Michigan Press.
2002   "Islam in Public: New Visibilities and New Imaginaries." *Public Culture* 14(1):173–90.

Graeber, David
2001   *Toward an Anthropological Theory of Value: The False Coin of Our Own Dreams*. New York: Palgrave.

Greenhouse, Carol J.
1996   *A Moment's Notice: Time Politics across Cultures*. Ithaca, NY: Cornell University Press.
2002   "Altered States, Altered Lives." In *Ethnography in Unstable Places: Everyday Lives in Contexts of Dramatic Political Change*, Carol J. Greenhouse, Elizabeth Mertz, and Kay B Warren, eds. Durham, NC: Duke University Press.

Gueye, Cheikh
2001   "Touba: The New *Dairas* and the Urban Dream." In *Associational Life in African Cities: Popular Responses to the Urban Crisis*, Arne Tostensen, Inge Tvedten, and Mariken Vaa, eds. Uppsala: Nordiska Afrikainstitutet.

Guyer, Jane I.
1995   *Money Matters: Instability, Values, and Social Payments in the Modern History of West African Communities*. Portsmouth, NH: Heinemann.
1999   "Comparisons and Equivalencies in Africa and Melanesia." In *Money and Modernity: State and Local Currencies in Melanesia*, D. Akin and J. Robbins, eds. Pittsburgh, PA: University of Pittsburgh Press.
2004   *Marginal Gains: Monetary Transactions in Atlantic Africa*. Chicago: University of Chicago Press.

Guyer, Jane I., LaRay Denzer, and Adigun Agbaje, eds.
2002   *Money Struggles and City Life: Devaluation in Ibadan and Other Urban Centers in Southern Nigeria, 1986–1996*. Portsmouth, NH: Heinemann.

Habermas, Jürgen
1984   *The Theory of Communicative Action, Volume One*. Boston: Beacon Press.

1996   "Further Reflections on the Public Sphere." In *Habermas and the Public Sphere*, Craig Calhoun, ed. Cambridge, MA: MIT Press.

Hansen, Thomas Blom, and Finn Stepputat
2005   *Sovereign Bodies: Citizens, Migrants, and States in the Post-colonial World*. Princeton, NJ: Princeton University Press.

Hardt, Michael, and Antonio Negri
2000   *Empire*. Cambridge, MA: Harvard University Press.
2004   *Multitude: War and Democracy in the Age of Empire*. New York: Penguin.

Harrison, Christopher
1988   *France and Islam in West Africa, 1860–1960*. Cambridge: Cambridge University Press.

Harrow, Kenneth W.
2007   "Nyo Ko Bok: A Year under Globalization in Senegal." *Africultures*, March 20. Available at http://www.africultures.com.

Hart, Keith
1973   "Informal Income Opportunities and Urban Employment in Ghana." *Journal of Modern African Studies* 11:61–89.

Harvey, David
1989   *The Condition of Postmodernity: An Inquiry into the Origins of Cultural Change*. New York: Blackwell.
2003   *The New Imperialism*. New York: Oxford University Press.

Hayek, F. A.
1944   *The Road to Serfdom*. Chicago: University of Chicago Press.

Hebdige, Dick
1996   *Subculture: The Meaning of Style*. London: Routledge [1979].

Heidegger, Martin
1962   *Being and Time*. Trans. John Mcquarrie and Edward Robinson. New York: Harper and Row [1927].

Hesse, Brian J.
2004   "The Peugeot and the Baobab: Islam, Structural Adjustment and Liberalism in Senegal." *Journal of Contemporary African Studies* 22(1):4–12.

Herzfeld, Michael
2005   *Cultural Intimacy: Social Poetics in the Nation-State*. New York: Routledge.

Hibou, Béatrice
1999   "The 'Social Capital' of the State as an Agent of Deception." In Jean-François Bayart, Stephen Ellis, and Béatrice Hibou, *The Criminalization of the State in Africa*. Bloomington: Indiana University Press.

Hirschkind, Charles
2001a   "Civic Virtue and Religious Reason: An Islamic Counterpublic." *Cultural Anthropology* 16(1):3–34.

2001b   "Hearing Modernity: Egypt, Islam, and the Pious Ear." Paper
            presented at the conference "Media, Religion, and the Public
            Sphere," Amsterdam, December 2001.
2006   *The Ethical Soundscape: Cassette Sermons and Islamic
            Counterpublics.* New York: Columbia University Press.
Hock, Carsten
1998   "Muslimische Reform und staatliche Autorität in der Repub-
            lik Mali seit 1960." Ph.D. diss., University of Bayreuth.
Hopkins, A. G.
1973   *An Economic History of West Africa.* New York: Columbia
            University Press.
Huizinga, Johan
1950   *Homo Ludens: A Study of the Play Element in Culture.*
            Boston: Beacon Press.
Human Rights Watch
2008   *"The Best School": Student Violence, Impunity, and the
            Crisis in Côte d'Ivoire.* Report 15–64323–129–, May.
Hunt, Lynn
1993   *The Family Romance of the French Revolution.* Berkeley and
            Los Angeles: University of California Press.
Hunwick, John O.
1999   "Islamic Financial Institutions: Theoretical Structures and
            Aspects of Their Application in Sub-Saharan Africa." In *Credit,
            Currencies and Culture: African Financial Institutions in
            Historical Perspective,* Endre Stiansen and Jane I. Guyer, eds.
            Uppsala: Nordiska Afrikainstitutet.
Iliffe, John
1967   "The Organization of the Maji Maji Rebellion." *Journal of
            African History* 8(3):495–512.
International Organization for Migration
2003   "Challenges and Responses for People on the Move." *World
            Migration Report Series,* vol. 2. Geneva.
Irele, F. Abiola
2001   *The African Imagination: Literature in Africa and the Black
            Diaspora.* Oxford and New York: Oxford University Press.
Jackson, Stephen
2001   "Nos Richesses sont pillées: Economies de guerre et rumeurs
            de crime dans les Kivus, République démocratique du Congo."
            Politique africaine 84(December):117–35.
2002   "Making a Killing: Criminality and Coping in the Kivu
            War Economy." *Review of African Political Economy*
            29(93/94):517–36.
2003a   "Fortunes of War: The Coltan Trade in the Kivus." In *Power,
            Livelihoods and Conflict: Case Studies in Political Economy
            Analysis for Humanitarian Action.* ODI Humanitarian

Policy Group Report no. 13, Sarah Collinson, ed. London: Overseas Development Institute (ODI).

2003b   *War Making: Uncertainty, Improvisation, and Involution in the Kivu Provinces, DR Congo, 1997–2002.* Ph.D. diss., Princeton University.

2004   " 'The State Didn't Even Exist': Non-Governmentality in Kivu, Eastern DR Congo." In *Between a Rock and a Hard Place: African NGOs, Donors, and the State,* Tim Kelsall and Jim Igoe, eds. Durham, NC: Carolina Academic Press.

2005   "Protecting Livelihoods in Violent Economies." In *Peaceful Profits: Approaches to Managing the Resource Dimensions of Armed Conflict,* Karen Ballentine, ed. Boulder, CO: Lynne Rienner.

2006   "Sons of Which Soil? The Language and Politics of Autochthony in Eastern D.R. Congo." *African Studies Review* 49(2):95–123.

2007   "Of 'Doubtful Nationality': Political Manipulation of Citizenship in the D.R. Congo." *Citizenship Studies* 11(5):481–500.

Kaba, Lansiné
1974   *The Wahhabiyya: Islamic Reform and Politics in French West Africa.* Evanston, IL: Northwestern University Press.

Kane, Ousmane
1997   "Muslim Missionaries and African States." In *Transnational Religion and Fading States,* Susan Hoeber Rudolph and James Piscatori, eds. Boulder, CO: Westview Press.

Kapchan, Deborah
1996   *Gender on the Market: Moroccan Women and the Revoicing of Tradition.* Philadelphia: University of Pennsylvania Press.

Kellogg, P.
1987   "Goodbye to the Working Class?" *International Socialism* 2(36):105–12.

Kelly, John
2003   "U.S. Power, after 9/11 and before It: If Not an Empire, Then What?" *Public Culture* 15(2):347–69.

Kenyatta, Jomo
1962   *Facing Mount Kenya.* New York: Vintage Books.

Khan, Firoz, and Edgar Pieterse
2004   "The Homeless People's Alliance: Purposive Creation and Ambiguated Realities." Research report for the project on Globalisation, Marginalisation & New Social Movements in Post-Apartheid South Africa. Durban: Centre for Civil Society and School of Development Studies, University of KwaZulu-Natal.

Khuri, Fuad I.
1978   "The Dynamics of War in Lebanon and the Militarization of Civilians." Paper presented at the meetings of the International Sociological Association (ISA).

Klein, Naomi
2007   *Shock Doctrine: The Rise of Disaster Capitalism.* New York: Metropolitan Books.

Kohlhagen, Dominik
2006   "Frime, escroquerie et cosmopolitisme: Le Succès du 'Coupé-Décalé' en Afrique et ailleurs." *Politique africaine* 100:92–105.

Konaté, Yacouba
2002   "Génération zouglou." *Cahiers d'etudes africaines* 42(4):777–96.
2003   "Les Enfants de la balle: De la Fesci aux mouvements de patriotes." *Politique africaine* 89:49–70.

Kraxberger, Brennan M.
2005   "The United States and Africa: Shifting Geopolitics in an "Age of Terror." *Africa Today* 51(1):47–68.

Landes, Joan
1995   "The Public and the Private Sphere." In *Feminists Read Habermas: Gendering the Subject of Discourse*, J. Meehan, ed. New York: Routledge.

Larkin, Brian
2004   "Degraded Images, Distorted Sounds: Nigerian Video and the Infrastructure of Piracy." *Public Culture* 16(2):289–314.

Lash, Scott, and John Urry
1987   *The End of Organized Capitalism.* Madison: University of Wisconsin Press.

Launay, Robert
1992   *Beyond the Stream: Islam and Society in a West African Town.* Berkeley and Los Angeles: University of California Press.

Launay, Robert, and Marie Miran
2000   "Beyond Mande Mory: Islam and Ethnicity in Côte d'Ivoire." *Paideuma* 46:63–84.

Launay, Robert, and Benjamin Soares
1999   "The Formation of an 'Islamic Sphere' in French Colonial West Africa." *Economy and Society* 28(3):467–89.

LeBlanc, Marie Nathalie
1999   "The Production of Islamic Identities through Knowledge Claims in Bouaké, Côte d'Ivoire." *African Affairs* 98(393):485–509.
2000   "Versioning Womanhood and Muslimhood: 'Fashion' and the Life Course in Contemporary Bouaké, Côte d'Ivoire." *Africa* 70(3):442–81.

Lee, Benjamin
1997   *Talking Heads: Language, Metalanguage, and the Semiotics of Subjectivity.* Durham, NC: Duke University Press.
Lee, Benjamin, and Edward LiPuma
2002   "Cultures of Circulation: The Imaginations of Modernity." *Public Culture* 14(1):191–213.
Lemarchand, René
2003   "The Democratic Republic of Congo: From Failure to Potential Reconstruction." In *State Failure and State Weakness in a Time of Terror,* Robert I. Rotberg, ed. Washington, DC: Brookings Institution Press.
Lemke, Thomas
2001   " 'The Birth of Bio-Politics': Michel Foucault's Lecture at the Collège de France on Neoliberal Governmentality." *Economy and Society* 30(2):190–207.
Le Pape, Marc, and C. Vidal, eds.
2002   *Côte d'Ivoire: L'Année terrible 1999–2000.* Paris: Karthala.
Lichtblau, Eric
2003   "A Nation at War: Legal Issues; 1996 Statute Becomes the Justice Department's Anti-Terror Weapon of Choice." *New York Times,* April 6, B15.
Lipsitz, George
2006   "Learning from New Orleans: The Social Warrant of Hostile Privatism and Competitive Consumer Citizenship." *Cultural Anthropology* 21(3):451–68.
LiPuma, Edward, and Thomas Koelble
2004   "Democracy, Freedom, and the Vise of Encompassment." *Identities: Global Studies in Culture and Power* 11:99–112.
LiPuma, Edward, and Benjamin Lee
2004   *Financial Derivatives and the Globalization of Risk.* Durham, NC: Duke University Press.
Locke, John
1980   *Second Treatise of Government.* Ed. C. B. Macpherson. Indianapolis, IN: Hackett Publishing Company [1690].
Loimeier, Roman
1997   *Islamic Reform and Political Change in Northern Nigeria.* Evanston, IL: Northwestern University Press.
2003   "Patterns and Peculiarities of Islamic Reform in Africa." *Journal of Religion in Africa* 33(3):237–62.
Lü, Xiaobo
2000   *Cadres and Corruption: The Organizational Involution of the Chinese Communist Party.* Stanford, CA: Stanford University Press.

Lüdtke, Alf

1995 "Introduction: What Is the History of Everyday Life and Who Are Its Practitioners?" In *The History of Everyday Life: Reconstructing Historical Experiences and Ways of Life*, Alf Lüdtke, ed.; W. Templer, trans. Princeton, NJ: Princeton University Press.

Luxemburg, Rosa

2003 *Accumulation of Capital.* New York: Routledge [1913].

MacGaffey, Janet

1991 "Historical, Cultural, and Structural Dimensions of Zaire's Unrecorded Trade." In *The Real Economy of Zaire: The Contribution of Smuggling and Other Unofficial Activities to National Wealth*, Janet MacGaffey, ed. Philadelphia: University of Pennsylvania Press.

MacGaffey, Janet, and Remy Bazenguissa-Ganga

2000 *Congo-Paris: Transnational Traders on the Margins of the Law.* London: James Currey.

MacGaffey, Wyatt

1998 "Am I Myself? Identities in Zaire, Then and Now." *Transactions of the Royal Historical Society* 6(8):291–307.

MacLeod, Arlene Elowe

1991 *Accommodating Protest.* Cairo: The American University in Cairo Press.

Mahmood, Saba

2005 *Politics of Piety: The Islamic Revival and the Feminist Subject.* Princeton, NJ: Princeton University Press.

Maira, Sunaina

2000 "Henna and Hip Hop: The Politics of Cultural Production and the Work of Cultural Studies." *Journal of Asian American Studies* 3(3):329–69.

Makhulu, Anne-Maria

2010 "The Question of Freedom: Post-Emancipation South Africa in a Neoliberal Age." In *Politics, Publics, Personhood: New Ethnographies at the Limits of Neoliberalism*, Carol Greenhouse, ed. Philadelphia: University of Pennsylvania Press.

Malaquais, Dominique

2001 "Anatomie d'une arnaque: Feymen et feymania au Cameroun." *Les Études du CERI* 77.

Mamdani, Mahmood

1996 *Citizen and Subject: Contemporary Africa and the Legacy of Late Colonialism.* Princeton, NJ: Princeton University Press.

2004 *Good Muslim, Bad Muslim: America, the Cold War, and the Roots of Terror.* Dakar: CODESRIA.

Marchal, Roland
2004   "Islamic Political Dynamics in the Somali Civil War." In *Islam and Its Enemies in the Horn of Africa,* Alex De Waal, ed. Bloomington: Indiana University Press.

Marcus, Greil
1989   *Lipstick Traces: A Secret History of the Twentieth Century.* Cambridge: Harvard University Press.

Martin, Emily
1994   *Flexible Bodies: The Role of Immunity in American Culture from the Days of Polio to the Age of Aids.* Boston: Beacon Press.

Marx, Karl
1963   *The Eighteenth Brumaire of Louis Bonaparte.* New York: International Publishers [1852].
1990   *Capital.* Volume 1, part 8. Trans. Ben Fowkes. London: Penguin [1867].

Marx, Karl, and Frederick Engels
1970   *The German Ideology: Part One.* Ed. C. J. Arthur. New York: International Publishers [1845, unpubl.].

Masquelier, Adeline
1999   "Debating Muslims, Disputed Practices: Struggles for the Realization of an Alternative Moral Order in Niger." In *Civil Society and the Political Imagination in Africa: Critical Perspectives,* J. L. Comaroff and J. Comaroff, eds. Chicago: University of Chicago Press.

Mattes, Hanspeter
1989   *Die islamistische Bewegung des Senegal zwischen Autonomie und Außenorientierung.* Hamburg: Institut für Afrika-Kunde.

Mbembe, Achille
1992   "Provisional Notes on the Postcolony." *Africa* 62(1):3–37.
2001   *On the Postcolony.* Berkeley and Los Angeles: University of California Press.
2002   "African Modes of Self-Writing." *Public Culture* 14(1):239–73.
2003   "Necropolitics." *Public Culture* 15(1):11–40.
2004   "Aesthetics of Superfluity." *Public Culture* 16(3):373–405.
2005   "Sovereignty as a Form of Expenditure." In *Sovereign Bodies: Citizens, Migrants, and States in the Postcolonial World,* Thomas Blom Hansen and Finn Stepputat, eds. Princeton, NJ: Princeton University Press.
2006   "Variations on the Beautiful in Congolese Worlds of Sound." In *Beautiful/Ugly: African and Diaspora Aesthetics,* Sarah Nuttall, ed. Durham, NC: Duke University Press.

Mbembe, Achille, and Sarah Nuttall
2004   "Writing the World from an African Metropolis." *Public Culture* 16(3):347–72.

Mbodj, Mohamed

1991   "The Politics of Independence: 1960–86." In *The Political Economy of Senegal under Structural Adjustment*, C.L. Delgado and S. Jammeh, eds. New York: Praeger.

1993   "The State of the Groundnut Economy: A 30 Year Crisis." In *Senegal: Essays in Statecraft*, Momar Coumba Diop, ed. Dakar: CODESRIA.

Mbow, Penda

2008   "Senegal: The Return of Personalism." *Journal of Democracy* 19(1):156–69.

McGovern, Mike

2009   "Proleptic Justice: The Threat of Investigation as a Deterrent to Human Rights Abuses in Côte d'Ivoire." In *Mirrors of Justice: Law, Power and the Making of History*, K Clarke and M. Goodale, eds. Cambridge: Cambridge University Press.

Meillassoux, Claude

1968   *Urbanization of an African Community: Voluntary Associations in Bamako.* Seattle: University of Washington Press.

1971   *The Development of Indigenous Trade and Markets in West Africa.* London: Oxford University Press.

1981   *Maidens, Meal, and Money: Capitalism and the Domestic Community.* New York: Cambridge University Press.

Meintjes, Helen

2001   "'Washing Machines Make Lazy Women': Domestic Appliances in the Negotiation of Women's Propriety in Soweto." *Journal of Material Culture* 6(3):345–63.

Merrifield, Andy

2002   *Metromarxism: A Marxist Tale of the City.* New York: Routledge.

Meyer, Birgit

1998   "The Power of Money: Politics, Occult Forces, and Pentecostalism in Ghana." *African Studies Review* 41:15–37.

2004   "Praise the Lord: Popular Cinema, Pentecostalite Style in Ghana's New Public Sphere. *American Ethnologist* 31(1):92–100.

Millar, Kathleen

2002   "Financing Terror: Profits from Counterfeit Goods Pay for Attacks." *U.S. Customs Today.* Available at http://www.cbp.gov/xp/CustomsToday/2002/November/interpol.xml.

Miran, Marie

1998   "Le Wahhabisme à Abidjan: Dynamisme urbain d'un Islam reformiste en Côte d'Ivoire contemporaine (1960–1996)." *Islam et Sociétés au Sud du Sahara* 12:5–74.

Mirza, Jasmin

2002   *Between Chaddor and the Market.* Oxford: Oxford University Press.

Mitchell, Timothy
    n.d.   "Violence and the Politics of Oil: A Conversation with Timothy Mitchell and Juan Cole." Eisenberg Institute for Historical Studies, University of Michigan, December 6, 2008.

Mitter, Sidhartta, Jesse Shipley, and Dominik Kohlhagen
    2007   "The Hip Hop Generation: Ghana's Hip Life and Ivory Coast's Coupé-Décalé." Available at http://www.afropop.org.

Miyazaki, Hiro
    2007   "Arbitraging Faith and Reason." American Ethnologist 34(3):430–32.

Moore, Henrietta L., and Todd Sanders, eds.
    2001   *Magical Interpretations, Material Realities: Modernity, Witchcraft and the Occult in Postcolonial Africa.* New York: Routledge.

Murray, Nancy
    2004   "Profiled: Arabs, Muslims and the Post-9/11 Hunt for the 'Enemy Within.'" In *Civil Rights in Peril*, Elaine C. Hagopian, ed. Chicago: Haymarket Books and Pluto Press.

Nattrass, Nicoli, and Jeremy Seekings
    2001   "Democracy and Distribution in Highly Unequal Economies: The Case of South Africa." *Journal of Modern African Studies* 39(3):471–98.

Navaro-Yashin, Yael
    2002   *Faces of the State: Secularism and Public Life in Turkey.* Princeton, NJ: Princeton University Press.

Newell, Sasha
    2006   "Estranged Belongings: A Moral Economy of Theft in Abidjan, Côte d'Ivoire." *Anthropological Theory* 6(2):179–203.
    [2007]   "Popular Culture, Urban Youth, and the Imagination of Ivoirité: Underlying Oppositions in the Ivorian Crisis." Paper presented at the annual meetings of the African Studies Association.

Nordstrom, Carolyn
    1997   *A Different Kind of War Story.* Philadelphia: University of Pennsylvania Press.

Nugent, Paul
    1995   *Big Men, Small Boys and Politics in Ghana: Power, Ideology and the Burden of History, 1982–1994.* New York: Pinter.

Nzongola-Ntalaja, Georges
    2002   *The Congo, from Leopold to Kabila.* London: Zed Books.

Obeng, Samuel
    1999   "Requests in Akan Discourse." *Anthropological Linguistics* 41(2):230–51.

206   /   *References Cited*

Ong, Aihwa
    1999   *Flexible Citizenship: The Cultural Logic of Transnationality.*
                Durham, NC: Duke University Press.
    2006   *Neoliberalism as Exception: Mutations in Citizenship and
                Sovereignty.* Durham, NC: Duke University Press.
Otayek, René
    1993   *Le Radicalisme islamique au sud du Sahara.* Paris, Talence:
                Éditions Karthala.
Panapress
    2006   "Côte d'Ivoire: Menaces sur les ressortissants ouest-africains,"
                October 4. Available at http://www.afrik.com.
Panos Institute
    1993   "Radio Pluralism in West Africa: A Survey Conducted by
                the Panos Institute." In *Paris and l'Union des Journalistes
                d'Afrique de l'Ouest,* vol. 3. Paris: Institut Panos and
                L'Harmattan.
Perry, Donna
    1997   "Rural Ideologies and Urban Imaginings: Wolof Immigrants
                in New York City." *Africa Today* 44(2):229–60.
Pillay, Pundy
    2006   "Human Resource Development and Growth: Improving
                Access to and Equity in the Provision of Education and Health
                Services in South Africa." *Development Southern Africa*
                23(1):63–83.
Polanyi, Karl
    2001   *The Great Transformation: The Political and Economic
                Origins of Our Time.* Boston: Beacon Press.
Polgreen, Lydia
    2002   "Secret Service Raid on a Factory Attacks CD Counterfeiting
                Ring." *New York Times,* December 12, A32.
Povinelli, Elizabeth
    2002   *The Cunning of Recognition: Indigenous Alterities and the
                Making of Australian Multiculturalism.* Durham, NC: Duke
                University Press.
Prashad, Vijay
    2003   *Keeping Up with the Dow Joneses: Debt, Prison, and Work-
                fare.* Cambridge, MA: South End Press.
Rahman, Saifur
    2007   "Senegal Welcomes Dubai Developers with Open Arms."
                Gulfnews.com, April 19. Available at http://gulfnews.com.
Reddy, Sanjay
    2004   "A Capability-Based Approach to Estimating Global Poverty."
                In *Dollar a Day: How Much Does It Say?,* a special issue of *In
                Focus.* Brasilia: International Poverty Centre, 6–8.

Reno, William

1995   *Corruption and State Politics in Sierra Leone.* New York: Cambridge University Press.

2001   "How Sovereignty Matters: International Markets and the Political Economy of Local Politics in Weak States." In *Intervention and Transnationalism in Africa: Global-Local Networks of Power,* T. Callaghy, R. Kassimir, and R. Latham, eds. Cambridge: Cambridge University Press.

Reveyrand-Coulon, Odile

1993   "Les Enoncés féminins de l'Islam." In *Religion et modernité politique en Afrique noire: Dieu pour tous et chacun pour soi,* Jean-François Bayart, ed. Paris: Karthala.

Riccio, Bruno

2004   "Transnational Mouridism and the Afro-Muslim Critique of Italy." *Journal of Ethnic and Migration Studies* 30(5):929.

Richardson, Clem

2004   "Help for Fed Up Street Vendors." *New York Daily News,* July 16.

Roberts, Allen

1996   "The Ironies of System D." In *Recycled, Re-Seen: Folk Art from the Global Scrap Heap,* C. Cerny and S. Seriff, eds. New York: Harry Abrams for the Museum of International Folk Art, Santa Fe.

Rodney, Walter

1972   *How Europe Underdeveloped Africa.* Washington, DC: Howard University Press.

Roitman, Janet L.

1990   "The Politics of Informal Markets in Sub-Saharan Africa." *Journal of Modern African Studies* 28(4):671–96.

2005   *Fiscal Disobedience: An Anthropology of Economic Regulation in Central Africa.* Princeton, NJ: Princeton University Press.

Rosander, Eva Evers

1997   "Le *Dahira* de Mam Diarra Bousso de Mbacké." In *Transforming Female Identities: Women's Organizational Forms in West Africa,* E. Evers Rosander, ed. Uppsala: Nordiska Afrikainstitutet.

1998   "Women and Muridism in Senegal: The Case of the Mam Diarra Bousso Daira in Mbacké." In *Women and Islamization: Contemporary Dimensions of Discourse on Gender Relations,* K. Ask and M. Tjomsland, eds. Oxford: Berg.

2003   "Mam Diarra Bousso: The Good Mother in Porokhane." Paper presented at the workshop "Modern Adaptations in Sufi-Based Islam," Berlin, Centre Modern Orient, April 2003.

Ross, Eric S.

1995   "Touba: A Spiritual Metropolis in the Modern World."
            Canadian Journal of African Studies 29(2):222–59.

Rotberg, Robert I.

2003   "Failed States, Collapsed States, Weak States: Causes and
            Indicators." In *State Failure and State Weakness in a Time
            of Terror*, Robert I. Rotberg, ed. Washington, DC: Brookings
            Institution Press.

Sachs, Susan

2002   "Immigrants Facing Strict New Controls on Cash Sent
            Home." *New York Times*, November 12, B1.

Salvatore, Armando

1999   "Global Influences and Discontinuities in a Religious Tradition:
            Public Islam and the 'New' Sari'a." *In Dissociation and Appro-
            priation: Responses to Globalization in Asia and Africa*, K.H.
            Füllberg-Stolberg and Schöne Ellinor Petra, eds. Berlin: Das
            Arabische Buch.

Salzbrunn, Monika

2004   "The Occupation of Public Space through Religious and Politi-
            cal Events: How Senegalese Migrants Became a Part of Harlem,
            New York." *Journal of Religion in Africa*, 34(4)468–92.

Sanankoua, Bintou

1991   "Les Associations féminines musulmanes à Bamako."
            In *L'Enseignement Islamique au Mali*, L. Brenner and
            B. Sanankoua, eds. Bamako: Editions Jamana.

Sánchez G., Gonzalo

2001   "Introduction: Problems of Violence, Prospects for Peace."
            In *Violence in Colombia, 1990–2000: Waging War and
            Negotiating Peace*, Charles Bergquist, Ricardo Peñaranda,
            and Gonzalo Sánchez G., eds. Wilmington, DE: SR Books.

Sassen, Saskkia, ed.

2002   *Global Networks, Linked Cities.* New York: Routledge.

Sayer, Andrew, and Richard Walker

1992   *The New Social Economy: Reworking the Division of Labour.*
            Cambridge, MA: Blackwell.

Scardino, A.

1987   "What, New York City Worry?" *New York Times*, May 3.

Schatzberg, Michael G.

1988   *The Dialectics of Oppression in Zaire.* Bloomington IN:
            Indiana University Press.

Schechner, Richard

1985   *Between Theatre and Anthropology.* Philadelphia: University
            of Pennsylvania Press.

Schulz, Dorothea

1999   In "Pursuit of Publicity: Talk Radio and the Imagination of a Moral Public in Mali." *Africa Spectrum* 99(2):161–85.

2001   *Perpetuating the Politics of Praise: Jeli Praise Singers, Radios and Political Mediation in Mali.* Köln: Rüdiger Köppe Verlag.

2003   "Political Factions, Ideological Fictions: The Controversy over the Reform of Family Law in Democratic Mali." *Islamic Law and Society* 10(1):132–64.

2004   "Islamic Revival, Mass-Mediated Religiosity and the Moral Negotiation of Gender Relations in Urban Mali." Habilitation thesis, Free University, Berlin.

2006   "Promises of (Im)mediate Salvation: Islam, Broadcast Media, and the Remaking of Religious Experience in Mali." *American Ethnologist* 33(2):210–29.

2007   "Competing Sartorial Assertions of Femininity and Muslim Identity in Mali." *Fashion Theory* 11(2/3):253–80.

2008   "'A Matter of Orthopraxy'? Muslim Women's 'Conversion Narratives' and the Controversial Construction of Sunni Identity in Mali." *Africa Today* 54(4):21–43.

Schulze, Reinhard

1993   "La Da'wa saoudienne en Afrique de l'Ouest." In *Le Radicalisme islamique au sud du Sahara*, R. Otayek, ed. Paris, Talence: Karthala.

Scott, David

2004   *Conscripts of Modernity: The Tragedy of Colonial Enlightenment.* Durham, NC: Duke University Press.

Seekings, Jeremy, and Nicoli Nattrass

2005   *Class, Race, and Inequality in South Africa.* New Haven: Yale University Press.

Sennett, Richard

2006   *The Culture of the New Capitalism.* New Haven: Yale University Press.

Sharma, Aradhana, and Akhil Gupta, eds.

2006   *The Anthropology of the State: A Reader.* Oxford: Blackwell.

Shipley, Jesse Weaver

2003   "National Audiences and Consuming Subjects: A Political Genealogy of Performance in Neoliberal Ghana." Ph.D. diss., University of Chicago.

n.d.   *Living and Preaching the Hiplife: Moral Citizenship, Popular Culture, and Transnational Media in Ghana* (manuscript in preparation).

Silverstein, Michael

1976   "Shifters, Linguistic Categories, and Cultural Description." In *Meaning in Anthropology*, Keith Basso and H. A. Selby Jr., eds. Albuquerque: University of New Mexico Press.

Simmel, Georg
1971   "Sociability." In *Georg Simmel: On Individuality and Social Forms*, Donald Levine, ed. Chicago: University of Chicago Press.
Simone, Abdoumaliq
1997   *Urban Processes and Change in Africa*. Dakar: CODESRIA.
2004   *For the City Yet to Come: Changing African Life in Four Cities*. Durham, NC: Duke University Press.
Simone, Abdoumaliq, and A. Abouhani, eds.
2005   *Urban Africa: Changing Contours of Survival in the City*. Dakar: CODESRIA.
Singer, P. W.
2003   *Corporate Warriors: The Rise of the Privatized Military Industry*. Ithaca, NY: Cornell University Press.
Smart, Carol
1992   "Disruptive Bodies and Unruly Sex: The Regulation of Reproduction and Sexuality in the Nineteenth Century." In *Regulating Womanhood: Historical Essays on Marriage, Motherhood and Sexuality*, C. Smart, ed. London: Routledge.
Smith, Adam
1977   *An Inquiry into the Nature and Causes of the Wealth of Nations*. Edwin Cannan, ed. Chicago: University of Chicago Press [1789].
Smith, Daniel
2007   *A Culture of Corruption: Everyday Deception and Popular Discontent in Nigeria*. Princeton, NJ: Princeton University Press.
Smith, James H., and Jeffrey W. Mantz
2007   "Do Cellular Phones Dream of Civil War? The Mystification of Production and the Consequences of Technology Fetishism in the Eastern Congo." In *Inclusion and Exclusion in the Global Arena*, Max Kirsch, ed. New York: Routledge.
Smith, Neil
2004   "After Iraq: Vulnerable Imperial Stasis." *Radical Philosophy* 127:2–7.
Soares, Benjamin
2004   "Islam and Public Piety in Mali." In *Public Islam and the Common Good*, Armando Salvatore and Dale Eickelman, eds. Leiden: Brill.
2005   *Islam and the Prayer Economy: History and Authority in a Malian Town*. Ann Arbor: University of Michigan Press.
Sontag, Susan
1966   "Notes on 'Camp.'" In *Against Interpretation*. New York: Anchor.

Spitulnik, Debra
   1996   "The Social Circulation of Media Discourse and the Media-
              tion of Communities." *Journal of Linguistic Anthropology*
              6(2):161–87.
Steinberg, Jonny
   2001   *Crime Wave: The South African Underworld and Its Foes.*
              Johannesburg: Witwatersrand University Press
Steinmetz, George
   2003   "The State of Emergency and the Revival of American
              Imperialism: Toward an Authoritarian Post-Fordism."
              Public Culture 15(2):323–45.
Stiansen, Endre, and Jane I. Guyer, eds.
   1999   *Credit, Currencies and Culture: African Financial Institutions*
              in Historical Perspective. Uppsala: Nordiska Afrikainstitutet.
Stoller, Paul
   1995   *Embodying Colonial Memories: Spirit Possession, Power,*
              and the Hauka in West Africa. London: Routledge.
   2002   *Money Has No Smell: The Africanization of New York City.*
              Chicago: University of Chicago Press.
Strange, Susan
   1997   *Casino Capitalism.* Manchester: Manchester University Press
              [1986].
Streiffeler, Friedhelm
   1994   "State Substitution and Market Liberalization in Northern
              Kivu, Zaire." *Sociologia Ruralis* 34(1):63–70.
Sule, Barbara, and Priscilla Starratt
   1991   "Islamic Leadership Positions for Women in Contemporary
              Kano Society." In *Hausa Women in the Twentieth Century,*
              C. Coles and B. Mack, eds. Madison: University of Wisconsin
              Press.
Sy, Tidiane
   2006   "Mother's Battle against Senegal Migration." *BBC News
              Dakar,* November 6. Available at http://news.bbc.co.uk.
Tall, Serigne Mansour
   2002   "Mouride Migration and Financing." *ISIM Newsletter,*
              September 9, 36.
Tambiah, Stanley
   1997   *Leveling Crowds: Ethnonationalist Conflicts and Collective*
              Violence in South Asia. Berkeley and Los Angeles: University
              of California Press.
Tansi, Sony Labou
   1990   *The Antipeople.* London: Marion Boyars.
Taussig, Michael
   1993   *Mimesis and Alterity: A Particular History of the Senses.*
              New York: Routledge.

Taylor, Charles
1992   *Sources of the Self: The Making of the Modern Identity.*
            Cambridge, MA: Harvard University Press.
2004   *Modern Social Imaginaries.* Durham, NC: Duke University
            Press.

Thioub, Ibrahima, Momar Coumba Diop, and Catherine Boone
1998   "Economic Liberalization in Senegal: Shifting Politics of
            Indigenous Business Interests." *African Studies Review*
            41(2):63–89.

Thomas, Karen
2006   "Madonna Speaks Out over Furor." *USA Today*, October 26.
            Available at http://www.usatoday.com.

Thürer, Daniel
1999   "The 'Failed State' and International Law." *International
            Review of the Red Cross* 836:731–61.

Tostensen, Arne, Inge Tvedten, and Mariken Vaa
2001   "The Urban Crisis, Governance and Associational Life." In
            *Associational Life in African Cities: Popular Responses to
            the Urban Crisis*, Arne Tostensen, Inge Tvedten, and Mariken
            Vaa, eds. Uppsala: Nordiska Afrikainstitutet.

Toungara, Jeanne Maddox
1995   "Generational Tensions in the Parti Démocratique de Côte
            d'Ivoire." *African Studies Review* 38(2):11–38.

Triaud, Jean-Louis
1986a   "Le Thème confrérique en Afrique de l'Ouest: Essai historique
            et bibliographique." In *Les Ordres mystiques dans l'Islam:
            Cheminements et situation actuelle*, A. G. V. Popovitch, ed.
            Paris: Editions de l'EHESS.
1986b   "Abd al-Rahman l'Africain (1908–1957), pionneur et précur-
            seur du wahhabisme au Mali." In *Radicalismes islamiques*,
            vol. 2., O. Carré et Paul Dumont, eds. Paris: L'Harmattan.
1997   Introduction to *Le Temps des marabouts: Itinéraires et
            stratégies islamiques en Afrique occidentale française*,
            v. 1880–1960, D. T. Robinson, Jean-Louis Triaud, et Ghislaine
            Lydon, eds. Paris: Editions Karthala.

Trouillot, Michel-Rolph
2003   *Global Transformations: Anthropology and the Modern
            World.* New York: Palgrave Macmillan.

UNDP (United Nations Development Programme)
2006   *UNDP Human Development Report.* Archived at http://hdr
            .undp.org/en/reports/global/hdr2006/.

U.S. Department of Justice
2004   "Report from the Field: The USA PATRIOT Act at Work."
            Prepared remarks of Attorney General John Ashcroft.
            Archived at http://www.justice.gov.

U.S. House of Representatives

2003   "International Copyright Piracy: A Growing Problem with Links to Organized Crime and Terrorism." Hearing before the Subcommittee on Courts, the Internet, and Intellectual Property of the Committee on the Judiciary, House of Representatives, March 13.

van de Walle, Nicholas

2001   *African Economies and the Politics of Permanent Crisis, 1979–1999.* New York: Cambridge University Press.

Van Natta, Don, Jr.

2003   "Terrorists Blaze a New Money Trail." *New York Times,* September 28, section 4, 1.

van Schendel, Willem, and Itty Abraham

2005   *Illicit Flows and Criminal Things: States, Borders, and the Other Side of Globalization.* Bloomington: Indiana University Press.

Vansina, Jan

1990   *Paths in the Rainforest: Towards a History of Political Tradition in Equatorial Africa.* London: James Currey.

Vigh, Henrik Erdman

2008   "Crisis and Chronicity: Anthropological Perspectives on Continuous Conflict and Decline." *Ethnos* 73(1):5–25.

Warner, Michael

2002   "Publics and Counterpublics." *Public Culture* 14(1):49–90.

Watts, Michael

2006   "Empire of Oil: Capitalist Dispossession and the Scramble for Africa." *Monthly Review* 58(4):1–17.

Weiss, Brad

2002   "Thug Realism: Inhabiting Fantasy in Urban Tanzania." *Cultural Anthropology* 17(1):93–124.

Weiss, Herbert

1995   "Zaire: Collapsed Society, Surviving State, Future Polity." In *Collapsed States: The Disintegration and Restoration of Legitimate Authority,* I. William Zartman, ed. Boulder, CO: Lynne Rienner.

Weist, Katherine M.

1995   "Development Refugees: Africans, Indians and the Big Dams." *Journal of Refugee Studies* 8(2):163–84.

Werbner, Richard

1996   "Multiple Identities, Plural Arenas." In *Postcolonial Identities in Africa,* Richard Werbner and Terence Ranger, eds. London: Zed Books.

White, Bob W.

2000   "Soukouss Or Sell-Out? Congolese Popular Dance Music on the World Market." In *Commodities and Globalization:*

Anthropological Perspectives, Angelique Haugerud, ed. Lanham, MD: Rowman and Littlefield.

2008   *Rumba Rules: The Politics of Dance Music in Mobutu's Zaire*. Durham, NC: Duke University Press.

White, Hylton

2001   "Tempora et Mores: Family Values and the Possessions of a Post-Apartheid Countryside." *Journal of Religion in Africa* 31(4):457–79.

Williams, Raymond

1973   *The Country and the City*. New York: Oxford University Press.

1977   *Marxism and Literature*. Oxford: Oxford University Press.

Willis, Paul

1981   *Learning to Labor: How Working Class Kids Get Working Class Jobs*. New York: Columbia University Press [1977].

Wilson, Michael

2004   "Policing a City Where Streets Are Less Mean." *New York Times*, August 8, A1.

Wolf, Eric R.

1997   *Europe and the People without History*. Berkeley and Los Angeles: University of California Press [1982].

Wrong, Michela

2002   *In the Footsteps of Mr. Kurtz: Living on the Brink of Disaster in Mobutu's Congo*. New York: Harper Perennial.

Wynter, Alex

2006   "Deadly Passage." *The Magazine of the International Red Cross and Red Crescent Society* 2. Available at http://www.redcross.int.

Yankah, Kwesi

1995   *Speaking for the Chief: Okyeame and the Politics of Akan Royal Oratory*. Bloomington: Indiana University Press.

Zaloom, Caitlin

2006   *Out of the Pits: Trading and Technology from Chicago to London*. Chicago: University of Chicago Press.

Zartman, I. William, ed.

1995   *Collapsed States: The Disintegration and Restoration of Legitimate Authority*. Boulder: Lynne Rienner.

Zelizer, Vivian A.

1994   *The Social Meaning of Money: Pin Money, Paychecks, Poor Relief, and Other Currencies*. Princeton, NJ: Princeton University Press.

Contributors

BETH A. BUGGENHAGEN is an assistant professor of anthropology at Indiana University, Bloomington. Her field research in Senegal and the United States considers circulation and value, visual and material culture, and gender and Islam. She is currently working on a book on Muslim families in global Senegal.

SIMON GIKANDI is the Robert Schirmer Professor of English at Princeton University. He is the recipient of numerous awards from organizations such as the American Council of Learned Societies, the Andrew W. Mellon Foundation, and the John Simon Guggenheim Memorial Foundation. His many books include *Reading the African Novel; Reading Chinua Achebe; Writing in Limbo: Modernism and Caribbean Literature; Maps of Englishness: Writing Identity in the Culture of Colonialism;* and *Ngugi wa Thiong'o.* He is the general editor of *The Encyclopedia of African Literature* and co-editor of *The Cambridge History of African and Caribbean Literature.* His major fields of research and teaching are the Anglophone literatures and cultures of Africa, India, the Caribbean, and postcolonial Britain; the "black" Atlantic; and the African diaspora. He received his Ph.D in English from Northwestern University.

STEPHEN JACKSON is currently a senior political affairs officer with the United Nations Department of Political Affairs, specializing in the Great Lakes Region of Central Africa. Previously, he worked as the Special Adviser to the Deputy Special Representative of the Secretary-General with the United Nations Mission in the DR Congo, as the deputy director of the Conflict Prevention and Peace Forum at the Social Science Research Council in New York, and as the director of the International Famine Centre at the National University of Ireland, Cork. He holds a Ph.D. in cultural anthropology from Princeton University and has published widely on Central Africa. In 2006, he co-edited with Peter Geschiere a special issue of the *African Studies Review* entitled *Autochthony and the Crisis of Citizenship: Democratization, Decentralization, and the Politics of Belonging.*

ANNE-MARIA MAKHULU is an assistant professor of cultural anthropology and African and African American studies at Duke University. Her research interests, broadly speaking, cover questions of the city, urbanism, and finance capital in South Africa. She is currently completing a book that concerns the politics of urban space during and after apartheid with a particular focus on the history of squatting.

MIKE MCGOVERN is an assistant professor of anthropology at Yale University, working on West Africa. His book *Making War in Côte d'Ivoire* (2010) focuses on the dramaturgy, sociology, and political economy of the Ivorian civil conflict. He is now finishing the manuscript for a book on the Republic of Guinea, which traces the intertwined processes of state formation and ethnogenesis over the course of the twentieth century. From 2004 to 2006 he worked as the West Africa project director for the International Crisis Group, a Brussels-based think tank that analyzes the causes of armed conflict.

CHARLES PIOT is associate professor of cultural anthropology at Duke University, where he also has a joint appointment in African and African American studies. His new book, *Nostalgia for the Future: West Africa after the Cold War* (2010), explores shifts in Togolese political culture after 1990, a time when the state began to pull back from social and development fields and the NGOs and Pentecostal churches took over the biopolitical field.

DOROTHEA E. SCHULZ is professor of anthropology at the University of Cologne. Her research, publications, and teaching are centered on the anthropology of religion, Islam in Africa, gender studies, media studies, public culture, and the anthropology of the state. Her forthcoming book, *Pathways to God*, deals with Muslim revivalist groups in urban Mali that operate beyond the confines of the nation-state and promote a relatively new conception of publicly enacted religiosity, significantly displayed in feminized signs of piety.

JESSE WEAVER SHIPLEY is assistant professor of anthropology at Haverford College. He is completing two mongraphs both due out in 2011: *Speaking of Freedom* examines theater and political history in 20th century Ghana, and *Living and Preaching the Hiplife* explores the making of hiplife music as a genre in urban Ghana and among Africans abroad. He is also a filmmaker (see http://www.livingthehiplife.com). His feature nonfiction works include *Living the Hiplife* (2007), *Is It Sweet* (2010), and *Black Star* (in progress).

Index

Abidjan: immigrants in, 71–72; music industry in, 75, 79–80, 173n18; Nouchi culture in, 82–83, 173n15; youth violence in, 72–73, 87

Accra, 95; hiplife and politics in, 93–104

Accumulation by dispossession, 18

ADEMA (Alliance pour la Démocratie au Mali), 120, 177n3

Affi N'Guessan, Pascal, 84–85

African Brothers Band, 105–6

Afro-pessimism, xii, xiii–xiv

Agence France-Presse, 76

Agriculture, 4, 71, 137–38

AIDS, 7

Airports: Senegal, 17

Akan culture: public speaking in, 105, 106

Alliance pour la Démocratie au Mali (ADEMA), 120, 177n3

Alpha Blondy, 75, 173n6

Al Qaeda: extralegal economy, 147–48

AMUPI (Association Malienne pour l'Unité et le Progrès de l'Islam), 119–20

Angola, 4, 15

Anti-Terrorism and Effective Death Penalty Act (ATEDPA; U.S.), 145

Arabisants, 119–20, 178n17

Arabs: surveillance of, 144

Arcelor Mittal, 17

Arendt, Hannah, 168n6; *The Origins of Totalitarianism*, 33

Arms production, 15

Ashanti Kingdom, 105

Association Malienne pour l'Unité et le Progrès de l'Islam (AMUPI), 119–20

ATEDPA (Anti-Terrorism and Effective Death Penalty Act), 145

Authority, 13, 60, 176n12; trade regulation, 132–33

Banking, xiv, 11, 169n16; Murid system, 143, 144; savings and credit schemes and, 36, 37–38, 40–41

Banyamulenge (Congolese Tutsi), 51

Barakaat, al, 143–44

Bateson, Gregory, 81–82

Baule (ethnic group), 82

"Being-in-the-world," xiv, xvi, 2, 8

Bernstein, André: *Bitter Carnival*, 64–65

Binladin Group, 17

Blay, Eddie, 98, 111

Blé Goudé, Charles, 73, 81, 87–88, 89, 173n6

Boystown (South Africa), 39

Brooklyn, 5, 21

Burkina Faso, 163

Bush, George W., 143, 148, 149

Canary Islands: West African migrants in, 1, 3, 10, 165nn1,2

Cape Flats (South Africa), 31; housing in, 32–33; informal economy, 33–34

CPSIA information can be obtained at www.ICGtesting.com
Printed in the USA
BVOW041635301011

274800BV00001B/7/P